Trace, Log, Text, Narrative, Data

An Analysis Pattern Reference for
Information Mining, Diagnostics, Anomaly Detection
Fifth Edition

Dmitry Vostokov
Software Diagnostics Institute

OpenTask

Published by OpenTask, Republic of Ireland

Copyright © 2023 by OpenTask

Copyright © 2023 by Dmitry Vostokov

Copyright © 2023 by Software Diagnostics Institute

OpenTask books are available through booksellers and distributors worldwide. For further information or comments, send requests to press@opentask.com.

Product and company names mentioned in this book may be trademarks of their owners.

A CIP catalog record for this book is available from the British Library.

ISBN-13: 978-1-912636-58-7 (Paperback)

Revision 5.04 (November 2023)

Table of Contents

Preface to the Fifth Edition

28 new trace and log analysis patterns have been discovered since the publication of the fourth edition inspired by container technology, data engineering, stream processing, data analysis, artificial chemistry, topology, and category theory. In addition to 9 patterns from Memory Dump Analysis Anthology, Volume 14, this edition also includes 19 analysis patterns from the forthcoming Volume 15.

We again changed the title and subtitle to "Trace, Log, Text, Narrative, Data: An Analysis Pattern Reference for Information Mining, Diagnostics, Anomaly Detection" due to the increased scope of applicability of such analysis patterns.

For this edition, we updated diagram pictures, classification, and the list of narratological and mathematical influences and added the long-awaited introduction and two new appendixes.

Preface to the Fourth Edition

24 new trace and log analysis patterns have been discovered since the publication of the third edition more than a year ago. Memory Dump Analysis Anthology has also grown to 4,700 pages with the publication of volumes 12 and 13. Even more ideas from mathematics were introduced to software diagnostics theory that is reflected in the added analysis patterns. This edition also includes 5 analysis patterns from the forthcoming volume 14. The total number of analysis patterns in this edition is more than 200.

We again changed the title and subtitle to "Trace, Log, Text, Narrative: An Analysis Pattern Reference for Data Mining, Diagnostics, Anomaly Detection" due to the ever-widening scope of applicability of such analysis patterns.

We also updated classification, the bibliography, and the list of narratological and mathematical influences.

This reference book is a part of the streaming architecture of pattern-oriented software diagnostics publications:

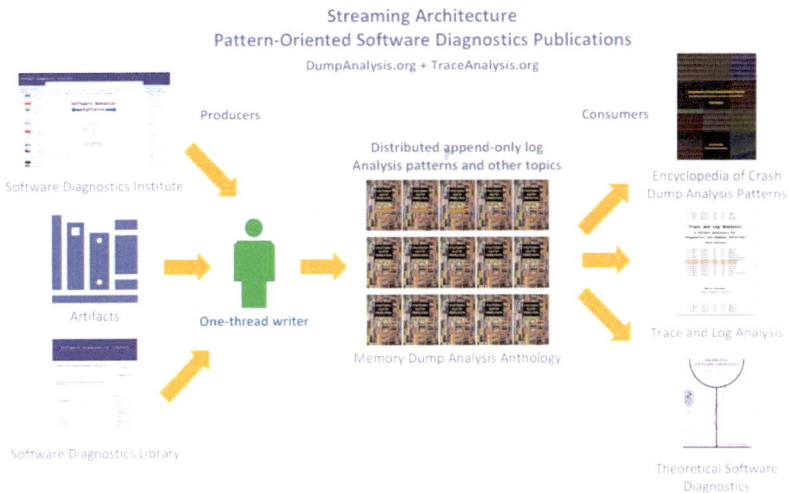

Streaming Architecture
Pattern-Oriented Software Diagnostics Publications
DumpAnalysis.org + TraceAnalysis.org

Preface to the Third Edition

44 new trace and log analysis patterns have been discovered since the publication of the second edition two and a half years ago. Memory Dump Analysis Anthology has also grown to 4,300 pages with the publication of volumes 10 and 11. More ideas from contemporary mathematics were introduced to software diagnostics theory that is reflected in the added analysis patterns. This edition also includes 11 analysis patterns from the forthcoming volume 12. We also added diagrams for several old analysis pattern descriptions.

Because the scope of applicability of such patterns is much wider than just software execution artifacts, we changed the title and subtitle to "Trace and Log Analysis: A Pattern Reference for Diagnostics and Anomaly Detection." We also included the following appendixes:

1. the analysis pattern classification;
2. the influence of narratology and contemporary mathematics on some pattern language names.

We also checked and corrected no longer available endnote links.

Preface to the Second Edition

33 new trace and log analysis patterns have been discovered since the publication of the first edition almost two years ago. Memory Dump Analysis Anthology has also grown to 3,800 pages with the publication of volumes 8b, 9a, and 9b. Significant advances were made in software diagnostics theory that is reflected in the added analysis patterns. This edition also features better index, minor corrections to the patterns from the first edition, and one pattern from the forthcoming volume 10a.

In addition to previous contact details, please also refer to Facebook trace analysis page, DA+TA group, and The Software Diagnostics Group on LinkedIn:

http://www.facebook.com/TraceAnalysis
http://www.facebook.com/groups/dumpanalysis
http://www.linkedin.com/groups/8473045

Preface to the First Edition

The need for this reference book arose when we started working on the next version of "Accelerated Windows Software Trace Analysis" training[1]. The previous version was two years old, and Software Diagnostics Institute[2] had already added 40 more trace and log analysis patterns to their catalog. All of them (almost 100 patterns in total) were scattered among 3,300 pages of various Memory Dump Analysis Anthology volumes (3 – 7, 8a), and a few found only in Software Diagnostics Library[3]. So we decided to reprint all these patterns and their illustrations in one small book and full color for easy reference. During editing, we also corrected various mistakes.

If you encounter any error, please send me a personal message using this contact e-mail:

dmitry.vostokov@dumpanalysis.org

Alternatively, via Twitter @ DumpAnalysis

About the Author

Dmitry Vostokov is an internationally recognized expert, speaker, educator, scientist, inventor, and author. He is the founder of the pattern-oriented software diagnostics, forensics, and prognostics discipline (Systematic Software Diagnostics), and Software Diagnostics Institute (DA+TA: DumpAnalysis.org + TraceAnalysis.org). Vostokov has also authored more than 50 books on software diagnostics, anomaly detection and analysis, software and memory forensics, root cause analysis and problem solving, memory dump analysis, debugging, software trace and log analysis, reverse engineering, and malware analysis. He has over 25 years of experience in software architecture, design, development, and maintenance in various industries, including leadership, technical, and people management roles. Dmitry also founded Syndromatix, Anolog.io, BriteTrace, DiaThings, Logtellect, OpenTask Iterative and Incremental Publishing (OpenTask.com), Software Diagnostics Technology and Services (former Memory Dump Analysis Services) PatternDiagnostics.com, and Software Prognostics. In his spare time, he presents various topics on Debugging.TV and explores Software Narratology, its further development as Narratology of Things and Diagnostics of Things (DoT), Software Pathology, and Quantum Software Diagnostics. His current interest areas are theoretical software diagnostics and its mathematical and computer science foundations, application of formal logic, artificial intelligence, machine learning and data mining to diagnostics and anomaly detection, software diagnostics engineering and diagnostics-driven development, diagnostics workflow and interaction. Recent interest areas also include cloud native computing, security, automation, functional programming, applications of category theory to software development and big data, and diagnostics of artificial intelligence.

Introduction

The primary goal of this reference is to assemble software trace and log analysis pattern language that can also be applied to narratives, texts, and data in general, classify analysis patterns into several categories and arrange them as a cross-referenced dictionary. So, in this introduction, we review essential fundamentals. Some examples are Windows-specific, although our pattern language is general and can also be used for other OS trace and log analysis, such as Linux and macOS.

We review basic concepts related to software traces and logs. These concepts include processes, threads, components (or modules), source code files, source code or API functions, and stack traces (or backtraces). However, one additional concept stays out. It is called **Adjoint Thread**, and we introduce and discuss it after we review threads. Together with threads, adjoint threads are essential for software trace and log analysis.

What is a software trace or log? For our purposes, it is just a sequence of formatted messages sent from running software. They are usually arranged by time and can be considered as a software narrative story.

Software Trace and Log

- A sequence of formatted messages
- Arranged by time
- A narrative story

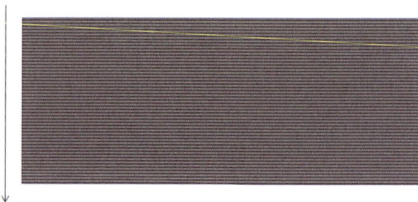

An operating system process is a container for resources such as memory, files, and synchronization objects. Even the OS kernel itself can be considered a process. Each process has its process identifier, PID, image name (for example, *notepad.exe*), and a list of associated loaded DLL modules (or shared libraries in Linux/macOS). An image name is also a module. It is important to remember that several processes can run in parallel, each having the same image name, for example, two instances of *notepad.exe*. For the latter example, most of the time, the list of shared libraries (DLLs) in both instances is identical. At the same time, one image name may correspond to completely different processes because, on the startup, a process may load different modules (shared libraries) for different purposes. Here a Windows example is the *svchost* executable. On a running Windows system, you can find many such *svchost* processes. When analyzing software logs, we can filter messages related to a specific PID or image name to find abnormal behavior according to the expected message flow. Here is a typical example: after the middle of the log, we no longer see any messages from a specific PID, not even any termination or process end messages.

Process

- PID
- Session
- Image Name
- Modules (DLLs, Shared Libraries)
- Examples:

svchost.exe   PID 1   PID 2

notepad.exe   PID 3   PID 4

In Windows and macOS, a thread is an execution unit owned by some process. In Linux, threads are almost the same as processes but share the same virtual memory. Remember that trace messages come from some thread because we must execute code to emit a trace message. Each thread is executed on some CPU and, in general, can have its CPU changed during execution history. Filtering by threads, for example, allows us to find any anomalous behavior, such as blocked execution activity and various execution delays. The pictorial example shows a discontinuity for TID 2 and a delay in TID 1.

Thread

- TID

- CPU

- Context

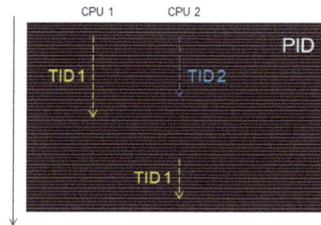

If a thread is a linear ordered flow of activities associated with a particular TID, as seen from a trace message perspective through time, we can also extend this flow concept and consider a linear flow of activities associated with some other parameter such as PID, CPU ID, or message text. Such messages have different TIDs but have some chosen constant parameter or column value in the trace viewing tool. The name **adjoint** comes from the fact that in threads of activity, TID stays the same, but other message attributes vary; in adjoint threads, we have the opposite. In Windows Process Monitor, we use exclusive and inclusive filtering to form adjoint threads. By applying complex filtering criteria, we get **Adjoint**

Threads from other adjoint threads, for example, an adjoint thread with specific PID and file activity formed after an inspection of an adjoint thread with the same image name, *svchost.exe*.

Adjoint Thread

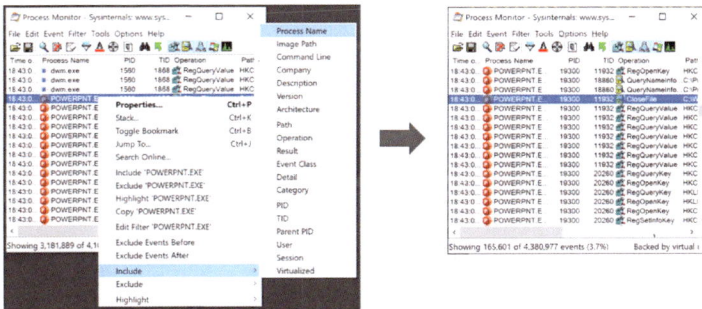

Trace messages come from a thread that belongs to a PID, but the code to emit them resides in source code files. Some source code files, such as static library code, can also be reused and included in different modules. Such DLL modules or shared libraries can also be loaded into different processes, for example, hooking modules. Therefore, Source or Module (in a simpler) case is another grouping of messages based on subsystem and functional division that may include several source code files. By module or source filtering, we can see subsystem activities.

Component / Module / Source

- Module Name
- Source Folder

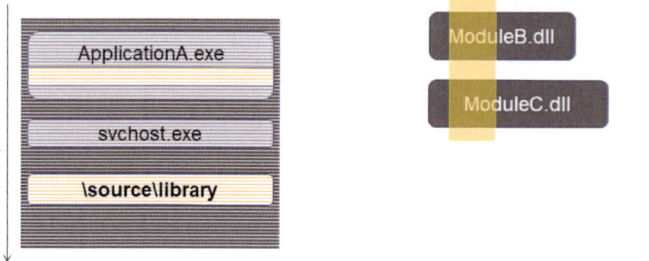

Source code consists of files, and each file has some functions inside that do the actual tracing. With a file or function filtering, we can see the flow of certain functionality that is more fine-grained than source or module adjoint thread.

File and Function

```
// MainApp.c
foo () {
    trace("foo: entry");
    // do stuff
    trace("foo: exit");
}
```

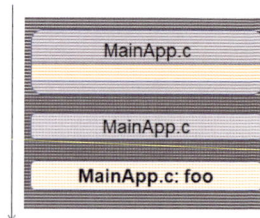

A formatted trace message is just a sentence with some invariant and variable parts. It is possible to trace invariant and variable parts, the so-called **Message Invariant** (page 198), and **Data Flow** (page 95) analysis patterns.

Trace Message

```
// MainApp.c
foo () {
  trace("foo: entry");
  int result = bar();
  trace("bar result: %");
  trace("foo: exit");
}
```

Invariant	Variable	Invariant	Variable	...

Because each trace message originated from some function in the source code, it has an associated stack trace similar to a live debugging scenario where we put a breakpoint at a trace message code location. Also, please note that stack traces (or backtraces) are read from bottom to top, as in a debugger.

Stack Trace

```
// MainApp.c
main() {
  trace("start");
  foo();
}

foo() {
  trace("foo: entry");
  bar();
}

bar() {
  trace("bar: entry");
  // do stuff
}
```

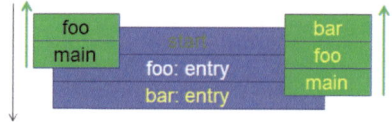

To illustrate trace analysis patterns graphically, we use the simplified abstract pictorial representation of a typical software trace or log. It has essential features such as message number, time, PID, TID, and message text. These and more complex diagrams constitute the so-called **Dia|gram** language. Sometimes, for illustration purposes, we provide trace fragments in a textual form where we include or exclude certain message attributes (or columns) such as message source or module, time, or date.

Minimal Trace Graphs

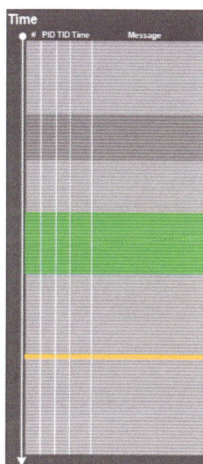

No	Module	PID	TID	Date	Time	Message
1	ModuleA	4280	1736	5/28/2012	08:53:50.496	Trace message 1
2	ModuleB	6212	6216	5/28/2012	08:53:52.876	Trace message 2
[..]						

Analysis patterns may be classified into several categories. The **Vocabulary** category consists of patterns related to a problem description from a user's point of view. The **Error** category covers general error distribution patterns. These patterns are related to error and failure messages, either explicitly stating an error or indirectly via an error code, abnormal function return value, or status values in the failure range. We also consider **Traces as Wholes** (here we ignore trace or log message contents and treat all messages statistically), their **Large Scale** structure (about the coarse grain structure of software traces and logs where the division unit is often a component or some high-level functionality), **Activity** patterns related to various software activities we see in logs and traces (most of them involve time dependency), patterns related to individual trace **Message** structure, patterns related to collections of messages (the so-called **Blocks**), and finally, patterns related to several traces and logs as a collection of artifacts from software incident (**Trace Set**). There are also **Memory**, **Text**, **Code**, and **Data** categories.

[This page intentionally left blank]

A

Abnormal Value

While preparing a presentation on malware narratives[4], we found that one essential pattern is missing from the current log analysis pattern catalog. Most of the time, we see some abnormal or unexpected value in a software trace or log, such as a network address outside the expected range, and this triggers a further investigation. The message structure may have the same **Message Invariant** (page 198), but the variable part may contain such values as depicted graphically:

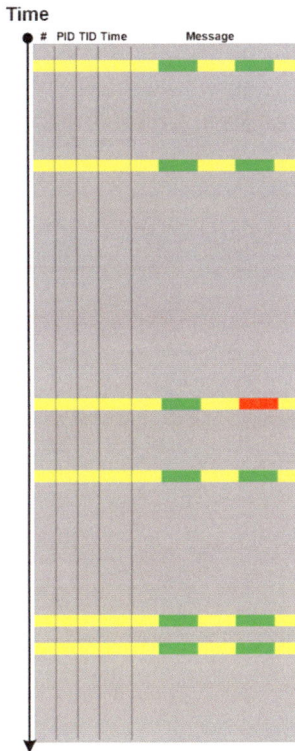

Please note that we also have **Significant Event** (page 270) pattern that is more general and also covers messages without variable parts or just suspicious log entries.

Activity Disruption

Sometimes a few **Error Messages** (page 123) or **Periodic Errors** (page 231) with low **Statement Density** (page 286) for specific **Activity Regions** (page 39) or **Adjoint Threads of Activity** (for a specific component, file, or function, page 48) may constitute **Activity Disruption**. If the particular functionality was no longer available at the logging time, then its unavailability may not be explained by such disruptions, and such messages may be considered **False Positive Errors** (page 134) in relation to the reported problem:

Time

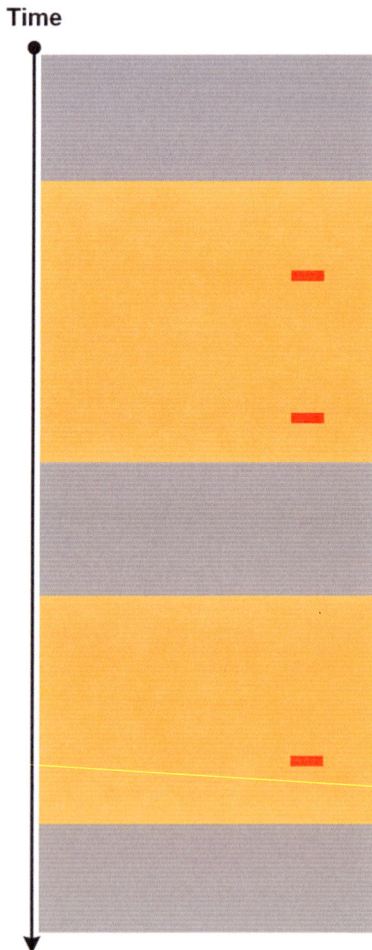

But, if we have **Periodic Message Blocks** (page 233) containing only **Periodic Errors** (page 231), **Activity Region** (page 39) or **Adjoint Thread** (page 48) **Discontinuity** (page 115), or simply **No Activity** (page 219), then we may have the complete cessation of activity that may correlate with the unavailable functionality:

Activity Divergence

Sometimes we have several **Threads of Activity** (page 296, for example, from the same process) visible for a certain period, and then suddenly, we see only one such thread till the end of a trace (or even none). It may be an indication of an application hang or some other abnormal behavior if several active threads doing logging are normal. If we consider such activities (including **Adjoint Threads**, page 48) as vectors running through some temporal "surface," we can use an analogy of a divergence[5]:

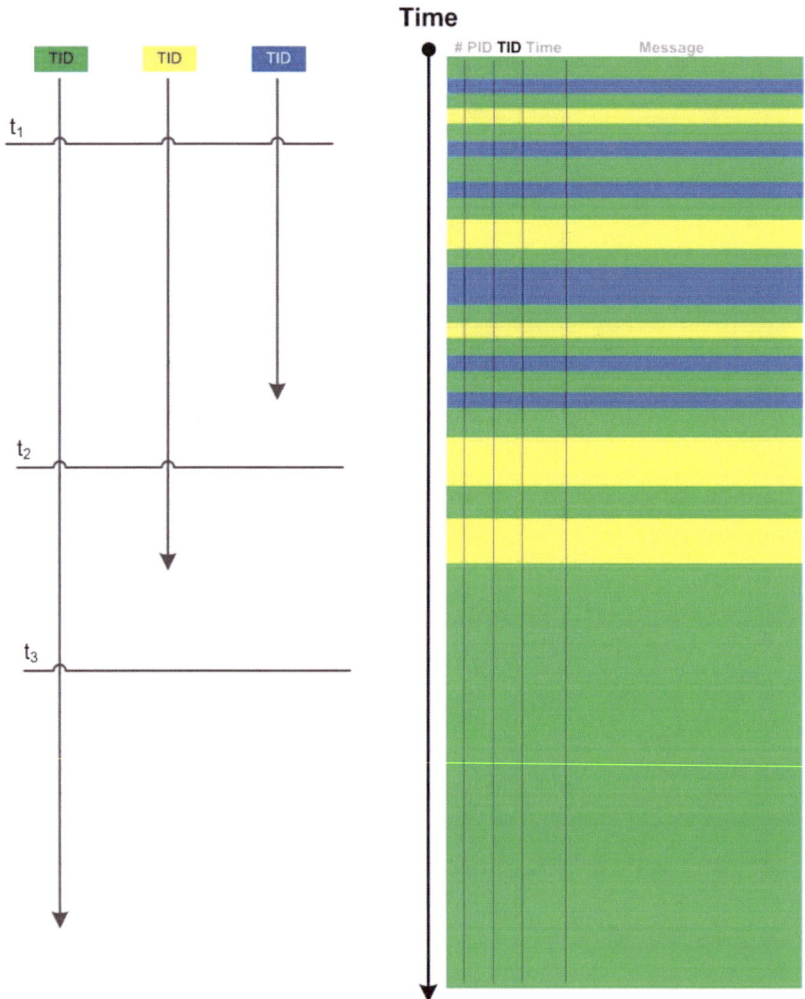

Activity Overlap

Sometimes specific parts of simultaneous **Use Case Trails** (page 354), blocks of **Significant Events** (page 270), or **Message Sets** (page 201) in general may overlap. It may point to possible synchronization problems such as race conditions (prognostics) or be visible root causes of them if such problems are reported (diagnostics). We call this pattern **Activity Overlap**:

For example, a first request may start a new session, and we expect the second request to be processed in the same already-established session:

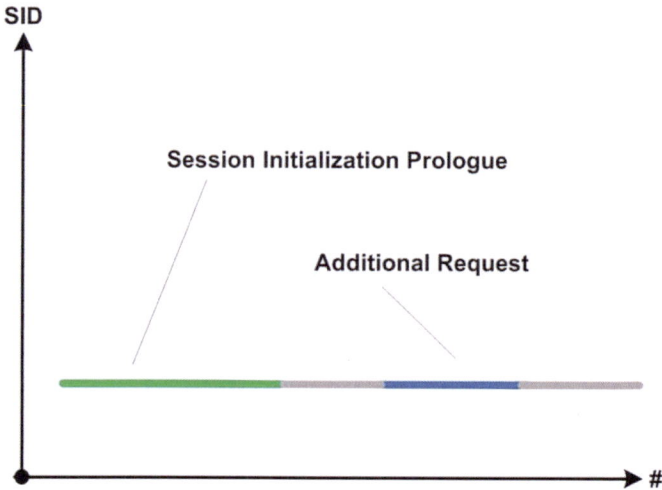

SID

Session Initialization Prologue

Additional Request

#

However, users report that the second session started upon the second request. If we filter the execution log by session id, we find out that session initialization prologs (**Trace Partition**, page 327) are overlapped. The new session started because the first session initialization was not completed:

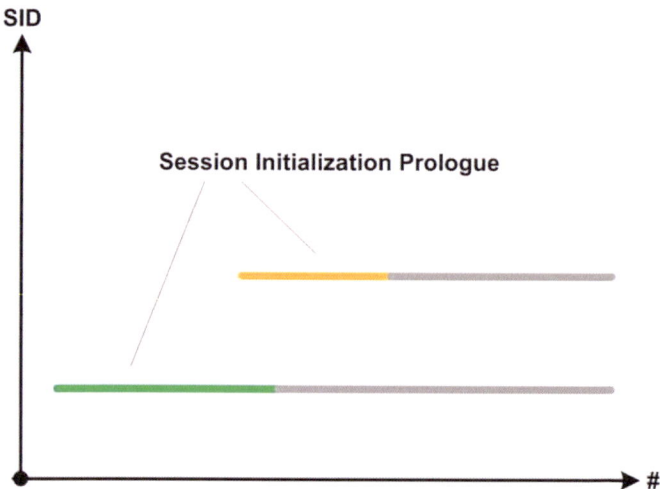

SID

Session Initialization Prologue

#

Activity Packet

Sometimes we are interested in **Message Set** (page 202) with the same time attribute value (or rounded to some digit). We call this analysis pattern **Activity Packet** by analogy with wave packets [6]. It may allow the identification of related threads and activities.

Time

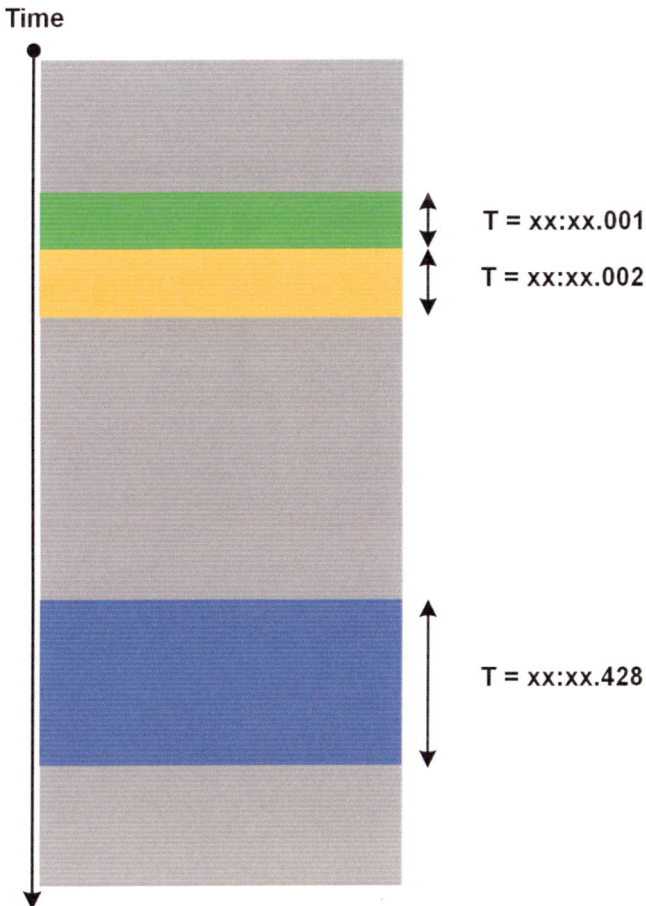

$T = xx:xx.001$

$T = xx:xx.002$

$T = xx:xx.428$

It differs from **Activity Quantum** (page 40) analysis pattern where the time attribute value may change for continuous **Message Set** with the same thread ID.

Activity Quantum

Having chosen a trace message, we are interested in its **Message Context** (page 191), which can span all "continuous" messages before and after from the same **Thread of Activity** (page 296). We call it **Activity Quantum,** which is variable and independent from the so-called CPU quantum. Different messages from **Activity Quantum** may be executed on different CPUs. The following diagram depicts this analysis pattern:

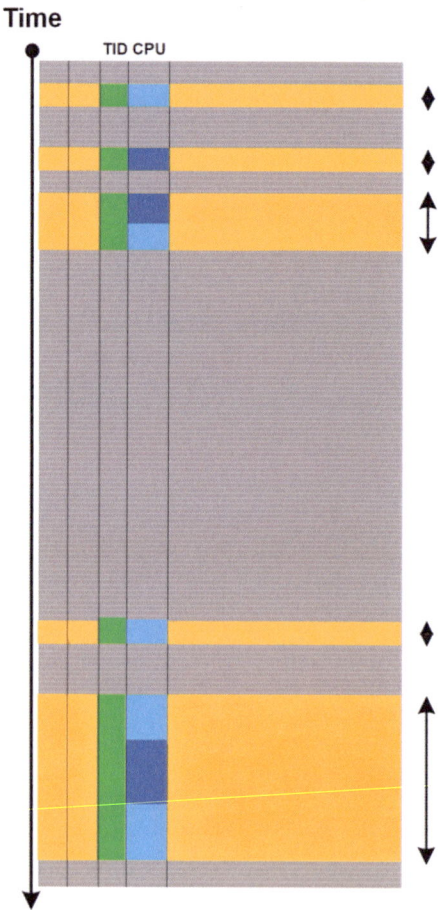

Activity Region

When looking at lengthy traces with thousands and millions of messages (trace statements), we can see regions of activity where the statement current (J_m, msg/s) is much higher than in surrounding temporal regions (**Statement Current**, page 286). Here is an illustration for a typical ETW[7] trace where a middle region of activity (J_{m2}) signifies a system performing some response function as a user session initialization and application launch:

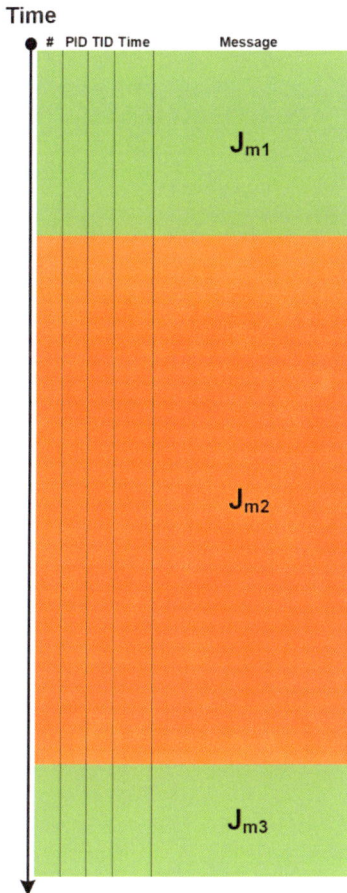

Statement current $J_{m2} > \max (J_{m1}, J_{m3})$

Activity Theatre

In addition to **Message Patterns** (page 201), there are higher-level patterns of specific activities and **Motives** (page 214). Such activities may or may not coincide with specific components (modules) because they may be grouped based on implementation messages, software internals semantics and not on architectural and design entities (as in **Use Case Trail** analysis pattern, page 354). Moreover, the same components may "play" different activity roles. Once assigned, **Activity Theatre** "scripts" can be compared with "scripts" from other traces and logs (**Inter-Correlation**, page 167) or different parts of the same log (**Intra-Correlation**, page 170). This pattern is illustrated in the following diagram:

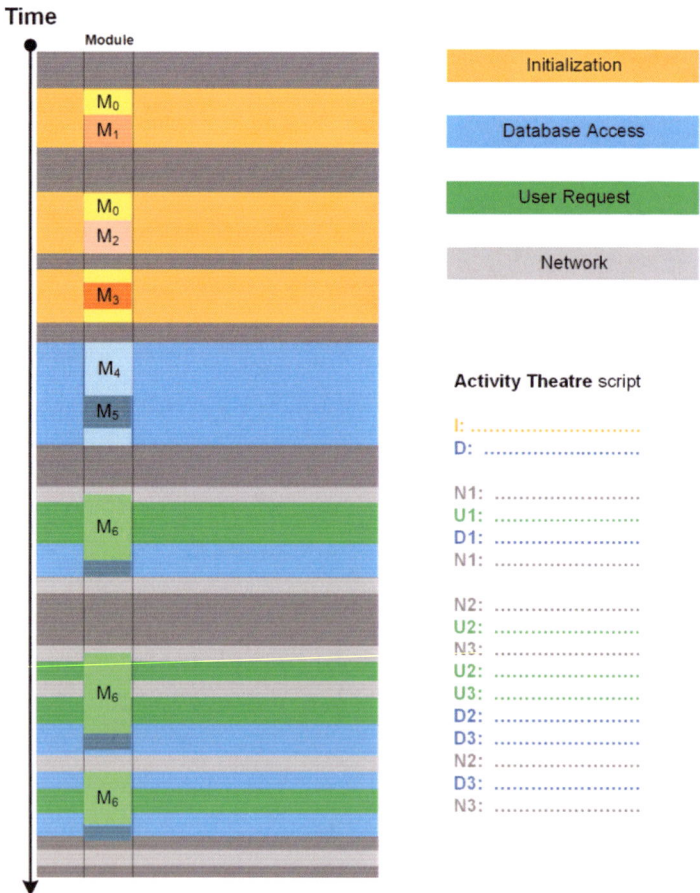

Adjoint Message

By analogy with **Adjoint Thread of Activity** (page 48), we introduce **Adjoint Message** analysis pattern. Most, if not all, analysis patterns focus on log message text and consider TID, PID, Module, source file, and function as its attributes. However, we can choose one of the attributes and consider it a message in its own right, with the original message text now consigned as another attribute. Then we can analyze the structure of the trace from the perspective of that newly selected message:

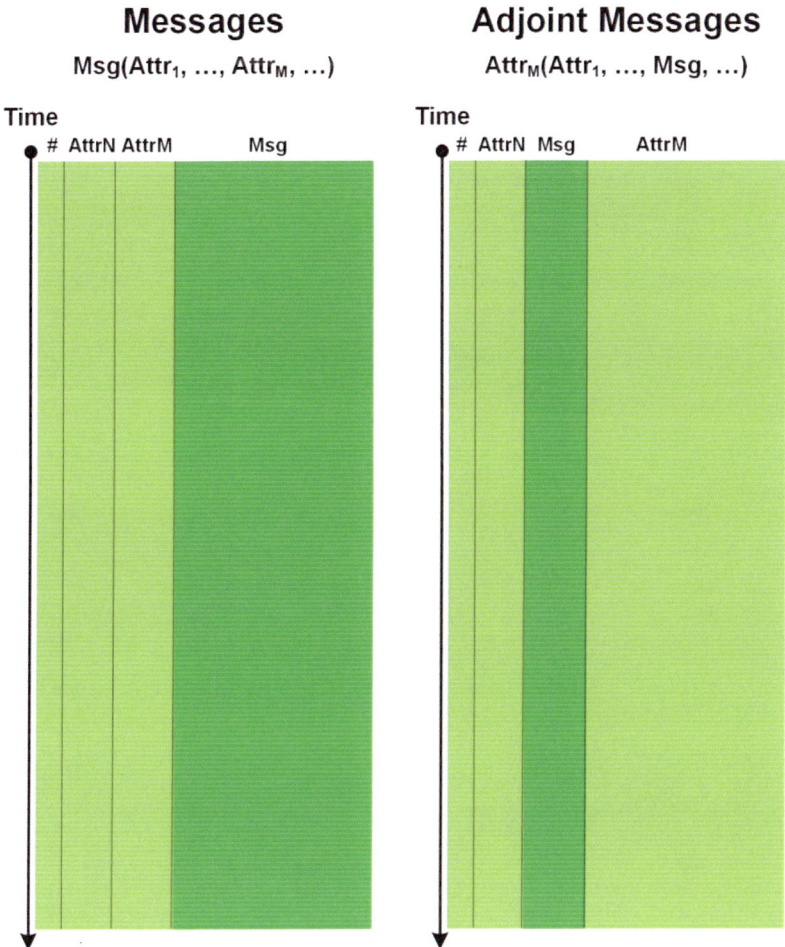

Messages

$Msg(Attr_1, ..., Attr_M, ...)$

Time

\# AttrN AttrM   Msg

Adjoint Messages

$Attr_M(Attr_1, ..., Msg, ...)$

Time

\# AttrN Msg   AttrM

Since the number of different message values now is smaller (for example, module names) compared to normal trace messages, we can use them in protein-like encoding and structure analysis schemes (see *Software Trace and Logs as Proteins*[8]). We metaphorically name **Adjoint Messages** as Amino-acid-Messages (**A-Messages**). We can also compress the same message sequences into one message, which may be useful for pattern matching (and even use different color intensities to represent message cardinalities):

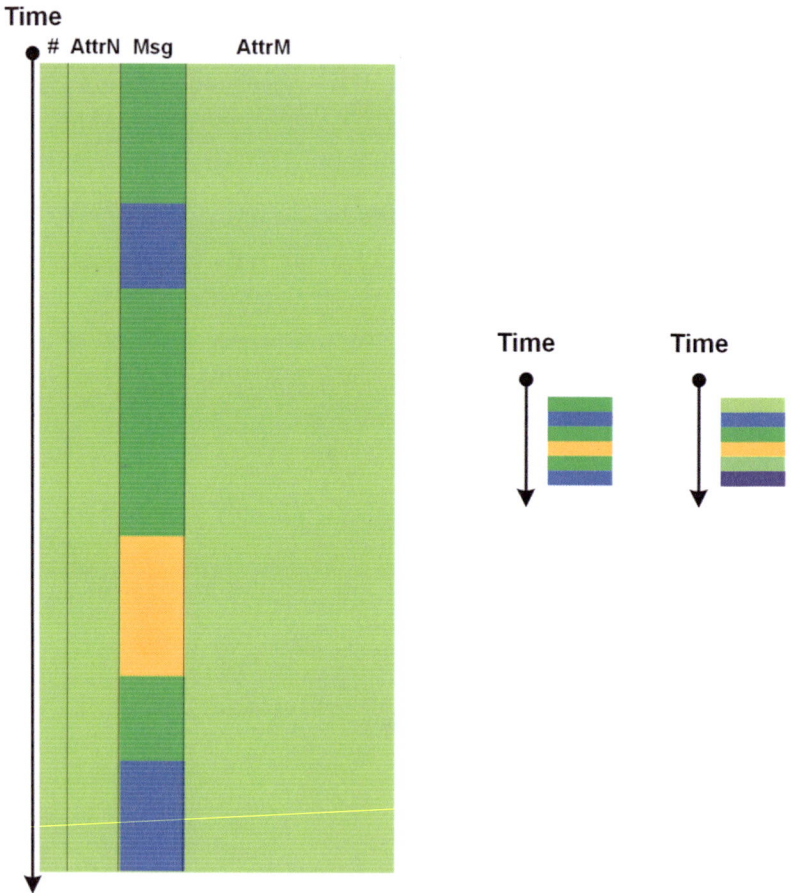

Adjoint Space

Sometimes we need memory reference information not available in software traces and logs, for example, to see the pointer dereferences and to follow pointers and linked structures. In such cases, memory dumps saved during logging sessions may help. In the case of process memory dumps, we can even have several **Step Dumps**[9]. We may force complete or kernel memory dumps after saving a log file. We call such pattern **Adjoint Space**:

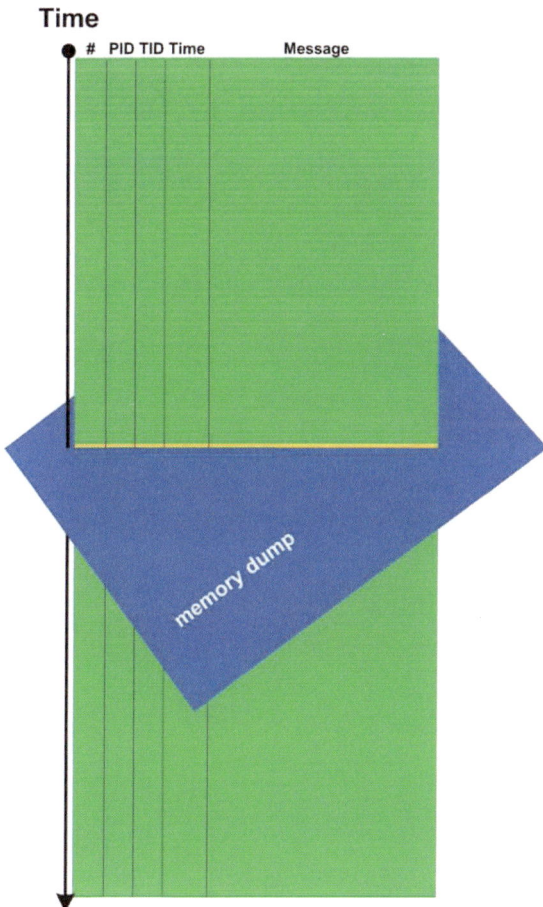

Then we can analyze logs and memory dumps together, for example, to follow pointer data further in memory space:

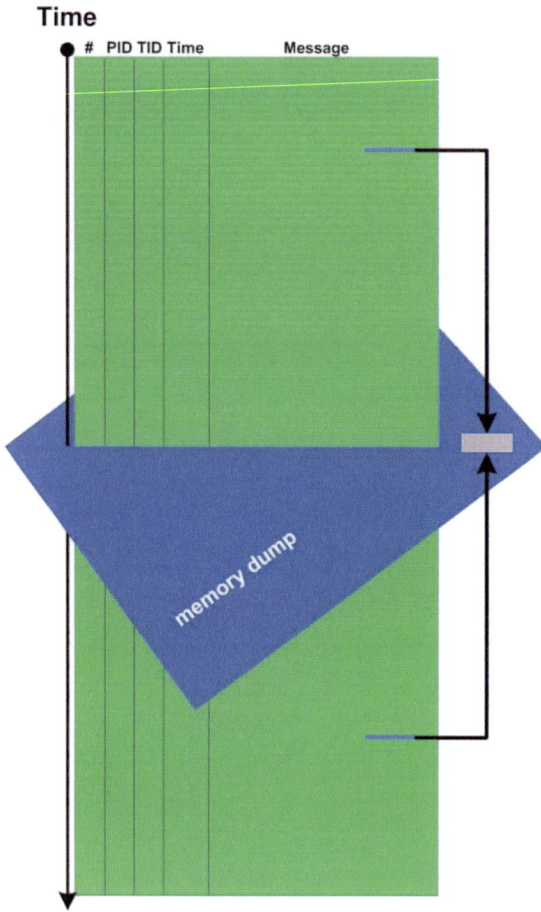

There is also a reverse situation when we use logs to see past data changes before memory snapshot time (**Paratext** memory analysis pattern[10]):

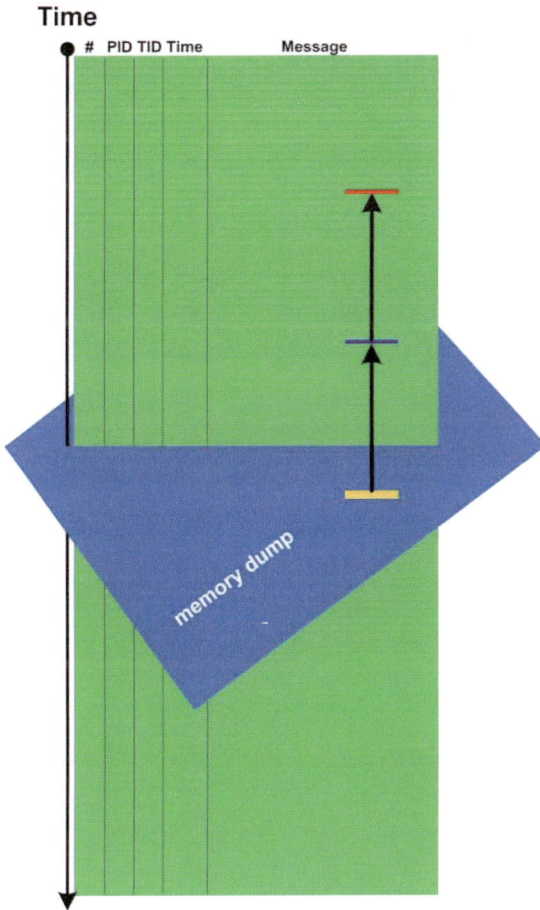

Adjoint Thread of Activity

This pattern is an extension of **Thread of Activity** (page 296) based on the concept of *multibraiding* (see below). There is also an article published in Debugged! MZ/PE magazine[11].

Having considered computational threads as braided strings[12] and after discerning software trace analysis patterns, we can see formatted and tabulated software trace output in a new light and employ the "fabric of traces" and braid metaphors for the **Adjoint Thread** concept. This new concept was motivated by reading about *Extended Phenotype*[13] and extensive analysis of ETW[14]-based traces. The word *Adjoint* was borrowed from mathematics[15] because the concept we discuss below resembles this metaphorical formula: (Thread A, B) = [A, Thread B]. Let me first illustrate adjoint threading using simplified trace tables. Consider this generalized software trace example (we omitted the date and time column for visual clarity):

#	Source Dir	PID	TID	File Name	Function	Message
1	\src\subsystemA	2792	5676	file1.cpp	fooA	Message text...
2	\src\subsystemA	2792	5676	file1.cpp	fooA	Message text...
3	\src\subsystemA	2792	5676	file1.cpp	fooA	Message text...
4	\src\lib	2792	5680	file2.cpp	barA	Message text...
5	\src\subsystemA	2792	5680	file1.cpp	fooA	Message text...
6	\src\subsystemA	2792	5676	file1.cpp	fooA	Message text...
7	\src\lib	2792	5680	file2.cpp	fooA	Message text...
8	\src\lib	2792	5680	file2.cpp	fooA	Message text...
9	\src\subsystemB	2792	3912	file3.cpp	barB	Message text...
10	\src\subsystemB	2792	3912	file3.cpp	barB	Message text...
11	\src\subsystemB	2792	3912	file3.cpp	barB	Message text...
12	\src\subsystemB	2792	3912	file3.cpp	barB	Message text...
13	\src\subsystemB	2792	3912	file3.cpp	barB	Message text...
14	\src\subsystemB	2792	3912	file3.cpp	barB	Message text...
15	\src\subsystemB	2792	2992	file4.cpp	fooB	Message text...
16	\src\subsystemB	2792	3008	file4.cpp	fooB	Message text...
...	...	...	...	...	...	...

We see several threads in a process PID 2792. We can filter trace messages that belong to any column, and if we filter by TID, we get a view of any **Thread of Activity** (page 296). However, each thread can "run" through any source directory, file name, or function. If a function belongs to a library, then multiple threads access it. This source location (we can consider it as a subsystem), file, or function view of activity is called an **Adjoint Thread.** For example, if we filter only the *subsystemA* column in the trace above, we get this table:

#	Source Dir	PID	TID	File Name	Function	Message
1	\src\subsystemA	2792	5676	file1.cpp	fooA	Message ...
2	\src\subsystemA	2792	5676	file1.cpp	fooA	Message ...
3	\src\subsystemA	2792	5676	file1.cpp	fooA	Message ...
5	\src\subsystemA	2792	5680	file1.cpp	fooA	Message ...
6	\src\subsystemA	2792	5676	file1.cpp	fooA	Message ...
7005	\src\subsystemA	2792	5664	file1.cpp	fooA	Message ...
10198	\src\subsystemA	2792	5664	file1.cpp	fooA	Message ...
10364	\src\subsystemA	2792	5664	file1.cpp	fooA	Message ...
10417	\src\subsystemA	2792	5664	file1.cpp	fooA	Message ...
10420	\src\subsystemA	2792	5676	file1.cpp	fooA	Message ...
10422	\src\subsystemA	2792	5680	file1.cpp	fooA	Message ...
10587	\src\subsystemA	2792	5664	file1.cpp	fooA	Message ...
10767	\src\subsystemA	2792	5680	file1.cpp	fooA	Message ...
11126	\src\subsystemA	2792	5668	file1.cpp	fooA	Message ...
11131	\src\subsystemA	2792	5680	file1.cpp	fooA	Message ...
11398	\src\subsystemA	2792	5676	file1.cpp	fooA	Message ...
11501	\src\subsystemA	2792	5668	file1.cpp	fooA	Message ...
11507	\src\subsystemA	2792	5668	file1.cpp	fooA	Message ...
11509	\src\subsystemA	2792	5664	file1.cpp	fooA	Message ...
11513	\src\subsystemA	2792	5680	file1.cpp	fooA	Message ...
11524	\src\subsystemA	2792	5668	file1.cpp	fooA	Message ...
...	...	...	...	...	...	...

We can graphically view the *subsystemA* as a braid string that "permeates the fabric of threads":

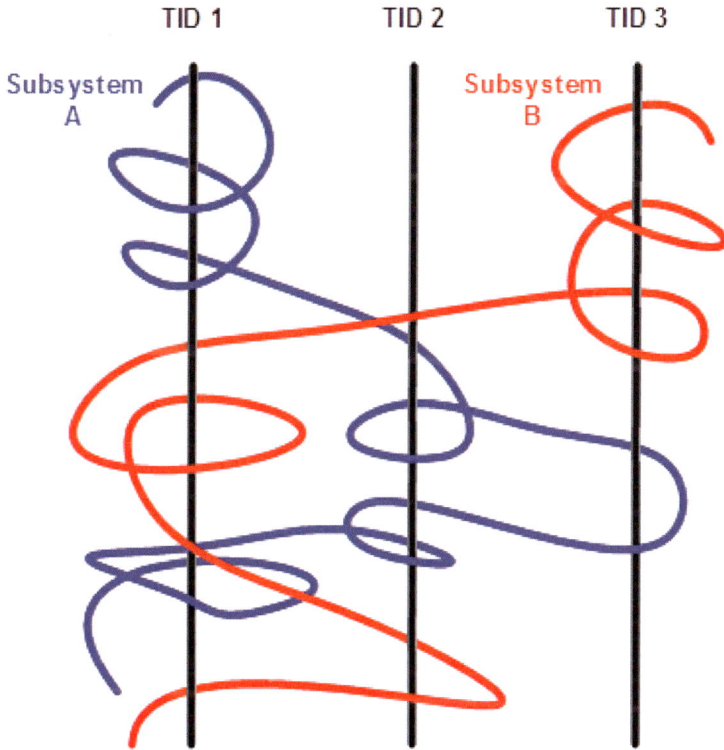

We can get many different braids by changing filters, hence *mult*braiding. Here is another example of a driver source file view initially permeating two process contexts and four threads:

#	Source Dir	PID	TID	File Name	Function	Message
41	\src\sys\driver	3636	3848	*entry.c*	DriverEntry	IOCTL …
80	\src\sys\driver	3636	3896	*entry.c*	DriverEntry	IOCTL …
99	\src\sys\driver	3636	3896	*entry.c*	DriverEntry	IOCTL …
102	\src\sys\driver	3636	3896	*entry.c*	DriverEntry	IOCTL …
179	\src\sys\driver	3636	3896	*entry.c*	DriverEntry	IOCTL …
180	\src\sys\driver	3636	3896	*entry.c*	DriverEntry	IOCTL …
311	\src\sys\driver	3636	3896	*entry.c*	DriverEntry	IOCTL …
447	\src\sys\driver	3636	3896	*entry.c*	DriverEntry	IOCTL …

448	\src\sys\driver	3636	3896	*entry.c*	DriverEntry	IOCTL ...
457	\src\sys\driver	2792	5108	*entry.c*	DriverEntry	IOCTL ...
608	\src\sys\driver	3636	3896	*entry.c*	DriverEntry	IOCTL ...
614	\src\sys\driver	3636	3896	*entry.c*	DriverEntry	IOCTL ...
655	\src\sys\driver	3636	3896	*entry.c*	DriverEntry	IOCTL ...
675	\src\sys\driver	3636	3896	*entry.c*	DriverEntry	IOCTL ...
678	\src\sys\driver	3636	3896	*entry.c*	DriverEntry	IOCTL ...
680	\src\sys\driver	3636	3896	*entry.c*	DriverEntry	IOCTL ...
681	\src\sys\driver	3636	3896	*entry.c*	DriverEntry	IOCTL ...
1145	\src\sys\driver	3636	4960	*entry.c*	DriverEntry	IOCTL ...
1153	\src\sys\driver	3636	4960	*entry.c*	DriverEntry	IOCTL ...
1154	\src\sys\driver	3636	4960	*entry.c*	DriverEntry	IOCTL ...
...	...	...	...	...	...	...

The following diagram illustrates **Adjoint Thread of Activity** for a selected message:

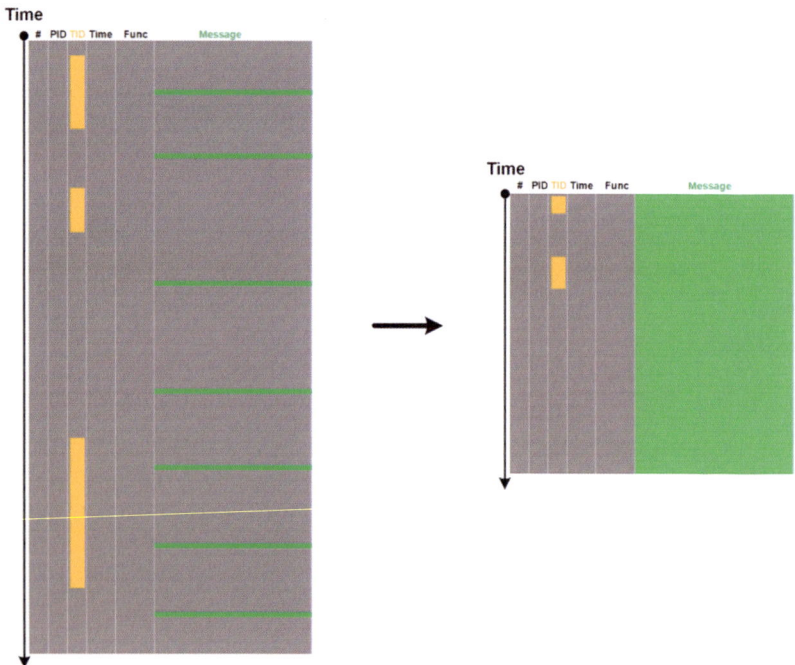

Anchor Messages

When a software trace is lengthy, it is useful to partition it into several regions based on a sequence of **Anchor Messages**. We can determine their choice by **Vocabulary Index** (page 362) or **Adjoint Thread of Activity** (page 48). For example, an ETW trace with almost 900,000 messages recorded during a desktop connection for 6 minutes can be split into 14 segments by the adjoint thread of the DLL_PROCESS_ATTACH message (the message was generated by *DllMain* of an injected module, not shown in the trace output for formatting clarity):

```
#       PID  TID  Time          Message
24226   2656 3480 10:41:05.774  AppA.exe: DLL_PROCESS_ATTACH
108813  4288 4072 10:41:05.774  AppB.exe: DLL_PROCESS_ATTACH
112246  4180 3836 10:41:05.940  DllHost.exe: DLL_PROCESS_ATTACH
135473  2040 3296 10:41:12.615  AppC.exe: DLL_PROCESS_ATTACH
694723  1112 1992 10:44:23.393  AppD.exe: DLL_PROCESS_ATTACH
703962  5020 1080 10:44:42.014  DllHost.exe: DLL_PROCESS_ATTACH
705511  4680 3564 10:44:42.197  DllHost.exe: DLL_PROCESS_ATTACH
705891  1528 2592 10:44:42.307  regedit.exe: DLL_PROCESS_ATTACH
785231  2992 4912 10:45:26.516  AppE.exe: DLL_PROCESS_ATTACH
786523  3984 1156 10:45:26.605  powershell.exe: DLL_PROCESS_ATTACH
817979  4188 4336 10:45:48.707  wermgr.exe: DLL_PROCESS_ATTACH
834875  3976 1512 10:45:52.342  LogonUI.exe: DLL_PROCESS_ATTACH
835229  4116 3540 10:45:52.420  AppG.exe: DLL_PROCESS_ATTACH
```

Each region can be analyzed independently for any anomalies, for example, to look for the answer to a question about why *wermgr.exe* was launched. We illustrate partitioning in the following schematic diagram:

It is also possible to make different trace segmentation by interleaving regions above with another set of **Anchor Messages** (page 53) comprising of the adjoint thread of the DLL_PROCESS_DETACH message:

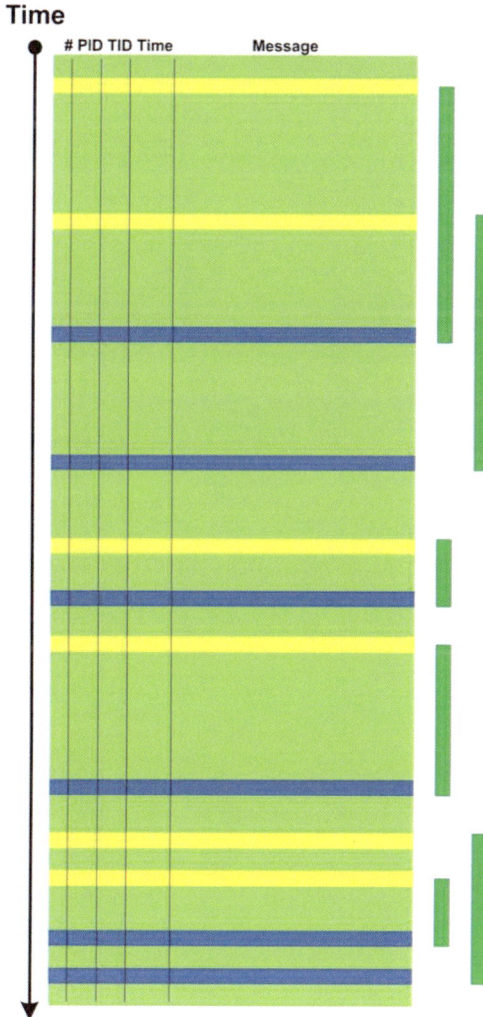

B

Back Trace

Usually, when we analyze traces and find **Anchor Message** (page 53) or **Error Message** (page 123), we backtrack using a combination of **Data Flow** (page 95) and **Message Sets** (page 201). Then we select the appropriate log messages to form **Back Trace** leading to a possible root cause message:

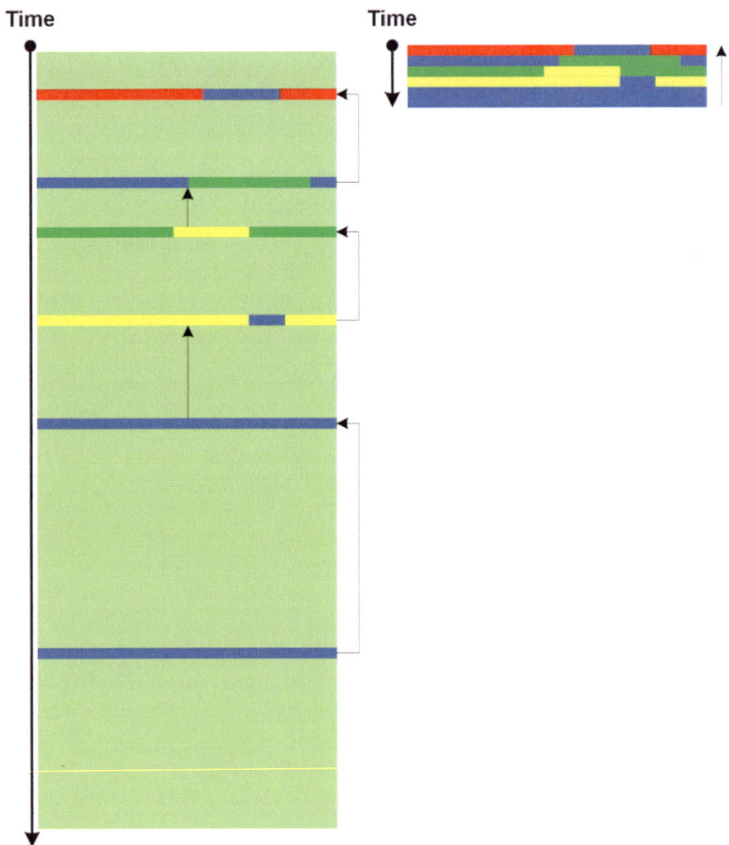

This pattern differs from **Error Thread** (page 124) pattern that just backtracks messages with the same TID (or, in general, ATID[16]). It also differs from **Exception Stack Trace** (page 129) pattern, which is just a serialized stack trace from a memory snapshot.

Background and Foreground Components

A metaphorical bijection [17] from the literary narratology to software narratology [18] provides a pattern of **Background and Foreground Components**. We can easily illustrate it on pseudo-trace color diagrams. For example, suppose we troubleshoot a graphical issue using an ETW trace containing the output from all components of the problem system. Graphics components and their messages are considered foreground for a trace viewer (a person) against numerous background components (for example, database, file, and registry access, shown in shades of green):

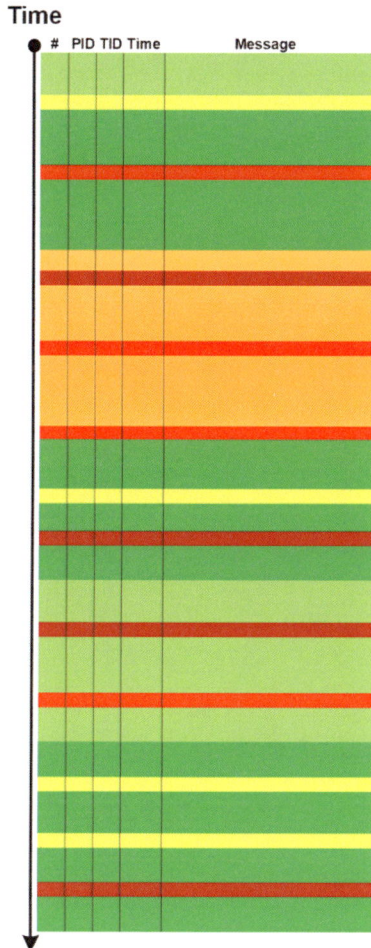

Some race viewers (for example, Process Monitor) can filter out background component messages and present only foreground modules (that I propose to call the *component foregrounding*):

Of course, this process is iterative and parts of what once was foreground become background and candidate for further filtering:

Basic Facts

A typical trace is a detailed narrative accompanied by a problem description that lists essential facts. For this reason, the first task of any trace analysis is to check the presence of **Basic Facts** in the trace. If they are not visible or do not correspond, the trace was possibly not recorded during the problem occurrence or was taken from a different computer or under different conditions. Here is an example. A user "test01" cannot connect to a published application in a terminal services environment. We look at the trace and find this statement:

```
No   PID  TID  Date      Time         Statement
[...]
3903 3648 5436 4/29/2009 16:17:36.150 User Name: test01
[...]
```

At least we can be sure that this trace was taken for the user *test01*, especially when we expect this or similar trace statements. If we do not see this trace statement, we may suppose that the trace was taken at the wrong time, for example, when the problem had already happened.

We suggest the following taxonomy of **Basic Facts**:

- Functional facts: *Expected a dialog to enter data.*
- Non-functional facts: *CPU consumption is 100%.*
- Identification facts: *Application name, PID, username.*

Bifurcation Point

The following two software traces from working and non-working software environments are a perfect example of the pattern. We borrow the name of this pattern from catastrophe theory[19]:

Working trace (the issue is absent):

```
#    PID  TID  Message
[...]
25   2768 3056 Trace Statement A
26   3756 2600 Trace Statement B
27   3756 2600 Trace Statement C
[...]
149  3756  836 Trace Statement X (Query result: XXX)
150  3756  836 Trace Statement 150.1
151  3756  836 Trace Statement 151.1
152  3756  836 Trace Statement 152.1
153  3756  836 Trace Statement 153.1
[...]
```

Non-working trace (the issue is present):

```
#    PID  TID  Message
[...]
27   2768 3056 Trace Statement A
28   3756 2176 Trace Statement B
29   3756 2176 Trace Statement C
[...]
151  3756 5940 Trace Statement Y (Query result: YYY)
152  3756 5940 Trace Statement 152.2
153  3756 5940 Trace Statement 153.2
154  3756 5940 Trace Statement 154.2
155  3756 5940 Trace Statement 155.2
[...]
```

First, we notice that in both traces, PIDs are the same (2768 and 3756), and we can conclude for this reason that, most likely, both traces came from the same environment and session. Second, messages A, B, C, and further are identical up to messages X and Y. The latter two messages differ greatly in their query results, XXX and YYY. After that, message distribution differs greatly in both size and content. Despite the same tracing time, 15 seconds, **Statement Current** (page 286) is 155 msg/s for working and 388 msg/s for the non-working case.

We can easily observe **Bifurcation Points** when the tracing noise ratio is small, and, for example, in the case of terminal services environments, we can achieve that by selecting appropriate tracing modules based on problem description or filtering irrelevant modules from full traces.

The following diagram illustrates **Bifurcation Point**:

Blackout

We recently analyzed a Process Monitor log that had a several-hour gap that we call **Blackout**. If you see such a pattern, it might have the following possible causes:

- Some files from **Split Trace** (page 282) are missing;
- **Split Trace** file set was artificially created;
- The tracing scope system was paused or frozen (for example, a virtualized system), or restarted;
- The tracing itself was paused.

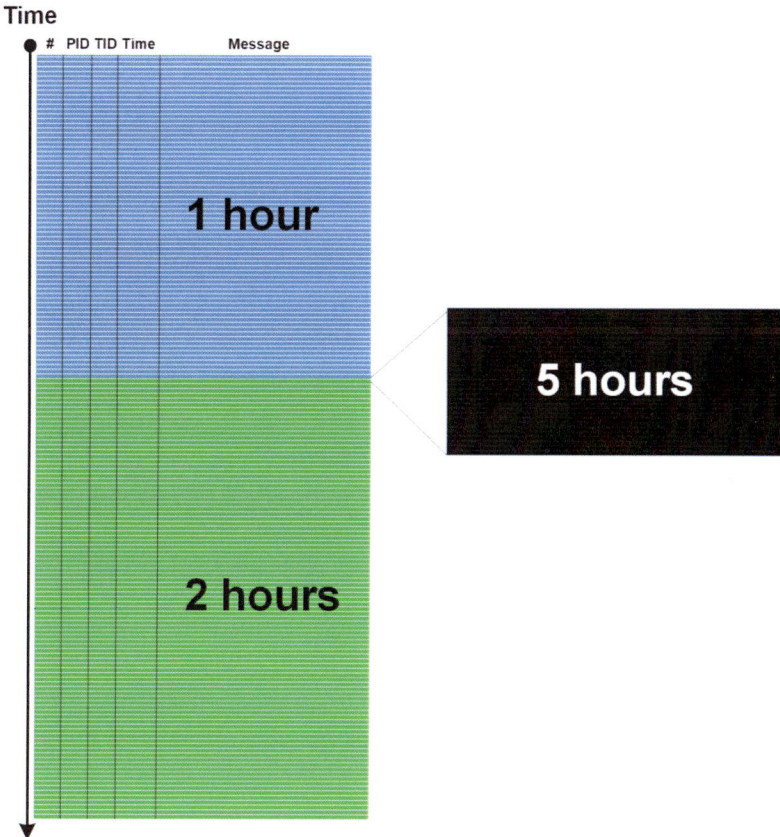

The **Blackout** pattern differs from Visibility Limit (page 360), where the latter is about the inherent inability to trace, but the former is only a temporary inability due to the abovementioned circumstances. It is also different from the **Discontinuity** (page 115) pattern, where the latter is about gaps in individual **Threads of Activity** (page 296) or **Adjoint Threads of Activity** (page 48).

Braid Group

One of the trace attributes we didn't pay much attention to in the past is the CPU. This column is present in some ETW-based trace implementations. As any trace attribute, it can be used to form an **Adjoint Thread of Activity** (page 48, as all messages from code are executed on that particular CPU). As we already considered threads as braids[20], we use braid groups[21] as a further metaphor. In our case, we combine CPUs and threads into one group, which uses permutation for CPU scheduling. Instead of permutations, twists may be modeled as changes of threads. The **Braid Group** analysis pattern is illustrated in the following diagram:

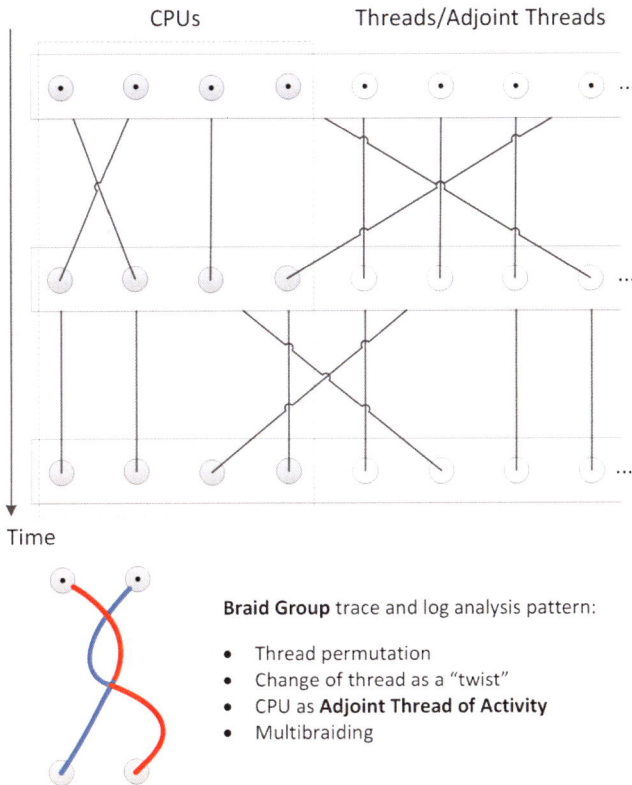

Braid Group trace and log analysis pattern:

- Thread permutation
- Change of thread as a "twist"
- CPU as **Adjoint Thread of Activity**
- Multibraiding

It is a preliminary description of the analysis pattern. For example, instead of multithreading, we can use *multibraiding*[22].

Braid of Activity

If we consider a log as a text, ignore its column structure, and search for the particular attribute value (for example, PID), we get **Message Set** (page 202) consisting of messages having that attribute value as a column (**Adjoint Thread of Activity**, page 48) and messages having that attribute value referenced in their message text. We call this pattern **Braid of Activity** because metaphorically, it looks like **Adjoint Threads of Activity** cross each other (like *multibraiding*[23]):

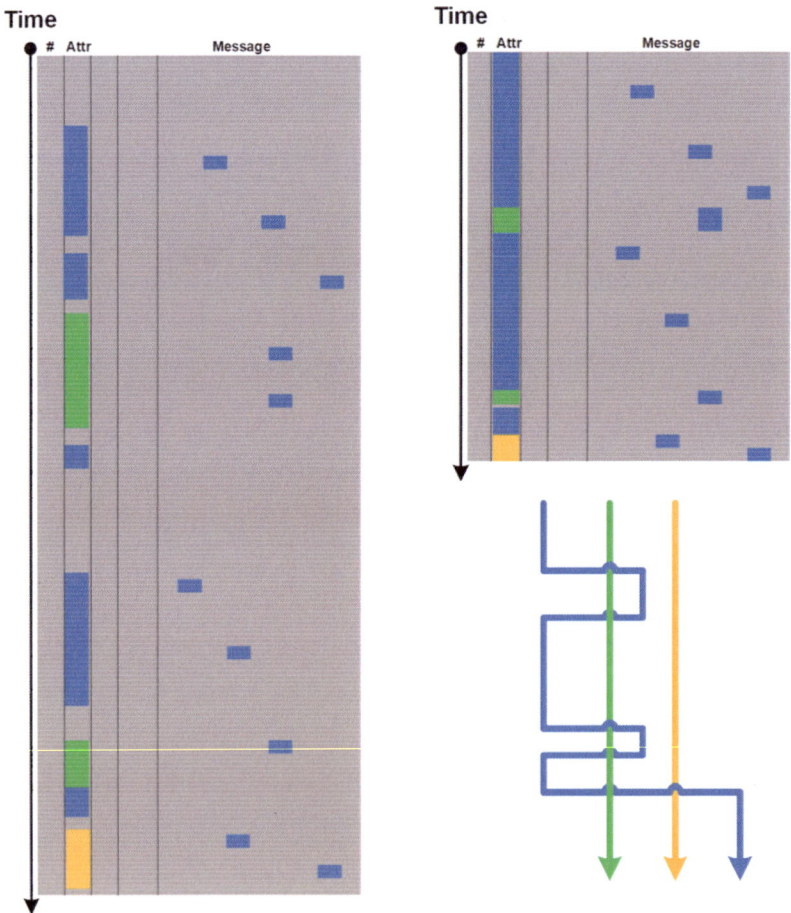

Break-in Activity

This analysis pattern is a message or a set of messages that surface just before the end of **Discontinuity** (page 115) of **Adjoint Thread** (page 48) and possibly triggered it:

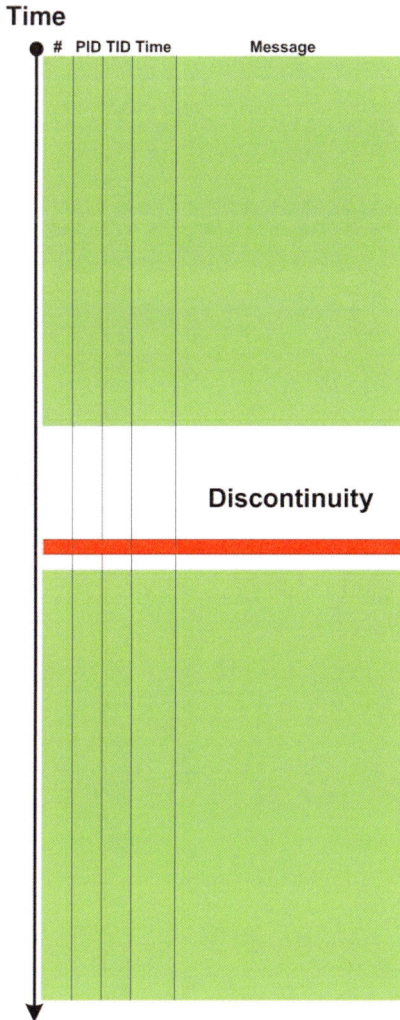

C

Calibrating Trace

Multiple traces and logs are usually collected for diagnosing distributed systems. Different tools and tracing settings (circular, sequential, file size limit) may be used, systems may be unsynchronized, and individual system tracing may be started at different times due to manual tracing setup and switching between systems. There may be **Blackouts** (page 63), **Circular** (page 78), and **Truncated** (page 351) traces. When we analyze such a trace set (**Inter-Correlation**, page 167), we usually select one trace or log used as **Calibrating Trace**. It is used for measuring all other traces against **Basic Facts** (page 60), such as start and end tracing times and the time of the problem. One such scenario is illustrated in the following diagram:

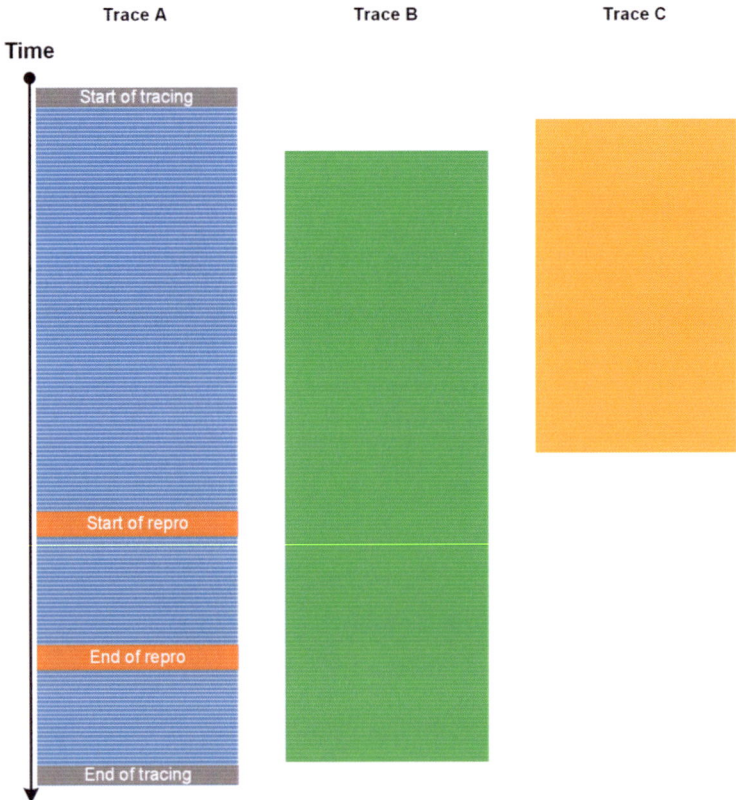

Cartesian Trace

Cartesian Trace analysis pattern has its analogical roots in a cartesian product[24]. It covers a case where we have a long trace and a few **Small DA+TA** (page 276) configuration traces (files). The former trace messages are associated with the latter messages (content or content changes), as depicted in the following diagram:

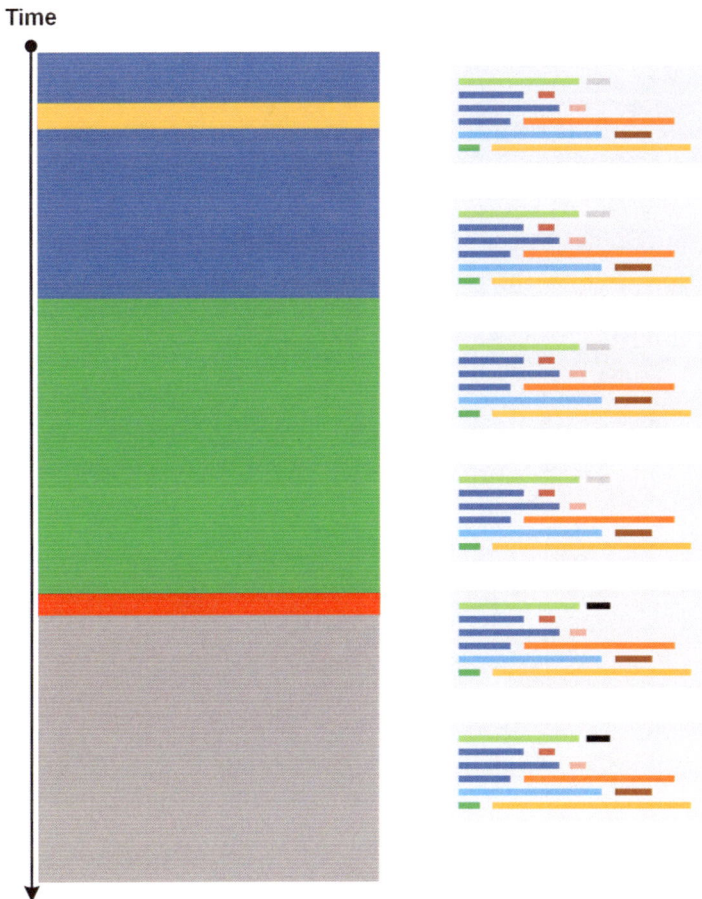

Think about a rectangle as a product of two-line fragments or a cylinder as a product of a circle and a line fragment. Both traces are completely independent in comparison to **Fiber Bundle** (page 136), **Trace Presheaf** (page 330), or **Trace Extension** (page 311).

Case Messages

Often, we have **Basic Facts** (page 60) but are unsure 100% if particular trace messages are relevant or not. We borrow the idea of the **Case Messages** analysis pattern from fuzzy sets[25] where we have a degree of membership function. It is illustrated in the following diagram:

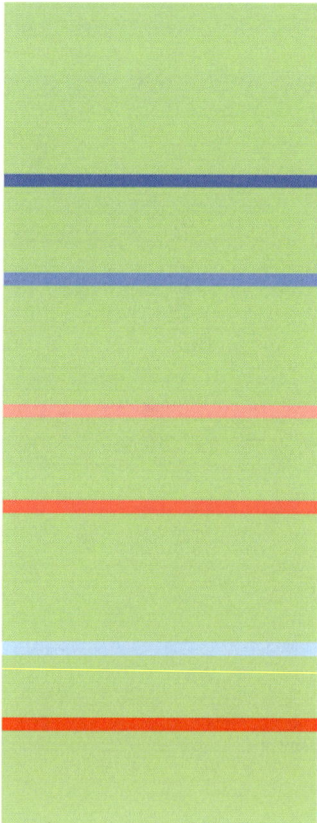

$$\{\, m_{\#} \mid \mu_{\text{Fact A}}(m_{\#}) > 0 \text{ or } \mu_{\text{Fact B}}(m_{\#}) > 0 \,\}$$

In comparison, **Message Set** (page 202) analysis pattern is about crisp sets where the degree of membership is either 0 or 1.

Causal Chains

The relations between **Causal History** (page 73) messages (0-chains) can be abstracted as **Causal Chains** (1-chains). Two relations can be linked if an endpoint of one is also a beginning point of another:

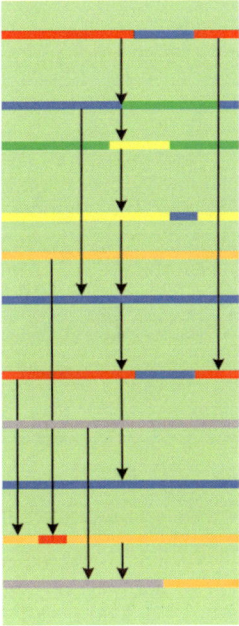

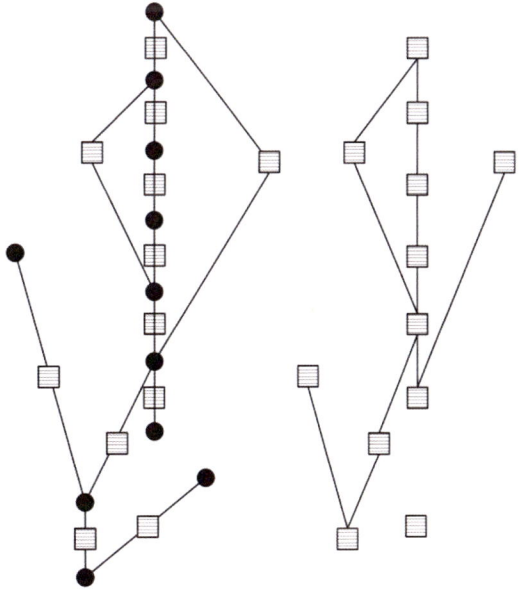

The relations of 1-chains can be abstracted as 2-chains and so on (n-chains):

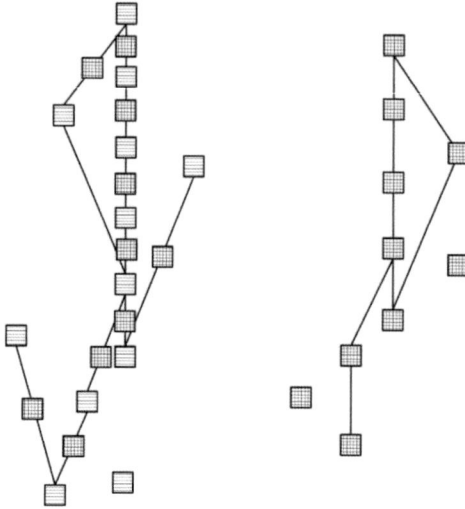

We took the idea of relation spaces and chains from the Discreet Causal Theory[26] book. **Causal chain**[27] terminology is also used in philosophy.

Causal History

Trace Paths (page 329) and **Back Traces** (page 56) form **Causal History** of the log where arrows point in the direction of possible causation:

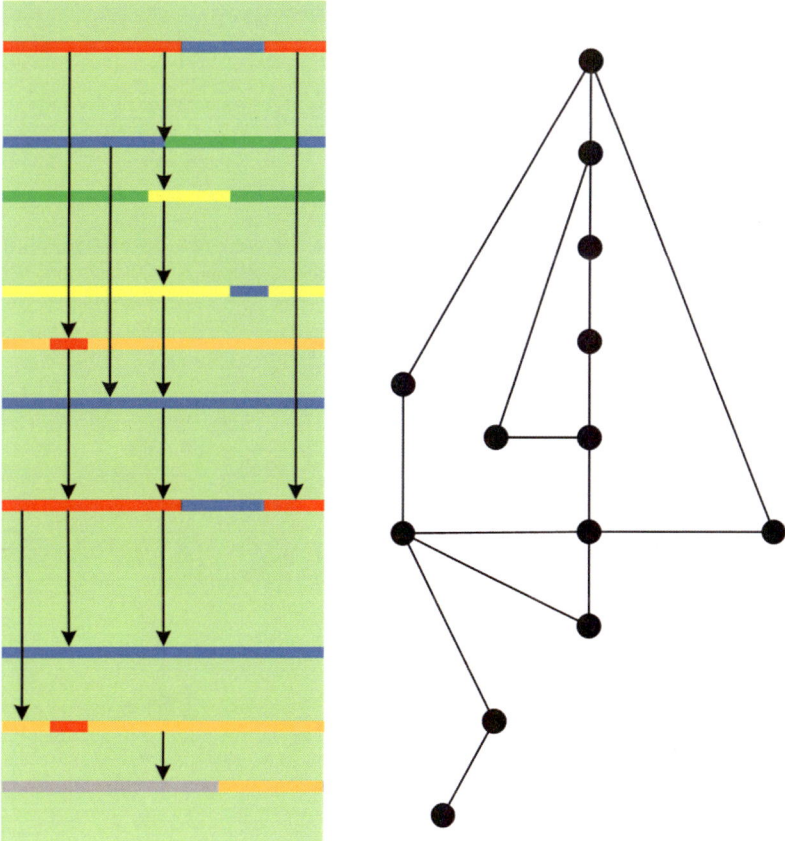

Here we borrow the notion of **causal sets** [28] from physics and corresponding mathematics. The left diagramming idea was taken from the Discrete Causal Theory book[29] and **Hasse diagrams**[30] (which is inverted in our picture). Also, such graphs are internal to software narratives compared to the more **general external space**[31] we proposed earlier.

We omit **Time** arrow as it is possible to consider general traces and logs[32] with their causality markers.

Causal Messages

When looking at **Causal History** (page 71) mesh, we can choose **Causal Messages** (not necessarily the top ones):

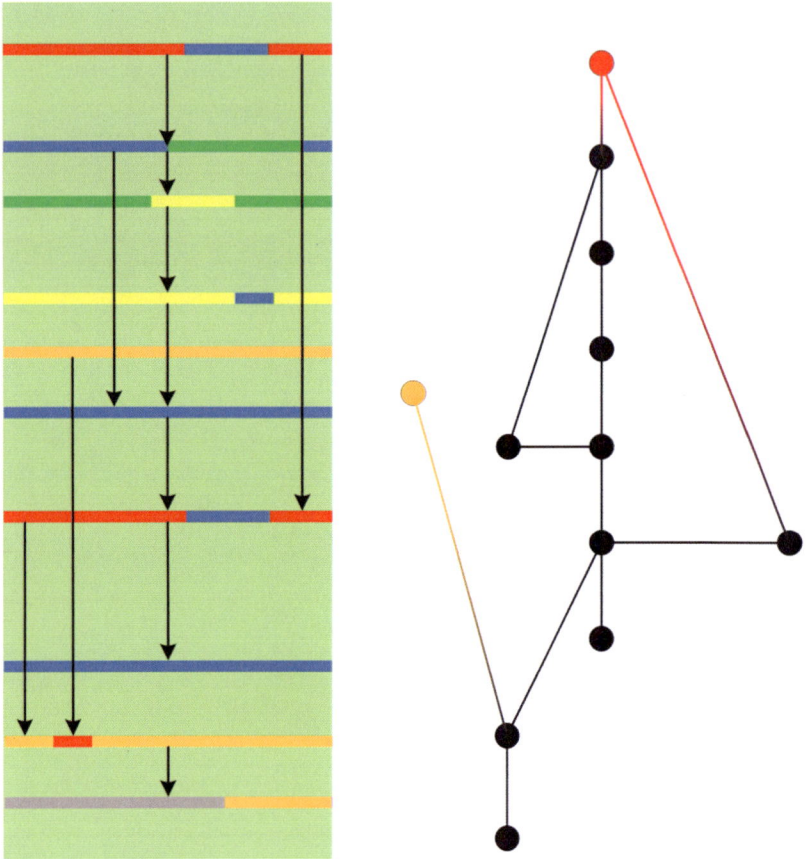

    Causal Messages may not overlap with the trace **Defect Group** (page 105), which may not have any causal relevance being only correlation messages.

Characteristic Message Block

Bird's eye view of software traces[33] makes it easier to see their coarse blocked structure:

The further finer structure is discernible, and we can even see nested blocks:

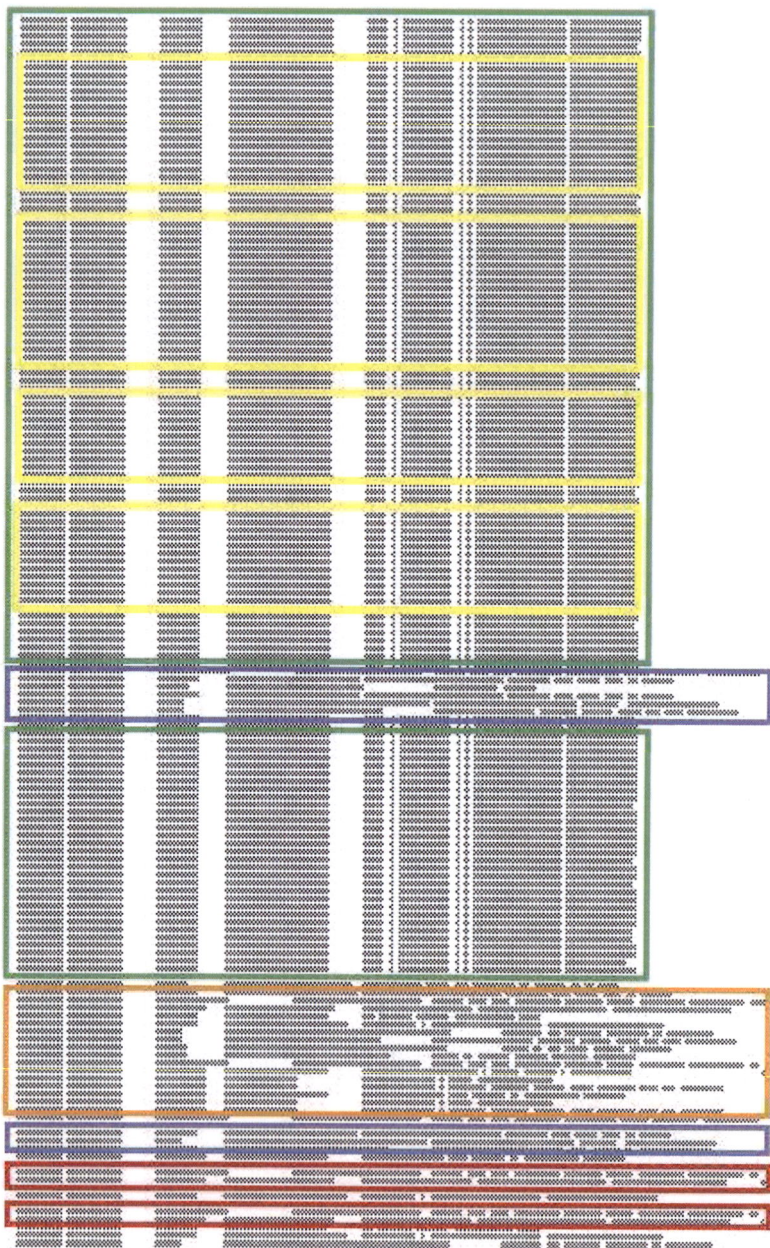

We can see some blocks of output when scrolling a trace viewer window, but if a viewer supports zooming, it is possible to get an overview and jump directly into **Characteristic Message Block**, for example, debug messages of repeated attempts to query a database. If a viewer supports message coloring, it also helps here. Sometimes, the latter technique is useful when we want to ignore bulk messages and start an analysis around block boundaries.

Circular Trace

It is an obvious structural trace analysis pattern. Sometimes, the information about circularity is missing in the problem description, or the trace metadata does not reflect it. Then **Circular Traces** can be detected by trace **File Size** (page 139) (usually large) and from timestamps, like this 100Mb trace snippet:

```
No      Module  PID  TID  Date       Time         Statement
[Begin of trace listing]
1       ModuleA 4280 1736 5/28/2009 08:53:50.496 [... Trace statement 1]
2       ModuleB 6212 6216 5/28/2009 08:53:52.876 [... Trace statement 2]
3       ModuleA 4280 4776 5/28/2009 08:54:13.537 [... Trace statement 3]
[... Some traced exceptions that are helpful for analysis ...]
3799    ModuleA 4280 3776 5/28/2009 09:15:00.853 [... Trace statement 3799]
3800    ModuleA 4280 1736 5/27/2009 09:42:12.029 [... Trace statement 3800]
[... Skipped ...]
[... Skipped ...]
[... Skipped ...]
579210 ModuleA 4280 4776 5/28/2009 08:53:35.989 [... Trace statement 579210]
[End of trace listing]
```

We can usually find the analysis region at the beginning of such traces because as soon as an elusive and hard-to-reproduce problem happens, the tracing is stopped:

Time

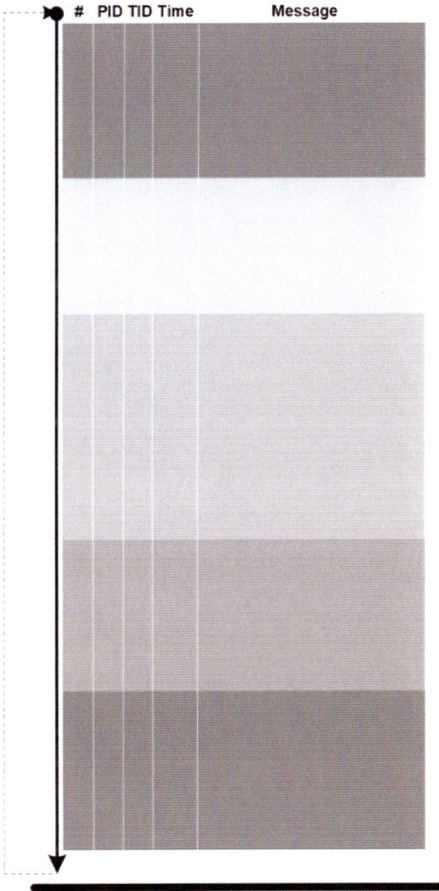

PID TID Time   Message

Problem
Repro

CoActivity

There's some kind of duality[34] between trace data and activity. For example, trace data corresponds to **CoData** (**CoTrace**, **CoLog**, page 88), the analysis activity. On the other hand, **Activity Regions** (page 41, and various Activity-related patterns such **Thread of Activity**, page 296) may contain data that itself may point to some activity (not necessarily the same), **CoActivity**. For example, some keyboard-related message data may contain values of passwords. This analysis pattern is illustrated schematically in the following diagram:

CoActivity is different from **Data Flow** (page 95), where the same or modified value is passed from one message to another, not necessarily inside the same activity.

Collapsed Message

Sometimes we want to collapse messages into one message while preserving content, for example, for grep. We call such an analysis pattern **Collapsed Message** (by an analogy for collapsing an internal directed graph edge, or edge contraction[35]). Several consecutive messages with the same attribute, for example, **Thread of Activity** (page 296) for **Exception Stack Trace** (page 129), may be collapsed into one longer trace message: a simple case of **Quotient Trace** (page 250) without compression or some transform. And this is different from **Motivic Trace** (page 215), which doesn't preserve message content.

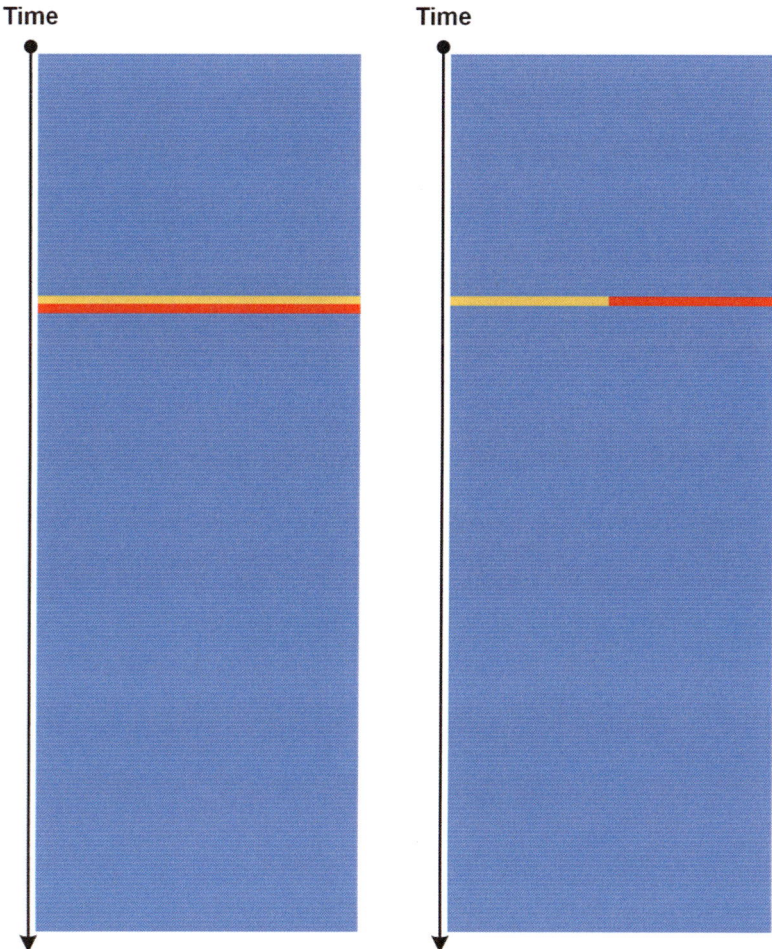

Combed Trace

A typical software trace or log (for example, from Process Monitor) lists messages from several processes and threads sequentially. However, such columns may be split into individual process ID or thread ID columns. The same can be done for any **Adjoint Thread** (page 48) and illustrated in the following diagram:

We call this analysis pattern **Combed Trace** by analogy with *multibraiding*[36].

Container Trace

The name of this pattern, **Container Trace**, originates from the logging style that is recommended as the best practice for containers (like Docker), where various components output their tracing and logging statements to the standard console output. Such components may have their incompatible **Trace Schemas** (page 333), for example, normal trace messages intermingled with **Exception Stack Traces** (page 129). However, in general, this pattern can be extended to any log file (a container for trace statements). This pattern is also different from **Trace Mask** (page 322), where individual traces come from separate files and have **Trace Schema** with some ATID (see **Adjoint Thread of Activity**, page 48) or FID (see **Feature of Activity**, page 135), such as time, that allows for blending them correctly. Furthermore, components that output their messages may not even have any internal **Trace Schema**. In such a case, **Container Trace** may simply be treated as **Text Trace** (page 294).

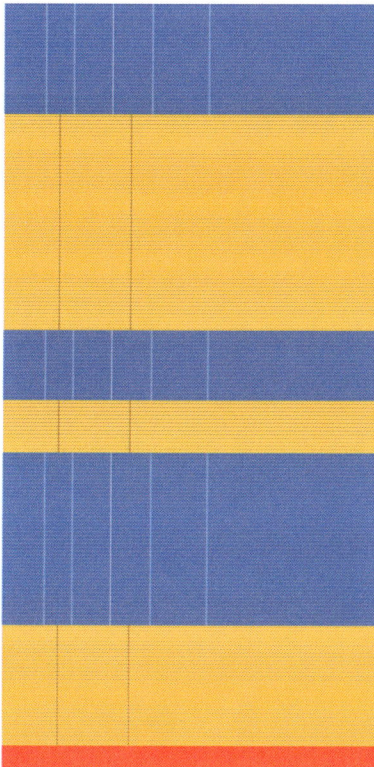

Cord of Activity

Several **Strands of Activity** (page 290) from different types of ATIDs (**Adjoint Threads of Activity**, page 48) combine into a **Cord of Activity**:

Time

Between cord and rope analogies, we chose cord as having "ord" (ordinal[37]) in it (and "c" as cardinal[38]). It is also possible to combine several **Cords of Activity** from different traces (**Trace Dimension**, page **309**) to form a "cable-laid rope." We don't introduce a separate pattern here since, in the resulting **Trace Mask** (page 322), we have a new **Cord of Activity** due to the additionally created ATID type referencing former separate traces and logs. Data references in messages may provide additional braiding via **Braids of Activity** (page 66).

We started with strands (we got the idea from the discussion of ethnomathematics where strand analysis[39] was mentioned), but then we found the following useful discussion on rope terminology: "Art and Science of Rope."[40]

Correlated Discontinuity

When analyzing **Inter-Correlation** (page 167) or **Intra-Correlation** (page 170) and finding **Discontinuities** (page 115) in a part of one trace or a different trace (for example, in client-server environments), it is useful to see if there are corresponding **Correlated Discontinuities** in another part of the same trace, for example, in a different **Thread of Activity**, page 296), or a different trace. Such a pattern may point to the underlying communication problem and suggest gathering a different trace (for example, a network trace) for further analysis.

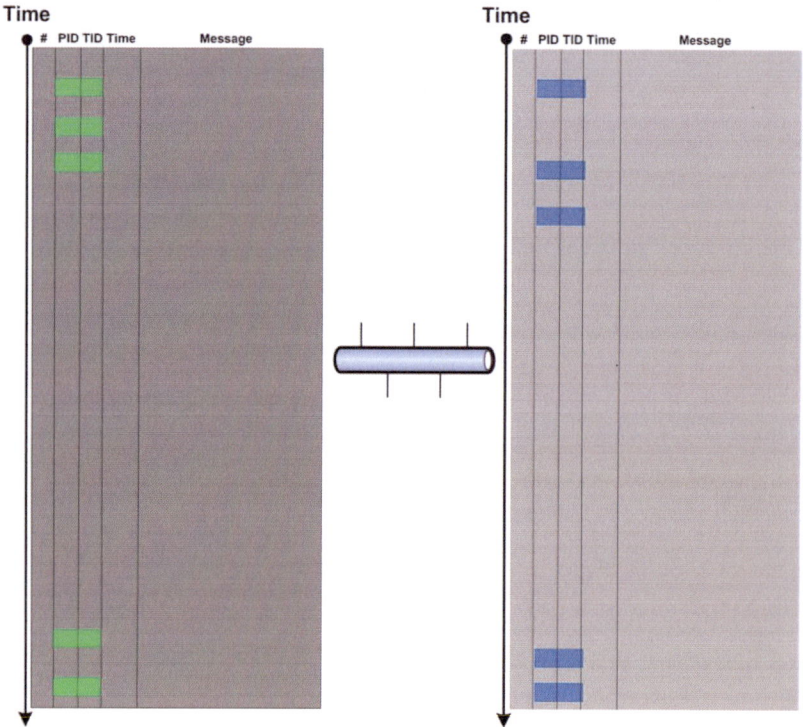

Corrupt Message

Sometimes log messages are formatted with mistakes; buffers are not cleared before copying; copied strings are truncated; tracing implementation and presentation contains coding defects. There can be internal corruption when messages are formed or "corruption" during a presentation, for example, default field conversion rules (like in Excel). We call this pattern **Corrupt Message**. Such messages may affect trace and log analysis where data search may not show fully relevant results. We then recommend double-checking findings using **Data Flow** (page 95) of a different **Message Invariant** (page 198).

Time

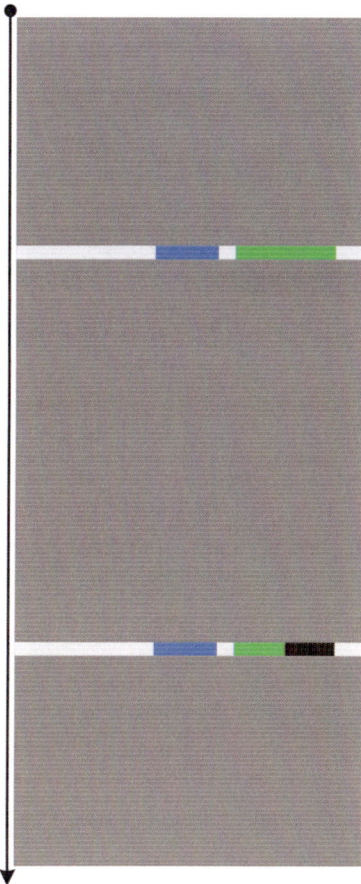

Examples:

Process name: Appáë±
Received TTONDOWN message
Time: 1.345E+93

CoTrace (CoLog, CoData)

When we do trace and log analysis (and software data in general), we look at specific messages found from search (**Message Patterns**, page 201), **Error Messages** (page 123), **Significant Events** (page 270), visit **Activity Regions** (page 41), filter **Message Sets** (page 202), walkthrough (**Adjoint**, page 48) **Threads of Activity** (page 296), and do other actions necessitated by trace and log analysis patterns. All these can be done in random order (starting from some analysis point), not necessarily representing the flow of Time or some other metric[41]:

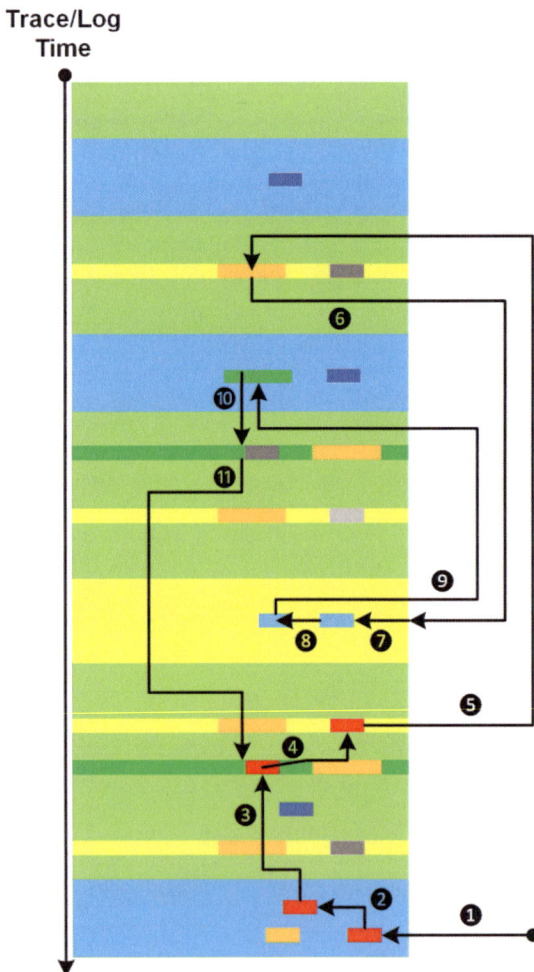

Analyzed messages form their own analysis trace that we call **CoTrace** (**CoLog**, **CoData**), where the prefix Co- denotes a space dual to trace (log, data) space:

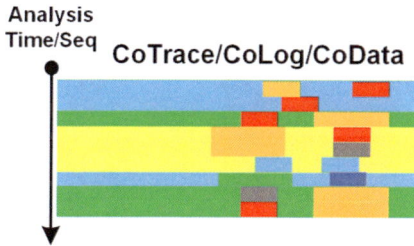

Instead of messages (or in addition to them), we can also form **CoTraces** consisting of visited **Activity Regions** or some other areas:

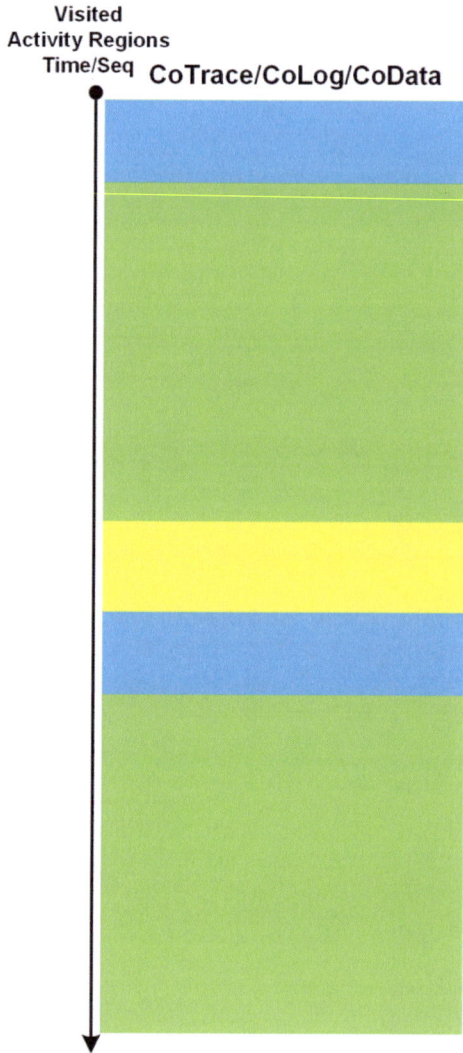

We can apply trace analysis patterns to **CoTraces** as well. The latter can also be used in the creation of higher-order pattern narratives[42].

Counter Value

This pattern covers performance monitoring and its logs. **Counter Value** is some variable in memory, for example, **Module Variable**[43] memory analysis pattern, that is updated periodically to reflect some aspect of state or calculated from different variables and presented in trace messages. We can organize such messages in a similar format as ETW-based traces we usually consider as examples for our trace patterns:

```
Source  PID TID   Function          Value
==================================================
[...]
System    0   0   Committed Memory 12,002,234,654
Process 844   0   Private Bytes     345,206,456
System    0   0   Committed Memory 12,002,236,654
Process 844   0   Working Set       122,160,068
[...]
```

Therefore, all other trace and log analysis patterns such as **Adjoint Thread** (page 48, can be visualized via different colors on a graph), **Focus of Tracing** (page 141), **Characteristic Message Block** (page 75, for graphs), **Activity Region** (page 41), **Significant Event** (page 270), and others can be applicable here. There are also some specific patterns, such as **Global Monotonicity** and **Constant Value,** that we discuss with examples in later reference editions.

Coupled Activities

Sometimes we need to know about the client-server interaction between components, threads, or processes to find out where the problem started. For example, if we have **Error Message** (page 123) or **Discontinuity** (page 115) in one PID **Adjoint Thread of Activity** (page 48), and we know that that process uses API from another PID, we can look at the latter PID **Adjoint Thread** to see if there are any **Error Messages** or other problems. The failure in the server can propagate to the client, as illustrated in the following diagram:

We call this pattern **Coupled Activities** similar to **Coupled Processes** memory analysis pattern [44]. It can help in **Intra-** (page 170) and **Inter-Correlation** (page 167) analysis, for example, in choosing **Adjoint Threads** from **Sheaf of Activities** (page 266).

Critical Point

Based on a mathematical analogy with critical points[45] in topology (Morse theory[46]), we introduce **Critical Points** in trace and log analysis where they signify the change of trace or log "shape" (topological or "geometric" properties) as illustrated in the following diagram:

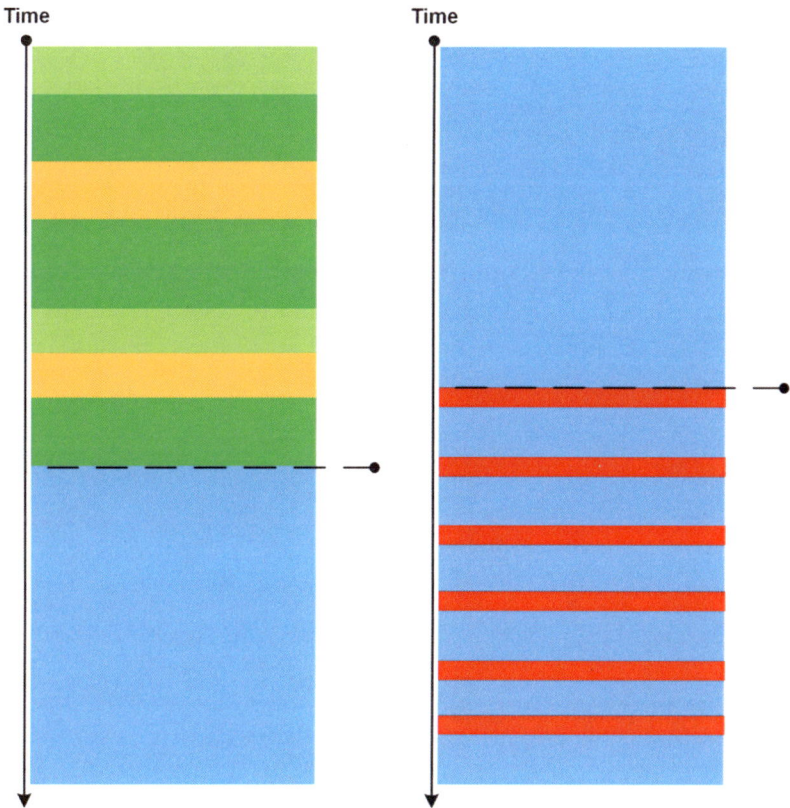

Such a point may be an individual message, its **Message Context** (page 191), or **Activity Region** (page 41).

Critical Points are examples of **Intra-Correlation** (page 170), whereas **Bifurcation Points** (page 61) are examples of **Inter-Correlation** (page 167).

D

Data Association

Sometimes we are interested in changes in particular {property, value} pairs or tuples $\{x_1, x_2, x_3, ...\}$ in general where x_i can be a number or a substring. It is a more general pattern than **Message Change** (page 187) because such tuples can be from different sources and belong to different messages:

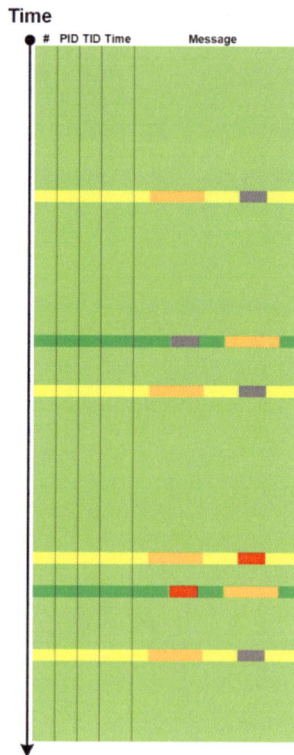

This pattern also differs from **Data Flow** (page 95), where a value stays constant across different sources and messages. It also differs from Gossip (page 148) pattern involving more semantic changes. Metaphorically we can think of this pattern as a partial derivative[47].

Data Flow

If trace messages contain some character or formatted data passed from module to module or between threads and processes, it is possible to trace that data and form a **Data Flow** thread similar to **Adjoint Thread** (page 48) we have when we filter by a specific message. However, in the former case, we have different message types.

Data Interval

When we have very large traces and **Basic Facts** (page 60) containing data values such as a user name, device name, or registry key value, we may use the **Data Interval** analysis pattern to select the trace fragment for the initial log analysis. The first and the last trace messages contain the selected data for the closed **Data Interval**. Depending on the trace size and other considerations, we can also choose open **Data Intervals**. It is illustrated in the following diagram where we use Analysis interval notation borrowed mathematics[48]:

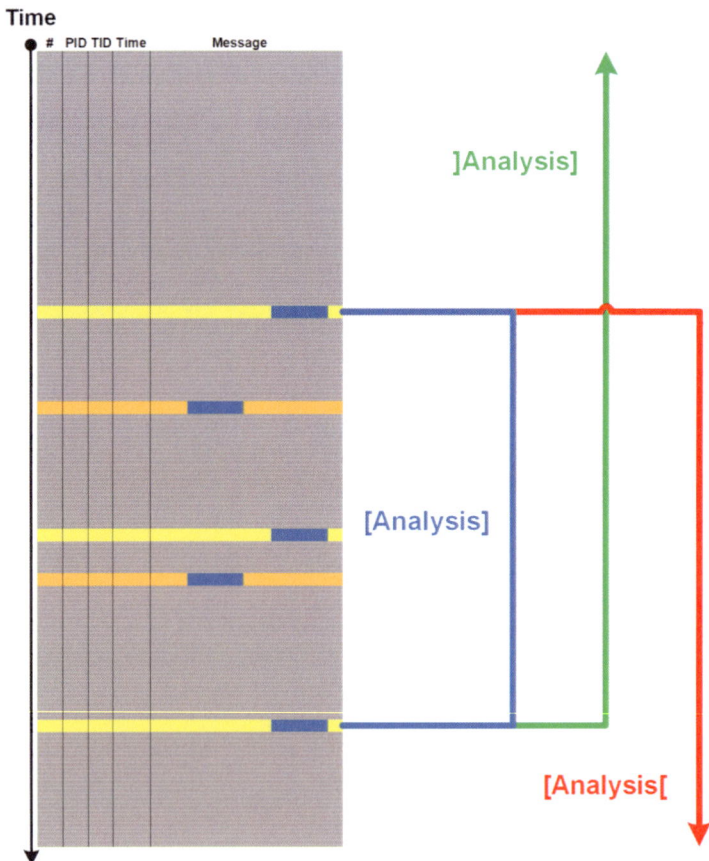

Interval boundary messages may also be used as **Trace Mask** (page 320) for another trace.

Data Reversal

Sometimes we notice that data values are in a different order than expected. We call this pattern **Data Reversal**. By data values, we mean some variable parts of a specific repeated message, such as the address of some structure or object. **Data Reversal** may happen for one message type:

However, it can also happen for some message types and not for others. A typical example here is *Enter/Leave* trace messages for nested synchronization objects such as monitors and critical sections:

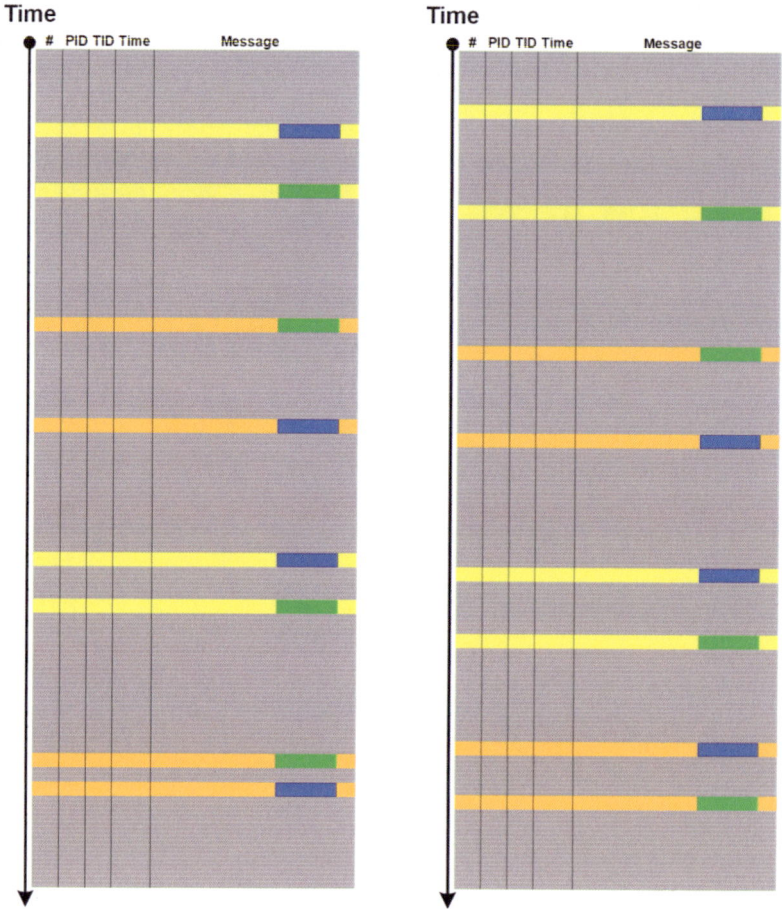

Since we talk about the same message type (the same **Message Invariant**, page 198), this pattern differs from **Event Sequence Order** (page 126).

In rare cases, we may observe **Data Reversal** inside one message with several variable parts, but this may also be a case of **Data Association** (page 94).

Data Selector

Data Selector is a variant of the **Inter-Correlation** (page 167) trace analysis pattern where we use data found in one trace to select **Message Set** (page 201) or **Adjoint** (page 48) **Thread of Activity** (page 296) in another trace. This analysis activity is depicted in the following picture, where we have a client log and a corresponding server log. In the server log, we have entries for many client sessions. To select messages corresponding to our client session, we use some data attributes in the client trace, for example, the username and **Linked Messages** (page 178) analysis pattern to find one of the messages in the server log that contains the same username. Then we find out which user session it belongs to and form its **Adjoint Thread** (page 48):

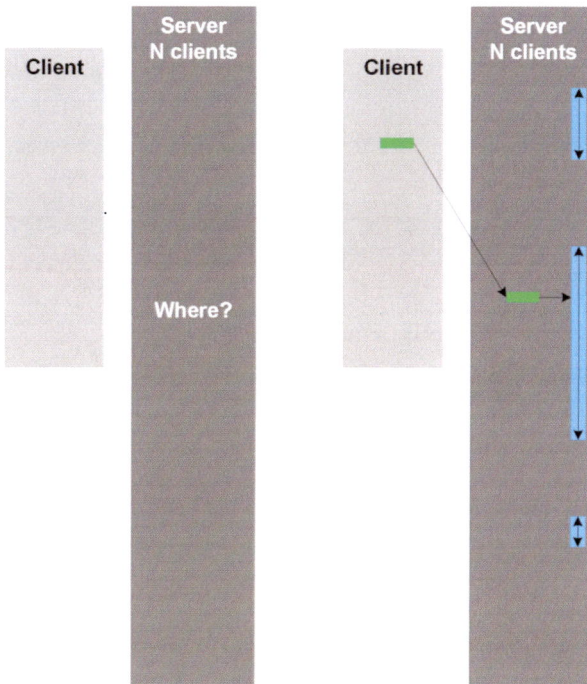

This pattern differs from **Identification Messages** (page 155), where we don't even know the object that emitted trace messages. In the **Data Selector** case, we know, in principle, what kind of messages we are looking for. We just need to select among many alternatives.

De Broglie Trace Duality

Recently we found a correlation between software trace with high **Statement Density and Current** (page 286) of **Periodic Error** (page 231) with uniform **Error Distribution** (page 121) and process heap **Memory Leak**[49] suspected from memory dump analysis. If we metaphorically view periodic errors as "frequency" and the size of a heap as "mass," we may see that the growth of "frequency" correlates with the growth of "mass" and vice versa. Since frequency is inversely proportional to wavelength, we see a metaphorical analog to Louis de Broglie's wave-particle duality[50]. In general, as we already pointed out in the discussion of narrativity and spatiality of software execution artifacts[51] (see also Software Trace and Memory Dump Analysis[52] seminar), software traces/logs and memory dumps can be seen as "dual" to each other according (metaphorically again) to de Broglie's "duality of the laws of nature." So we name this analysis pattern **De Broglie Trace Duality** since some memory dump regions can be considered of a general trace[53] nature. Our correlation can be depicted in this diagram:

Time

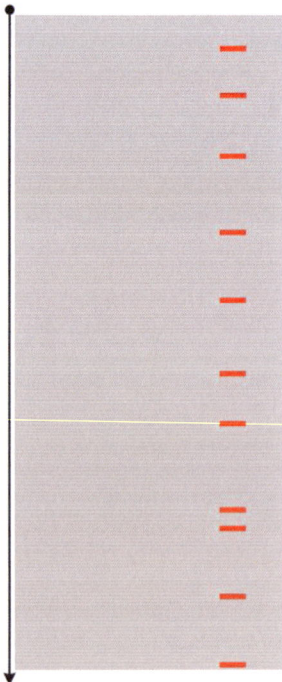 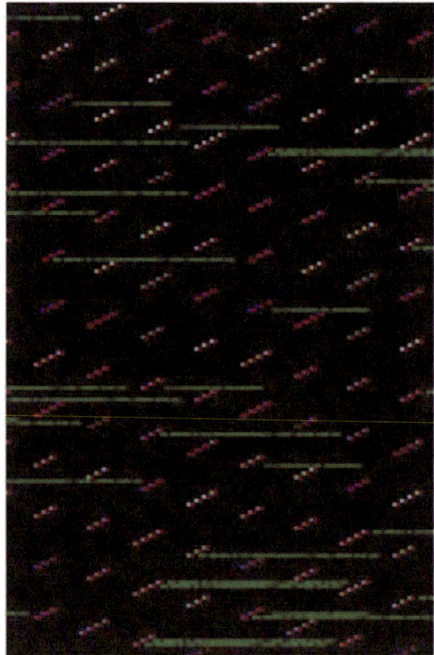

Practically, when we see *Memory Consumption Patterns*[54] (but don't know their source/root cause yet), we can ask for traces and logs, and in the case of frequent **Periodic Errors** found there, we can suggest troubleshooting steps that may serve as a resolution or workaround.

Declarative Trace

The trace statements in source code can be considered as **Declarative Trace** by analogy with variable declaration and definition in programming languages such as C and C++. Declaration of the variable doesn't mean that the variable is used. Some declared variables, such as arrays, expand in memory when used (as in .bss sections). The same is with trace messages from **Declarative Trace**. Some of them don't appear in the actual software execution trace, and some are repeated because of loops and multiple code reentrance. However, **Declarative Traces** are useful for studying the possibilities of tracing and logging design, implementation, and coverage (for example, **Sparse Trace**, page 279). Some trace analysis patterns are also applicable for **Declarative Traces,** such as **Message Sets** (page 201) and **Bifurcation Points** (page 61) among different source code versions. It is illustrated in the following picture:

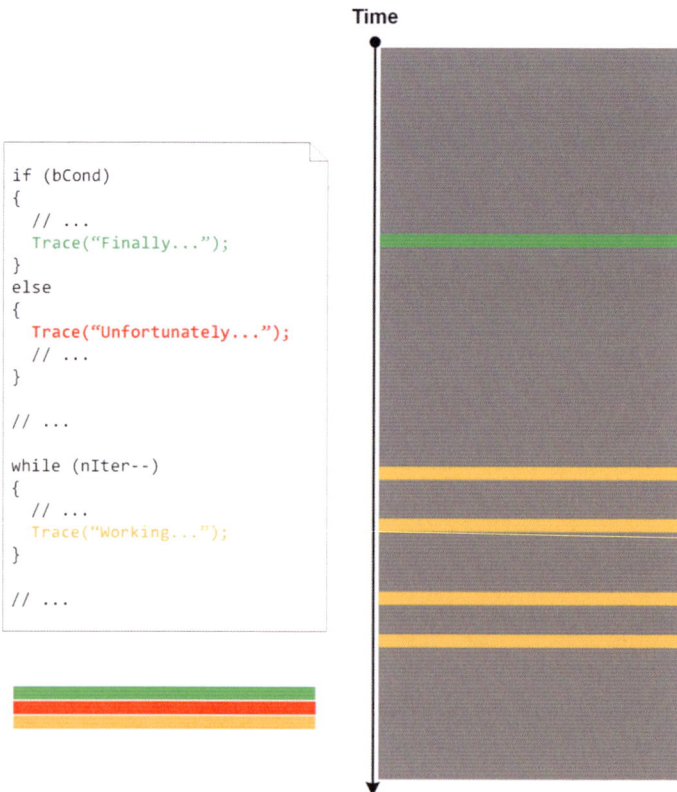

Defamiliarizing Effect

"Capturing delicate moments, one gives birth to a poetry of traces ..."

Ange Leccia, Motionless Journeys, by Fabien Danesi

In this pattern from software narratology,[55] we see sudden unfamiliar trace statements across the familiar landscape of **Characteristic Blocks** (page 68) and **Activity Regions** (page 41).

An example of a familiar trace:

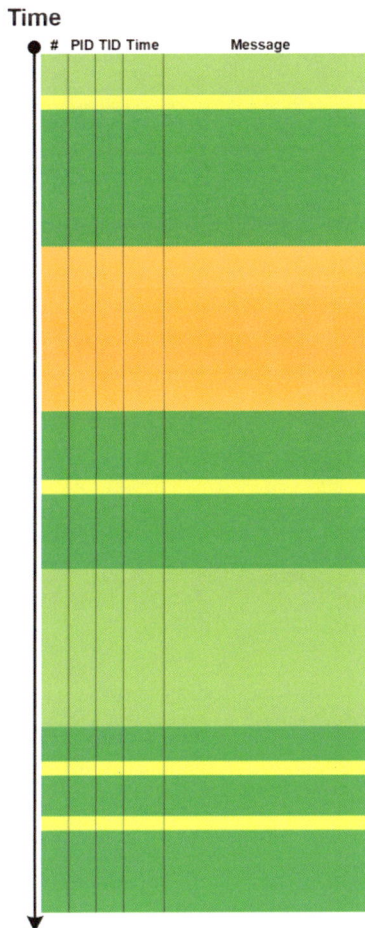

An example of the new trace from a problem system:

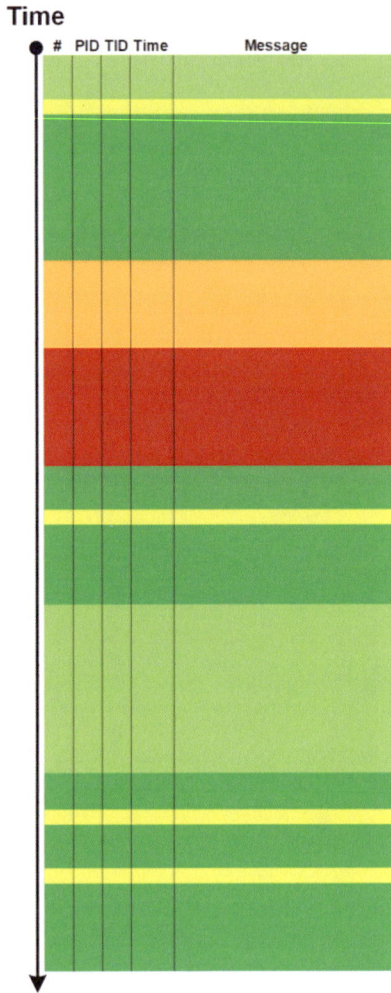

Defect Group

Defect Group analysis pattern addresses messages related to source code defects [56], problem descriptions, and **Inter-Correlation** (page 167) with wrong configuration files (**Small DA+TA**, page 276). It differs from **Message Set** (page 202) analysis pattern as a predicate to group them may not be easily available.

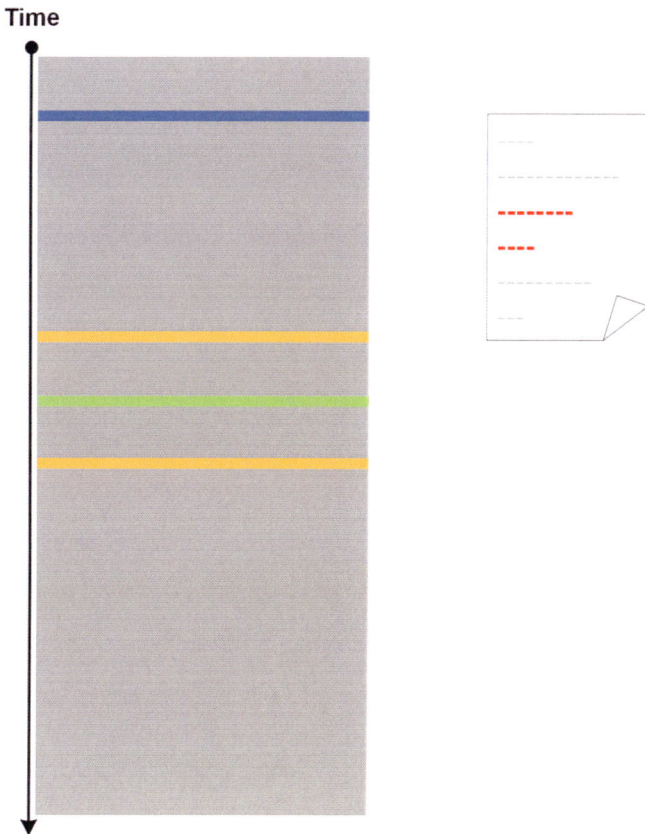

Such **Defect Groups** can be the results of previous analyses. The name of the analysis pattern came from the representation theory's **defect group of a block**[57], but at present, it is only a name analogy.

Definition Trace

Trace Schema (page 333) can be represented as **Schema Trace** or, avoiding naming confusion, **Definition Trace**. The resulting trace loses ordering (similar to unordered **Message Set**, page 202) but allows the application of trace and log analysis patterns, especially if some order is fixed, for example, alphabetical for names or original presentation column arrangement. Schema definition **Trace Schema** can be represented as another **Definition Trace** as illustrated in the following diagram:

Treated as unordered Message Sets

Delay Dynamics

Here we introduce the **Delay Dynamics** analysis pattern. It is not an oxymoron, and dynamics is referred to by what happens during the delay (**Discontinuity**, page 115 with **Time Delta**, page 298) in other **Threads of Activity** (page 296) as depicted in the following diagram:

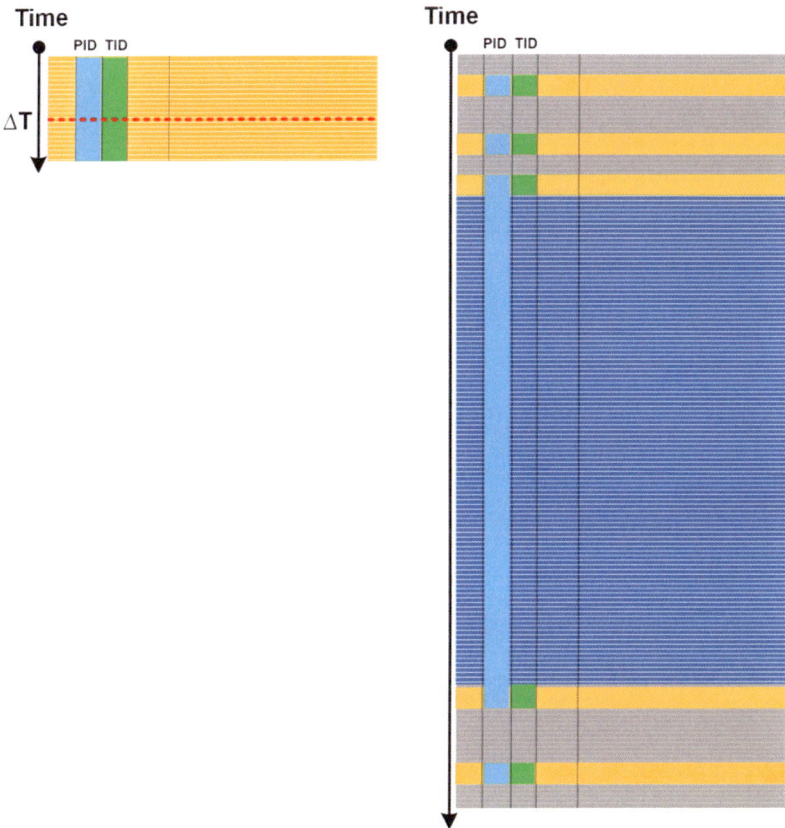

Instead of threads, various **Adjoint Threads of Activity** (page 48) may also be inspected.

Denormalized Message

If necessary, for example, for the conversion to **Text Trace** (page 294), individual trace messages may need to be converted to message text form blending various message constituents like ATIDs, **Message Invariants** (page 198), data, and **Trace Constants** (page 306) into some textual narrative form. We illustrate it in the following diagram:

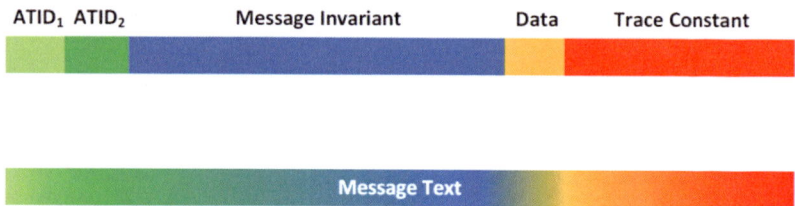

We call the resulting message text **Denormalized Message**. It is the reverse process of finding **Features of Activity** (page 135) and constructing structured messages conforming to some **Trace Schema** (page 333).

Density Distribution

Sometimes we find a grouping of some messages in one trace, and then we are interested in the same groupings either in the same trace (**Intra-Correlation**, page 170) or another trace (**Inter-Correlation**, page 162). We may consider such grouping as having some **local** density compared to the global **Statement Density** (page 286) pattern. Then we might be interested in that selected message grouping density distribution as illustrated on this minimal trace graph:

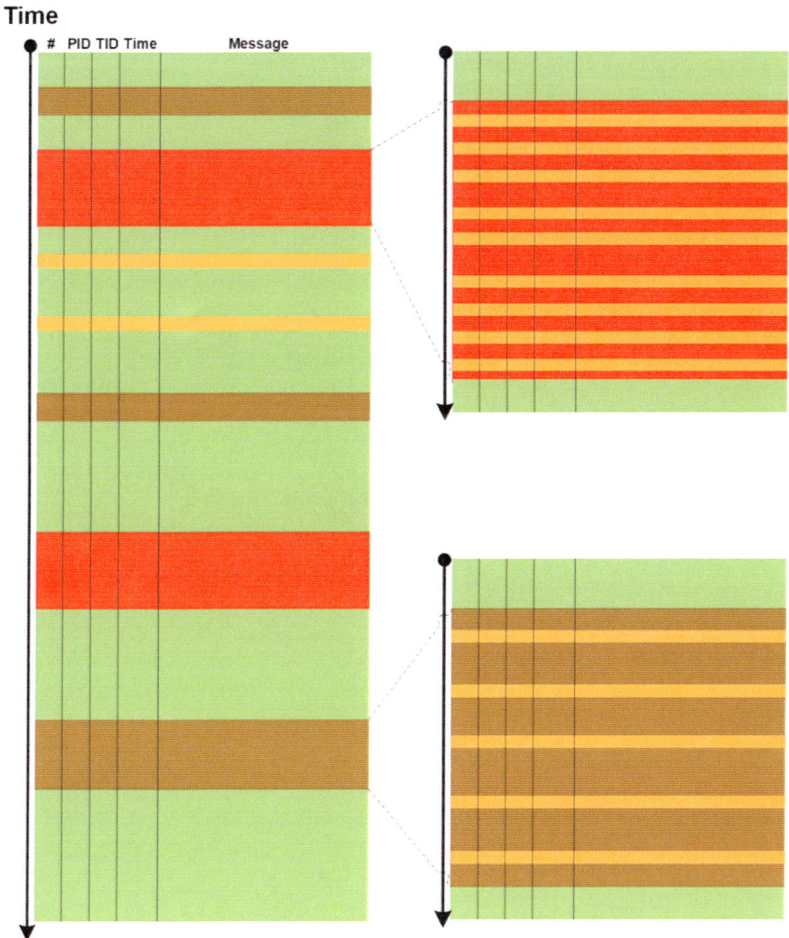

Dialogue

Dialogue is an important pattern, especially in network trace analysis. It usually involves a message source, a different message target (although both can be the same), and some alternation between them, as shown in this abstract trace diagram:

Message and source are not only IP addresses or port numbers but also window handles, for example. Sometimes, the roles of the source and target are played by different Process ID and Thread ID combinations (Client ID, CID). In such cases, some parts of a message text may signify a reply and response, as shown graphically:

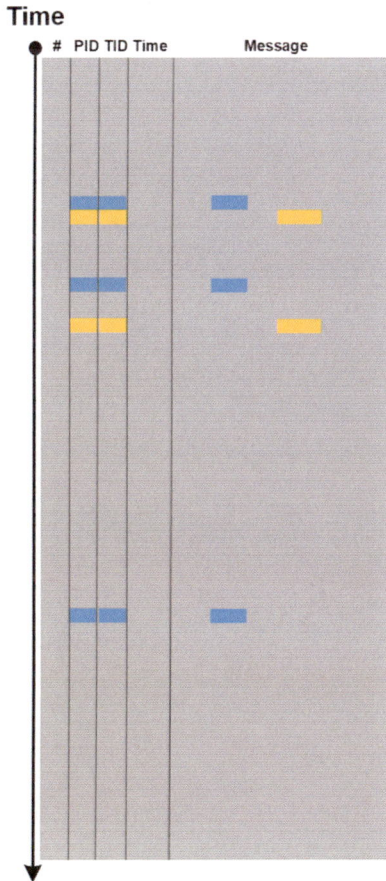

A similar illustration can be done for multi-computer trace, for example, when several traces from different servers are combined into one, where a combination of CID and a computer ID (Co) or just CO can play the roles of source and target.

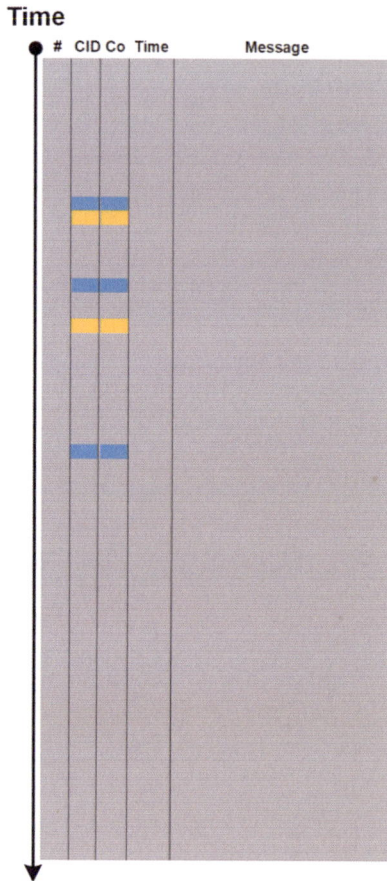

Note that on all illustrations above the 3rd request does not have a reply message: a possible **Incomplete History** (page 159) pattern.

Diegetic Messages

Like in literature (and in narratology, in general), we have components that trace themselves and the components that tell the story of computation, including status updates they query from other components and subsystems. This pattern gets its name from diegesis[58]. Here's the difference between diegetic (in blue) and non-diegetic trace messages:

```
PID    TID    TIME          MESSAGE
11864  11912  06:34:53.598  ModuleA: foo called bar. Status OK.
11620  10372  06:34:59.754  ModuleB: ModuleA integrity check. Status OK.
```

Some modules may emit messages that tell about their status, but from their message text, we know the larger computation story, like in a process startup sequence example[59].

The following diagram illustrates this analysis pattern:

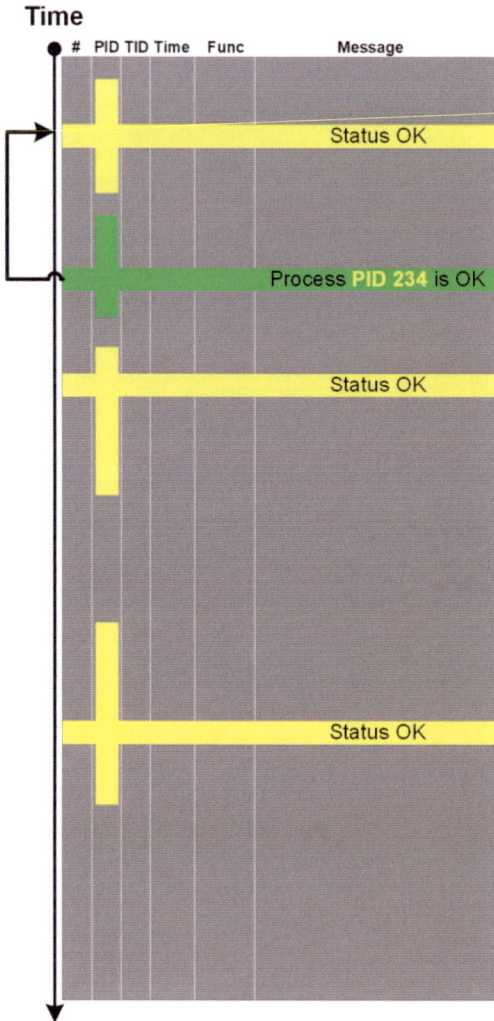

Discontinuity

Sometimes there are reported delays in application startup, session initialization, long response times, and simply the absence of response. All these problems can be reflected in software traces showing sudden gaps in **Threads of Activity** (page 48). This pattern is called **Discontinuity** per analogy with continuous and discontinuous functions in mathematics. Here is an example. One process had a long period of CPU spiking calculation, and we recorded a trace. When we open it, we see this **Periodic Error** (page 231):

```
N   PID  TID  Time         Message
[...]
326 2592 5476 08:17:18.823 OpenRegistry: Attempting to open [.. Hive path ..]
327 2592 5476 08:17:18.824 OpenRegistry: Failed: 2
[...]
```

However, when looking for any **Discontinuities** (page 115) for thread 5476, we see a gap of more than 7 minutes:

```
N    PID  TID  Time         Message
[...]
3395 2592 5476 08:17:19.608 OpenRegistry: Attempting to open [.. Hive path ..]
3396 2592 5476 08:17:19.608 OpenRegistry: Failed: 2
3461 2592 5476 08:24:31.137 OpenRegistry: Attempting to open [.. Hive path ..]
3462 2592 5476 08:24:31.137 OpenRegistry: Failed: 2
[...]
```

For this reason, we have three possibilities here:

1. The process twice did lengthy CPU spiking calculations involving registry access and was quiet between them.
2. Registry access belonged to some background activity and ceased for 7 minutes, and during that time, the process had CPU spiking intensive calculation.
3. This discontinuity is irrelevant because either the calculation module was not selected for tracing or it simply doesn't have relevant tracing statement coverage for the code that does the calculation.

The full case study is covered in the September 2009 issue of Debugged! MZ/PE magazine[60].

The following diagram illustrates **Discontinuity** analysis pattern:

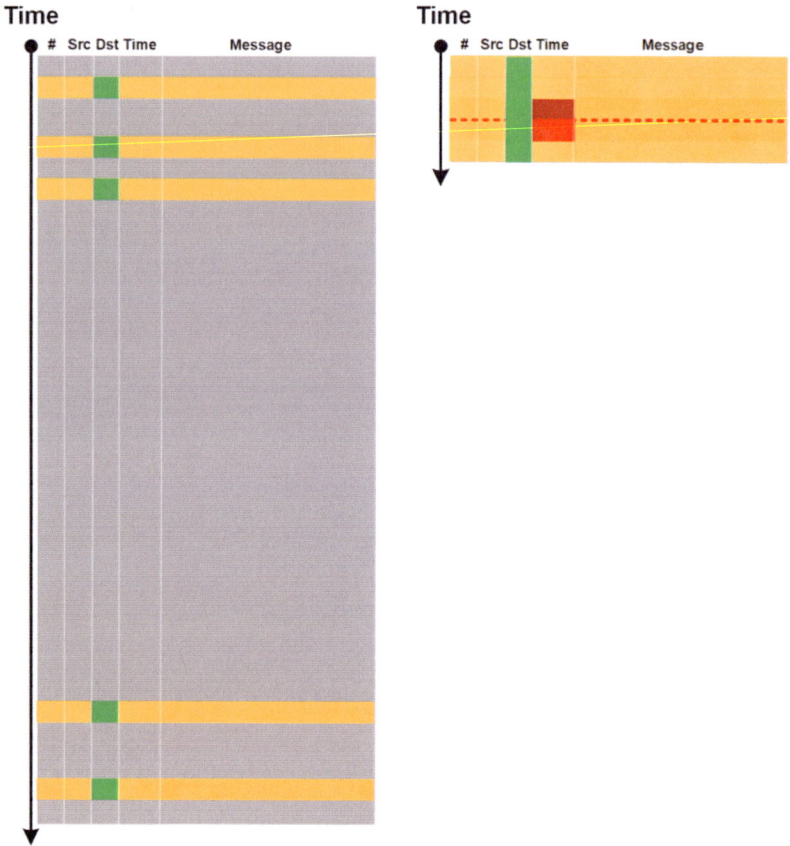

Dominant Event Sequence

Sometimes we have an insufficiently detailed problem description, or several similar parallel user activities are going on simultaneously; for example, several sessions are launched in a terminal services environment. In such cases, when tracing is done for the duration of specific user activity, this pattern may help. Here we select a full sequence of events or event sequence based on some **Basic Facts** (page 60). For example, if a session ID was missing in the problem description, we can choose the longest and fullest process launch sequence[61] and assume that its session ID was the one missing:

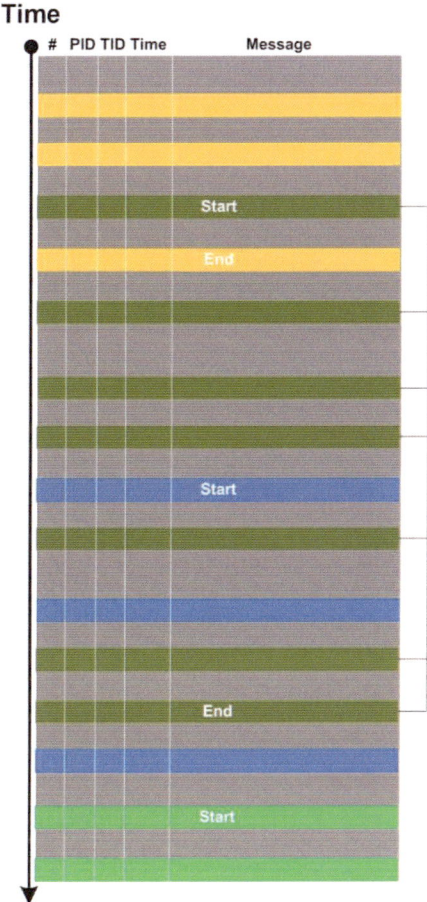

Drone Message

Sometimes we see a constantly repeated message throughout a trace or log (a trivial **Periodic Message Block**, page 233) with constant **Time Delta** (page 298). In certain trace forms (without explicit timing information), such messages may indicate internal time references, as illustrated in the following diagram:

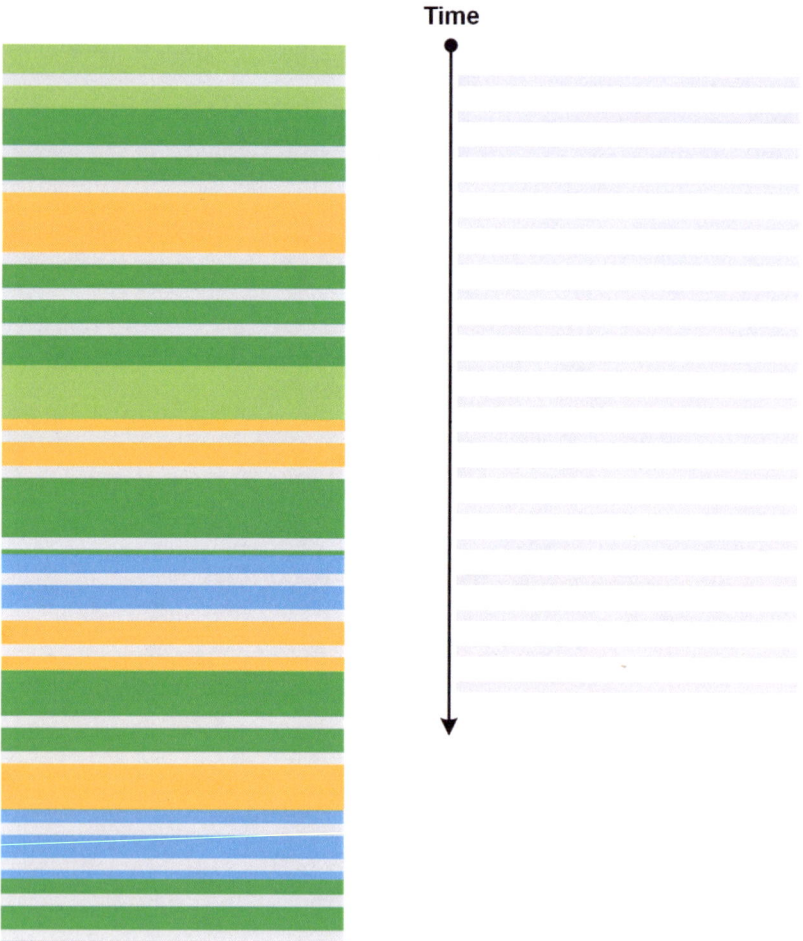

We name this pattern **Drone Message** based on an analogy with the Drone effect[62] in music.

E

Embedded Trace

Trace embedding usually happens when some external tracing or logging framework or library is used. In this case, a trace message becomes part of an outer trace message which may have its own uniform **Trace Schema** (page 333). In this case, **Embedded Trace** analysis pattern differs from **Container Trace** (page 83), where outer **Trace Schemas** may vary.

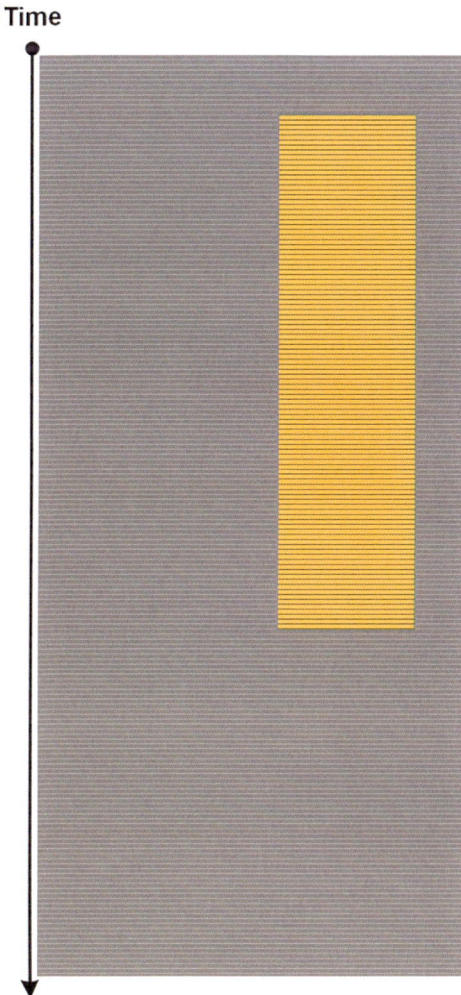

Empty Trace

Empty Trace is another trivial missing pattern that we need to add to make the software log analysis pattern system complete. It ranges from an empty trace message list where only a meta-trace header (if any) describing the overall trace structure is present to a few messages where we expect thousands. It is also an extreme case of **Truncated Trace** (page 352), **No Activity** (page 219), and **Missing Component** (page 207) patterns for a trace taken as a whole. Note that an empty trace file does not necessarily have a zero file size because a tracing architecture may preallocate some file space for block data writing.

Equivalent Messages

Some trace and log messages may have different grammatical structure and content but similar semantics. Therefore, we can create a table listing equivalent messages (using some equivalence relation [63]) and use it to construct simpler traces and logs as depicted in this picture:

One trivial example of **Equivalent Messages** analysis pattern is **Quotient Trace** (page 250). Another example is **Inter-Correlational** (page 167) analysis of logs that have different structure and format. In such a case, **Equivalent Messages** simplify the analysis of higher **Trace Dimensions** (page 309).

Error Distribution

Sometimes we need to pay attention to **Error Distribution,** for example, the distribution of the same error across a software log space or different **Error Messages** (page 123) in different parts of the same software log or trace (providing effective partition):

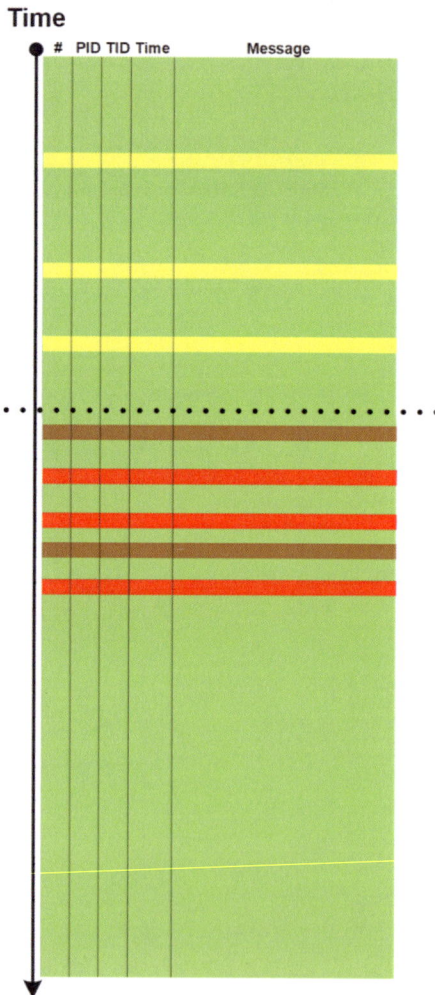

Error Message

While working on Accelerated Windows Software Trace Analysis training,[64] we discovered some missing patterns needed for completeness despite their triviality. One of them is called **Error Message**. Here an error is reported either explicitly ("operation failed") or implicitly as an operation status result such as 0xC00000XX. Sometimes, a trace message designer specifies that the number value is supplied for information only and should be ignored. Some **Error Messages** may contain information irrelevant to the current software incident, the so-called **False Positive Errors** (page 134). Some tracing architectures and tools include a message information category for errors, where we can filter by error category[65] to get **Adjoint Thread** (page 48). Please note that the association of a trace statement with an error category is left to the discretion of an engineer writing code. Also, information category messages may contain implicit errors, such as the last error and return status reports.

Error Powerset

A typical software trace may contain several **Error Messages** (page 123) with different error codes and different exception names with **Exception Stack Traces** (page 129). Searching for individual codes or exceptions in problem databases may show many matches. Searching for all of them may show nothing. Therefore, we can construct the set of all subsets of the set of codes and exceptions (a power set [66]) and perform analytic reasoning (and a search) based on certain subsets based on the problem description, **Trace Viewpoints** (page 344), such as **Use Case Trails** (page 354), **Motifs** (page 214), **Focus of Tracing** (page 141), **Foreground Components** (page 57), (**Adjoint**, page 48) **Threads of Activity** (page 296), and simply some **Activity Regions** (page 41) and **Message Sets** (page 201).

The following picture illustrates the **Error Powerset** analysis pattern with a trace that has four error messages where two messages have the same error code.

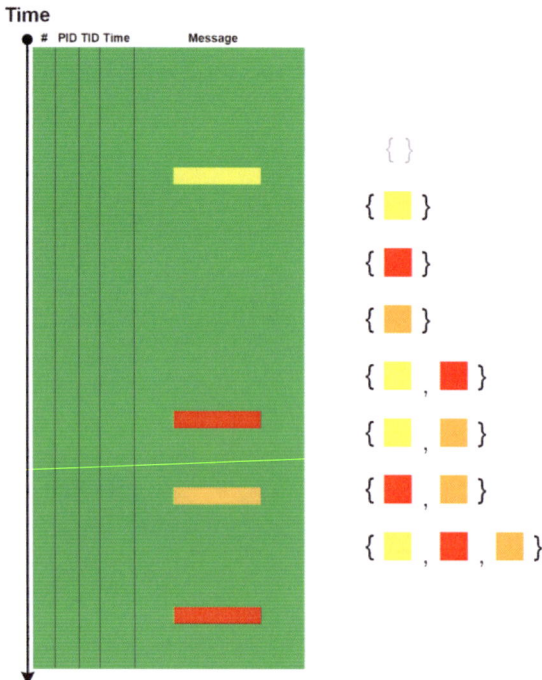

Error Thread

When we see **Error Message** (page 123) or **Exception Stack Trace** (page 129) in a log file, we might want to explore the sequence of messages from the same **Thread of Activity** (page 296) that led to the error. Such **Message Set** (page 201) has an analogy with memory analysis patterns such as **Execution Residue** (of partial stack traces without overwrites[67]) and **Stack Trace** (where the error message is a top stack frame[68]):

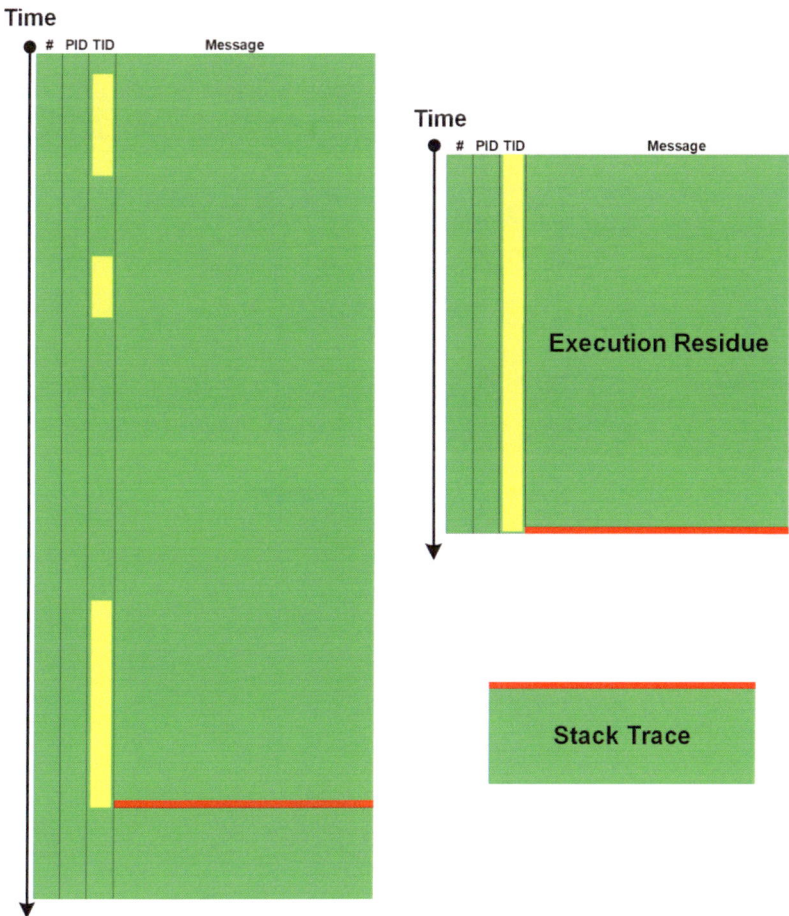

Event Sequence Order

In any system, this pattern is expected as a precondition to its normal behavior. Any out-of-order events should raise the suspicion bar as they might result in or lead to synchronization problems. It needs not to be a sequence of trace messages from different threads but also between processes. For example, image load events in ETW traces can indicate the wrong configuration of a service startup order. The following diagram depicts a possible pattern scenario:

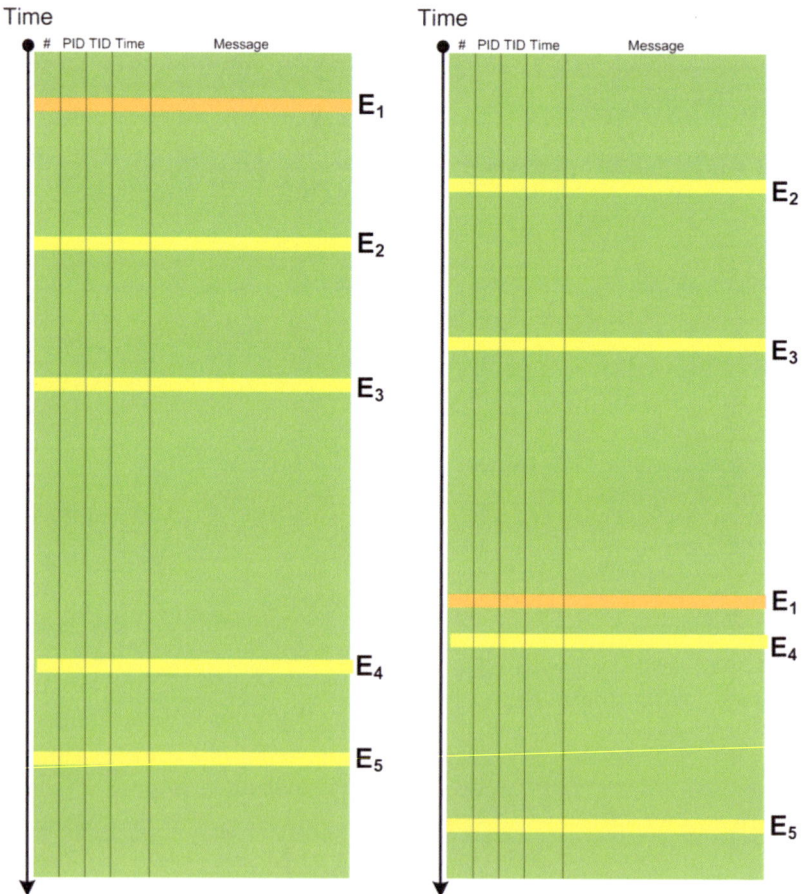

Event Sequence Phase

Sometimes we have several use case instances traced into one log file. Messages and **Activity Regions** (page 41) from many **Use Case Trails** (page 354) intermingle and make analysis difficult, especially with the absence of UCID (Use Case ID), any other identification tags, or **Linked Messages** (page 178). However, most of the time, we are initially interested in a sequence of **Significant Events** (page 270). After finding **Anchor Messages** (page 53), we can use **Time Deltas** (page 298) to differentiate between trace statements from different **Use Case Trails**. Here we assume the correct **Event Sequence Order** (page 126). We call this pattern the **Event Sequence Phase** by analogy with wave phases[69]. All such individual *"waves"* may have different *"shapes"* due to various delays between different stages of their use case and implementation narratives:

Time

Time

A or B or C?	C
A or B or C?	B
A or B or C?	C
Use case instance A	Use case instance A
Use case instance B	Use case instance B
Use case instance C	Use case instance C

φ

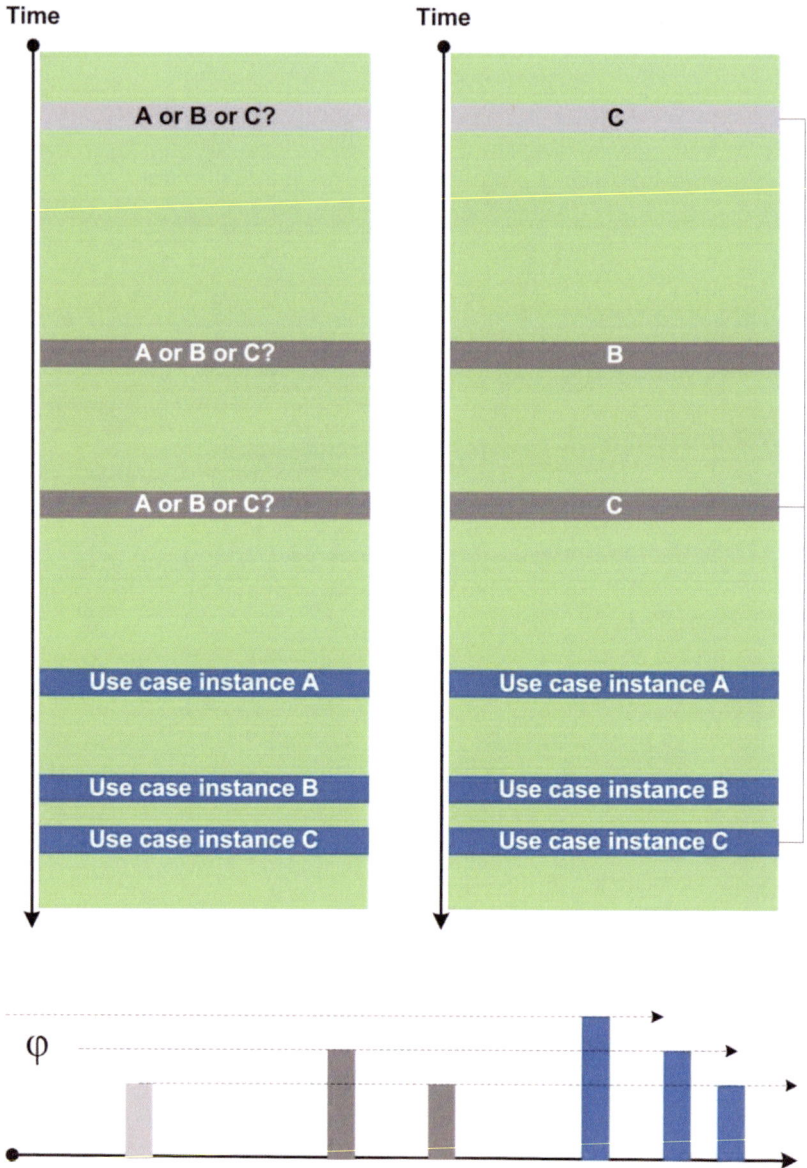

In the picture above, we also identified **Dominant Event Sequence** (page 117) for use case instance C.

Exception Stack Trace

Often the analysis of software traces starts with searching for short textual patterns, like a failure or an exception code, or simply the word "exception." Also, some software components can record their own exceptions or exceptions that were propagated to them, including full stack traces. It is all common in .NET and Java environments. Here is a synthetic and beautified example based on real software traces:

```
N     PID  TID  Message
[...]
265799 8984 4216 ComponentA.Store.GetData threw exception:
'System.Reflection.TargetInvocationException: DCOM connection to server failed with error:
'Exception from HRESULT: 0x842D0001' -> System.Runtime.InteropServices.COMException
(0x842D0001): Exception from HRESULT: 0x842D0001
   at ComponentA.GetData(Byte[] pKey)
   at System.RuntimeMethodHandle._InvokeMethodFast(Object target, Object[] arguments,
SignatureStruct& sig, MethodAttributes methodAttributes, RuntimeTypeHandle typeOwner)
   at System.RuntimeMethodHandle.InvokeMethodFast(Object target, Object[] arguments,
Signature sig, MethodAttributes methodAttributes, RuntimeTypeHandle typeOwner)
   at System.Reflection.RuntimeMethodInfo.Invoke(Object obj, BindingFlags invokeAttr, Binder
binder, Object[] parameters, CultureInfo culture, Boolean skipVisibilityChecks)
   at System.Reflection.RuntimeMethodInfo.Invoke(Object obj, BindingFlags invokeAttr, Binder
binder, Object[] parameters, CultureInfo culture)
   at ComponentB.Connections.ComInterfaceProxy.Invoke(IMessage message)'
265800 8984 4216 === Begin Exception Dump ===
265801 8984 4216 ComponentB.Exceptions.ConnectionException: DCOM connection to server failed
with error: 'Exception from HRESULT: 0x842D0001' ->
System.Runtime.InteropServices.COMException (0x842D0001): Exception from HRESULT: 0x842D0001
265802 8984 4216 at ComponentA.Store.GetData(Byte[] pKey)
[...]
265808 8984 4216 Exception rethrown at [0]:
265809 8984 4216 at System.Runtime.Remoting.Proxies.RealProxy.HandleReturnMessage(IMessage
reqMsg, IMessage retMsg)
265810 8984 4216 at System.Runtime.Remoting.Proxies.RealProxy.PrivateInvoke(MessageData&
msgData, Int32 type)
265811 8984 4216 at ComponentA.Store.GetData(Byte[] pKey)
265812 8984 4216 at ComponentA.App.EnumBusinessObjects()
[...]
265816 8984 4216 ===> InnerException:
265817 8984 4216 ** COM Exception Error Code: 0x842d0001
265818 8984 4216 System.Runtime.InteropServices.COMException (0x842D0001): Exception from
HRESULT: 0x842D0001
265819 8984 4216 at ComponentA.Store.GetData(Byte[] pKey)
265820 8984 4216 === End Exception Dump ===
[...]
```

In the embedded stack trace, we see that the App object tried to enumerate business objects and asked the Store object to get some data. The latter object was probably trying to communicate with the real data store via DCOM. The communication attempt failed with HRESULT.

In the previous pattern example, a stack trace was inside a single trace message but can also be split such as each frame has its own message (date and time columns were removed for clarity):

```
E/AndroidRuntime(31416): java.lang.NullPointerException
E/AndroidRuntime(31416):  at android.view.MotionEvent.writeToParcel(MotionEvent.java:1596)
E/AndroidRuntime(31416):  at
com.example.nullpointer.FullscreenActivity$1.onTouch(FullscreenActivity.java:139)
E/AndroidRuntime(31416):  at android.view.View.dispatchTouchEvent(View.java:3881)
E/AndroidRuntime(31416):  at android.view.ViewGroup.dispatchTouchEvent(ViewGroup.java:869)
E/AndroidRuntime(31416):  at android.view.ViewGroup.dispatchTouchEvent(ViewGroup.java:869)
E/AndroidRuntime(31416):  at android.view.ViewGroup.dispatchTouchEvent(ViewGroup.java:869)
E/AndroidRuntime(31416):  at android.view.ViewGroup.dispatchTouchEvent(ViewGroup.java:869)
E/AndroidRuntime(31416):  at android.view.ViewGroup.dispatchTouchEvent(ViewGroup.java:869)
E/AndroidRuntime(31416):  at com.android.internal.policy.impl.PhoneWindow$DecorView.
superDispatchTouchEvent(PhoneWindow.java:1750)
E/AndroidRuntime(31416):  at com.android.internal.policy.impl.PhoneWindow.
superDispatchTouchEvent(PhoneWindow.java:1135)
E/AndroidRuntime(31416):  at android.app.Activity.dispatchTouchEvent(Activity.java:2096)
E/AndroidRuntime(31416):  at com.android.internal.policy.impl.PhoneWindow$DecorView.
dispatchTouchEvent(PhoneWindow.java:1734)
E/AndroidRuntime(31416):  at android.view.ViewRoot.deliverPointerEvent(ViewRoot.java:2216)
E/AndroidRuntime(31416):  at android.view.ViewRoot.handleMessage(ViewRoot.java:1887)
E/AndroidRuntime(31416):  at android.os.Handler.dispatchMessage(Handler.java:99)
E/AndroidRuntime(31416):  at android.os.Looper.loop(Looper.java:130)
E/AndroidRuntime(31416):  at android.app.ActivityThread.main(ActivityThread.java:3687)
E/AndroidRuntime(31416):  at java.lang.reflect.Method.invokeNative(Native Method)
E/AndroidRuntime(31416):  at java.lang.reflect.Method.invoke(Method.java:507)
E/AndroidRuntime(31416):  at
com.android.internal.os.ZygoteInit$MethodAndArgsCaller.run(ZygoteInit.java:867)
E/AndroidRuntime(31416):  at com.android.internal.os.ZygoteInit.main(ZygoteInit.java:625)
E/AndroidRuntime(31416):  at dalvik.system.NativeStart.main(Native Method)
```

Explanation Trace

When we analyze a trace or log, we may produce **CoTrace** (page 88) of
analyzed messages and visited regions. But the ultimate goal of any trace
and log analysis is to construct the explanation of the observed behavior to
justify the root cause analysis and the proposed mechanism. There may be
several proposed explanations, each having a different set of messages from
the analyzed trace that illustrate them. We call them **Explanation Traces**.
This pattern is shown in the picture where we use the same trace from the
CoTrace analysis pattern.

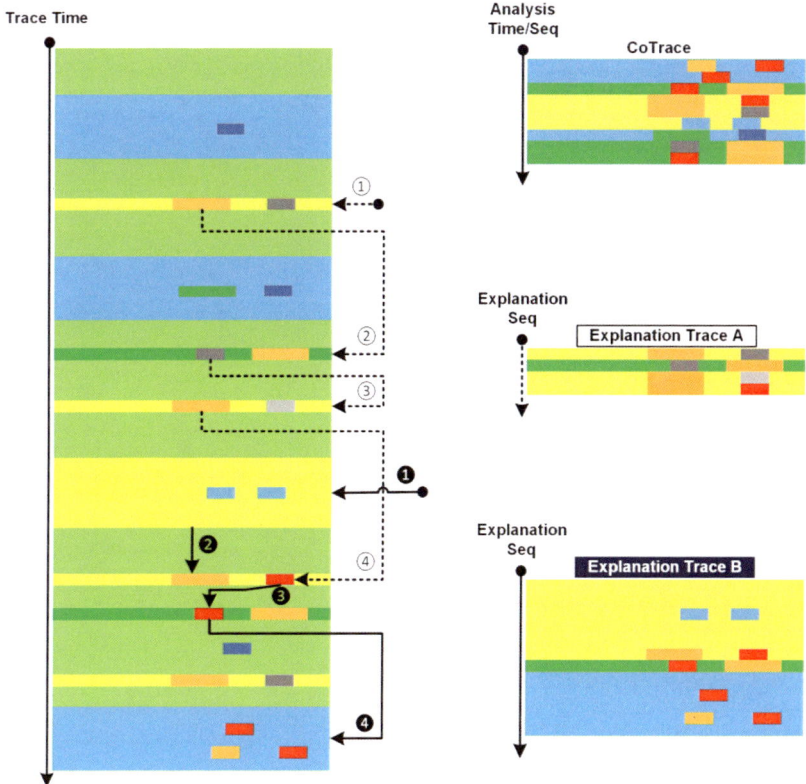

F

Factor Group

We borrowed the next trace and log analysis pattern name from factor groups in mathematics (or quotient groups[70]). Here a group is, of course, not a mathematical group[71] but just a group (or set) of log messages or trace statements. However, every trace message has variable and invariant parts (**Message Invariant**, page 198). Variable parts usually contain some values, addresses, or status bits. They can even be string values. Such values from a set can be partitioned into disjoint (non-overlapping) subsets. For example, a window foreground status can be either TRUE or FALSE. Also, we can group messages into disjoint factor groups, each one having either only true or only false foreground status. For example, the following trace graph illustrates a WindowHistory64[72] log where it was reported that one window was periodically losing and gaining focus:

$$\frac{|M/\blacksquare|}{|M/\blacksquare|} = 1$$

We found messages related to the reported process window title. We found another such group of messages for a different process window by using **Density Distribution** (page 105) pattern. Then a factor group was formed with two subgroups, and their **Relative Density** (page 251) was compared. For correlated alternating values, it was expected to be 1. It was a very simple case, of course, which was analyzed just by looking at a textual log, but in more complex cases, computer assistance is required. A member of a factor group can also be generalized as a message subset with messages having variable part values from some domain subset or even calculated from it (a predicate): $M_i = \{ m \mid P(m) \}$, where the original group of messages is a disjoint union of such message subsets: $M = \cup M_i$.

False Positive Error

We often see such errors in software traces recorded during deviant software behavior (often called non-working software traces). When we double-check their presence in normally expected software behavior traces (often called working traces), we find them there too. We already mentioned similar false positives when introducing the first software trace analysis pattern called **Periodic Error** (page 231). Here is an example that was taken from the real trace. In a non-working trace, we found the following error in the **Adjoint Thread** (page 48) of **Foreground Component** (page 57):

```
OpenProcess error 5
```

However, we found the same error in the working trace, continued looking and found several other errors:

```
Message request report: last error 1168, ...
[...]
GetMsg result -2146435043
```

The last one is 8010001D if converted to a hex status, but, unfortunately, the same errors were present in the working trace, too, in the same **Activity Regions** (page 41).

After that, we started comparing both traces looking for **Bifurcation Point** (page 61), and we found the error that was only present in a non-working trace with significant trace differences after that:

```
Error reading from the named pipe: 800700E9
```

On Windows, the WinDbg debugger can convert error and status values into descriptions:

```
0:000> !error 800700E9
Error code: (HRESULT) 0x800700e9 (2147942633) - No process is on the
other end of the pipe.
```

Feature of Activity

When looking at trace and log messages, we are usually interested in some features (for example, when doing **feature engineering**[73], but not limited to) which can be labeled via Feature IDs (FID). Messages with the same FID value constitute **Feature of Activity**, similar to **Thread of Activity**, page 296 (or **Adjoint Thread of Activity**, page 48).

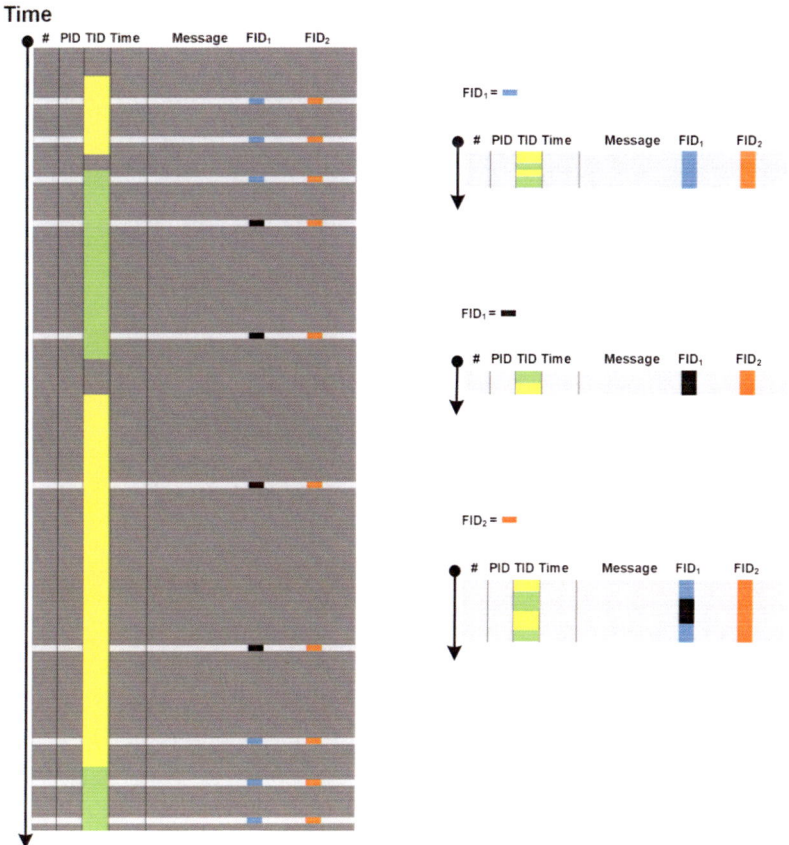

Such **Features of Activity** can span several (A)TIDs in contrast to **Fibers of Activity** (page 138) which are confined to the same (A)TID and may have different FID values. Therefore, inside (A)TID, there can be several **Features of Activity** having different FID values.

Fiber Bundle

Modern software trace recording, visualization, and analysis tools such as Process Monitor, Xperf, WPR, and WPA provide stack traces associated with trace messages. Consider stack traces as software traces that we have, in a more general case, traces (fibers) bundled together on (attached to) a base software trace. For example, a trace message that mentions an IRP can have its I/O stack attached, together with its thread stack trace with function calls leading to a function that emits the trace message. Another example is an association of different types of traces with trace messages, such as managed and unmanaged ones, or, for example, the so-called Mapped Diagnostic Context (MDC). This general trace analysis pattern needed a name, so we opted for **Fiber Bundle** as an analogy with a fiber bundle[74] from mathematics. Here's a graphical representation of stack traces recorded for each trace message where one message also has an associated I/O stack trace:

Trace
messages

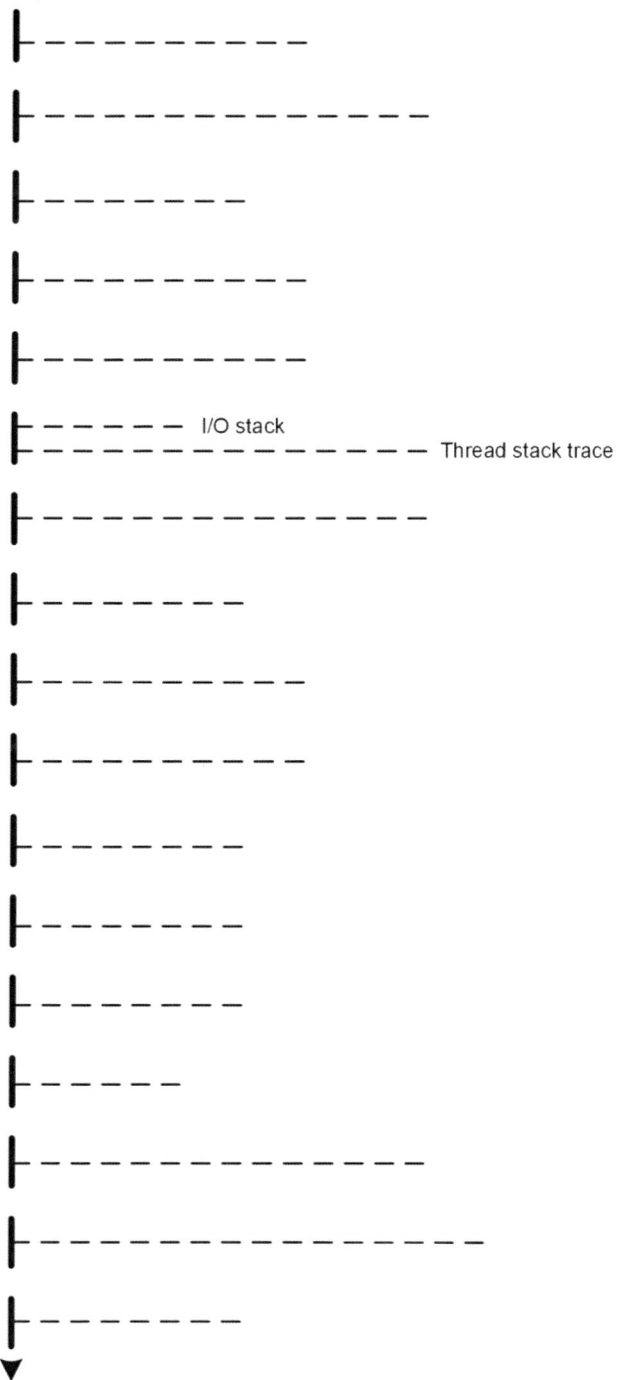

I/O stack

Thread stack trace

Fiber of Activity

When using complex trace and log analysis patterns such as **Fourier Activity** (page 142), we may be first interested in selecting all instances of a particular message type from a specific **Thread of Activity** (page 296) and then look for **Time Deltas** (page 298), **Discontinuities** (page 115), **Data Flow** (page 95), and other patterns. We call this analysis pattern **Fiber of Activity** by the analogy of fibers[75] (lightweight threads) since the individual thread execution flow is "co-operative" inside, whereas threads themselves are preempted outside. The following diagram from **Fourier Activity** analysis pattern example illustrates the concept by showing three fibers:

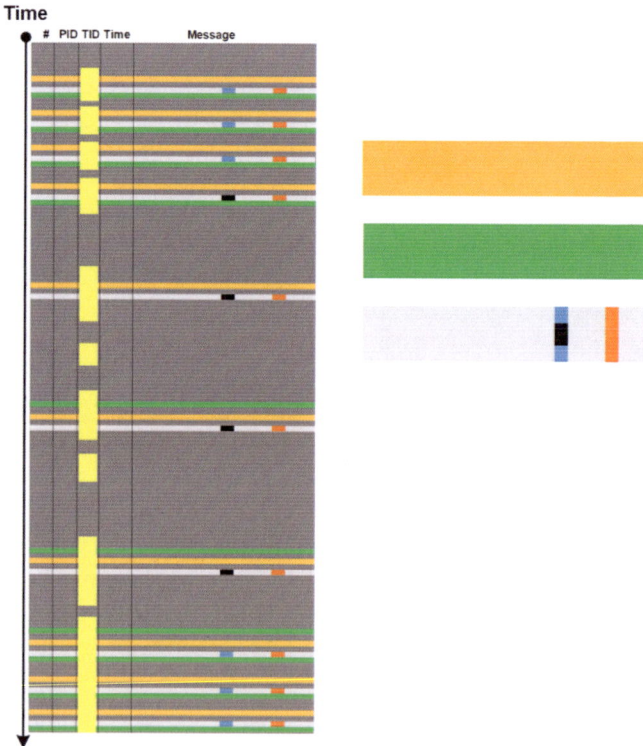

This analysis pattern differs from trace-wide **Sheaf of Activities** (page 266), where the latter is about selecting messages as **Adjoint Threads of Activity** (page 48), which may span several processes and threads.

File Size

Trace and log analysis starts with assessing artifact **File Size**, especially with multiple logging scenarios in distributed systems. For example, if all log files are the same size, we might have **Circular Traces** (page 78) or **Truncated Traces** (page 352). Both point to the wrong trace timing plan[76] or just using the default tracing tool configuration.

Software Problem A	Name: Client-A.log Size: 10MB	Name: Server-A.log Size: 10MB
Software Problem B	Name: Client-B.log Size: 10MB	Name: Client-B.log Size: 10MB
No Problem	Name: Client-C.log Size: 10MB	Name: Server-C.log Size: 10MB

Flag

Sometimes we may want to **Flag** a message or **Activity Region** (page 41), for example, using **Message Annotations** (page 185). In other cases, we may have **Activity Regions** that are sorted by their coordinate-wise inclusion. Or we have an inclusion of **Message Sets** (page 202). The analysis pattern name is borrowed from flag [77] filtration [78] in mathematics, where we consider subsets of messages and **Activity Regions** as subspaces. **Dia|gram** pictures [79] of **Flags** may even resemble flags of some countries.

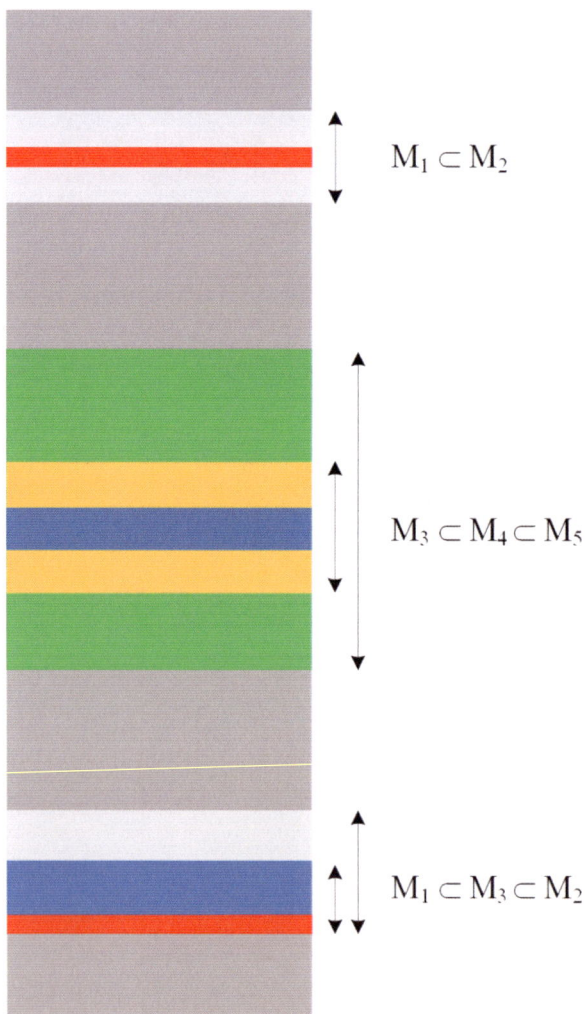

$$M_1 \subset M_2$$

$$M_3 \subset M_4 \subset M_5$$

$$M_1 \subset M_3 \subset M_2$$

Focus of Tracing

Activity Region pattern (page 41) highlights "mechanical" and syntactical aspects of trace analysis, whereas this pattern brings attention to changing the semantics of trace message flow, for example, in a terminal services environment, from login messages during session initialization to database search. Here is a graphical illustration of the pattern where the tracing focus region spans three regions of activity:

Activity regions: J_{m1}, J_{m2}, J_{m3}

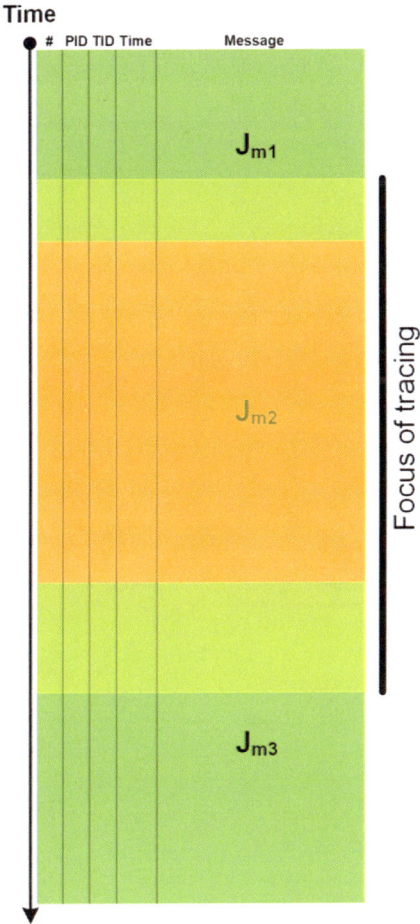

Fourier Activity

Sometimes we have trace and log messages that appear with a certain time frequency throughout all log activity or specific **Thread of Activity** (page 296). Such frequencies may fluctuate, reflecting varying system or process performance. Analyzing trace areas where such messages have different **Time Deltas** (page 298) may point to additional diagnostic log messages useful for root cause analysis. The following minimal trace graph depicts the recent log analysis for proprietary file copy operation where the frequency of internal communication channel entry/exit **Opposition Messages** (page 225) was decreasing from time to time. Such periods were correlated with increased time intervals between "entry" and "exit" messages. Analysis of messages between them revealed additional diagnostic statements missing in periods of higher frequency and corresponding **Timeouts** (page 300), adding up to overall performance degradation and slowness of copy operation.

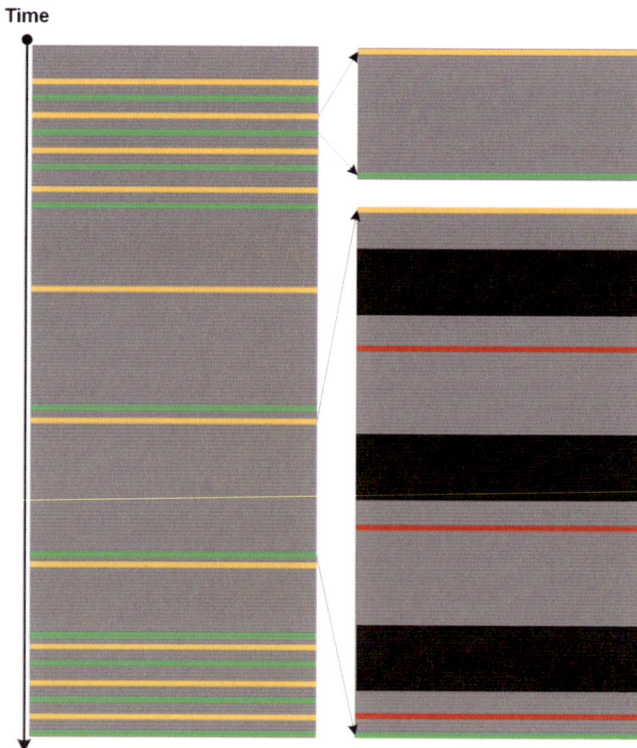

Additional analysis of **Data Association** (page 94) in a different message type between available communication buffers and the total number of such buffers revealed a significant frequency drop during constant **Data Flow** (page 95) of zero available communication buffers:

Time

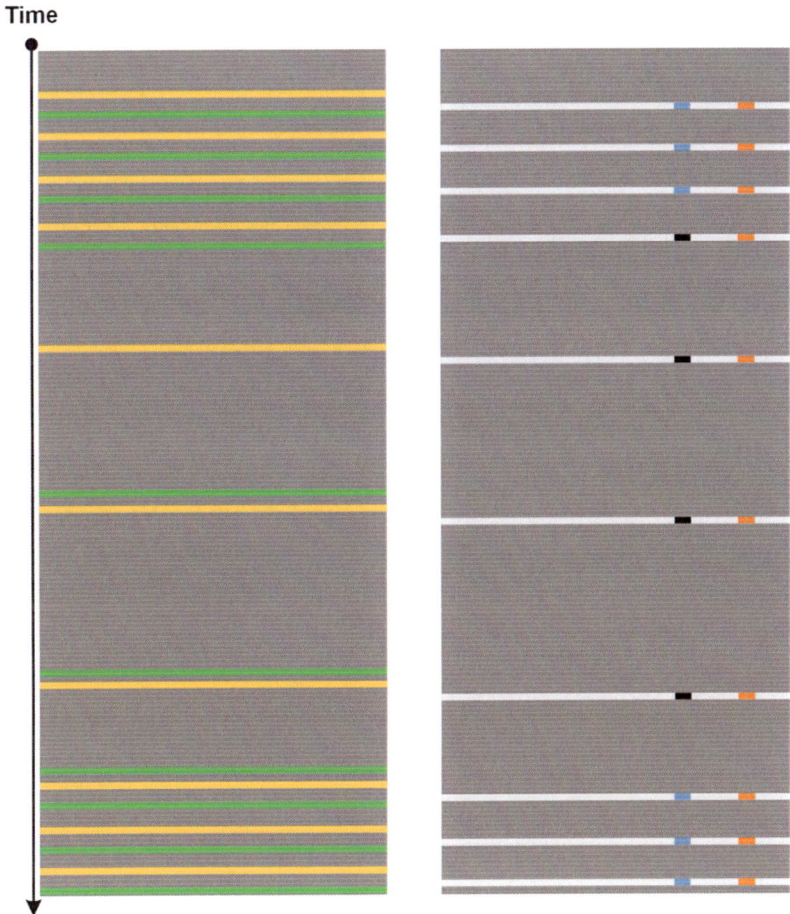

We call this analysis pattern **Fourier Activity** by analogy with the Fourier series[80] in mathematics. This pattern is for individual message types and can also be considered a fine-grained example of **Statement Current** (page 286) and **Trace Acceleration** (page 303) analysis patterns which can be used to detect areas of different frequencies in individual **Fibers** (**Adjoint Threads of Activities**, page 48, formed from the same **Thread of Activity**).

G

Galois Trace

When doing **Inter-Correlational** (page 167) analysis between different traces and logs, we can move simultaneously in time direction or backward (**Back Tracing**, page 56). In some cases, we may start our analysis by identifying **Significant Events** (page 270) in both logs and then move in opposite directions finding another pair of messages that can be useful for diagnostic identification. We call this analysis pattern **Galois Trace** by analogy with the Galois connection[81] in mathematics. In our case, moving from trace A to trace B and back corresponds to F and G functions with A and B as individual trace messages or their **Message Contexts** (page 191, as per monotone [82] definition). The analysis pattern is illustrated in the following diagram:

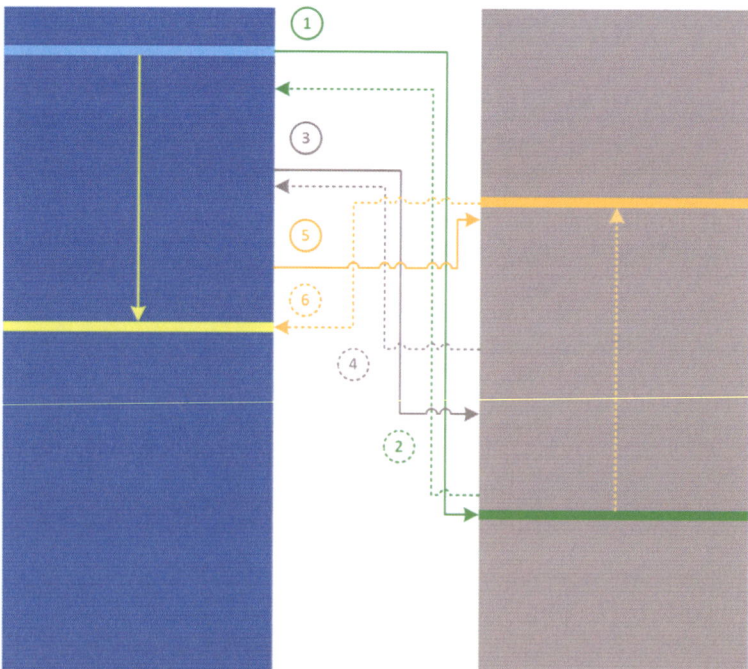

Significant Events (start of analysis)
Significant Events (end of analysis)

Generative Trace

Source code can be considered a type of **general trace** [83] from the corresponding **generative narrative plane** [84]. We call it **Generative Trace** since it can generate different traces of execution. If such a trace contains logging code statements, they form **Declarative Trace** (page 102) as a subset of messages. **Generative Trace** also overlaps with the corresponding **Moduli Trace** (page 211). We can apply many trace and log analysis patterns and even consider the line number axis as pseudo-time. The following diagram illustrates the **Linked Messages** (page 178) analysis pattern in the context of **Generative Trace** and generated traces:

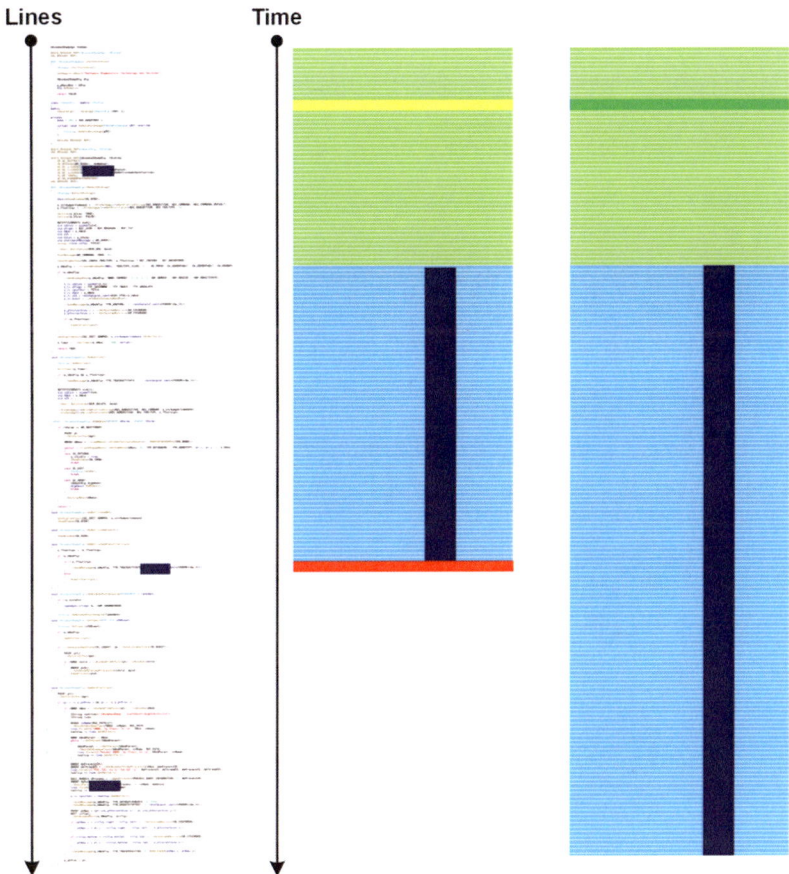

Glued Activity

Adjoint Thread (page 48) invariants like PID can be reused, giving rise to curious ETW traces where two separate execution entities are glued together in one trace. For example, in one trace, we see AppA and AppB sharing the same PID:

```
#       Module  PID  TID   Time       Message
[...]
242583 ProcMon 5492 9476 11:04:33 LoadImageEvent for ImageName: …\AppA.exe PID: 5492
256222 ProcMon 5492 9476 11:04:50 ProcessDestroyEvent for PPID: 12168 PID: 5492
274887 ProcMon 5492 1288 11:05:18 LoadImageEvent for ImageName: …\AppB.exe PID: 5492
[...]
```

Other similar examples may include different instances of components sharing the same name, source code, or even, in general, periodic tracing sessions appended to the end of the same trace file. Although, we think that the latter should be a different pattern. We named this pattern **Glued Activity** by an analogy of different thread strings glued together (in general, manifolds[85] glued along their boundaries). Another name might be along the line of **Adjoint Thread** ID reuse (ATID reuse).

The following diagram illustrates common scenarios for this analysis pattern:

Time

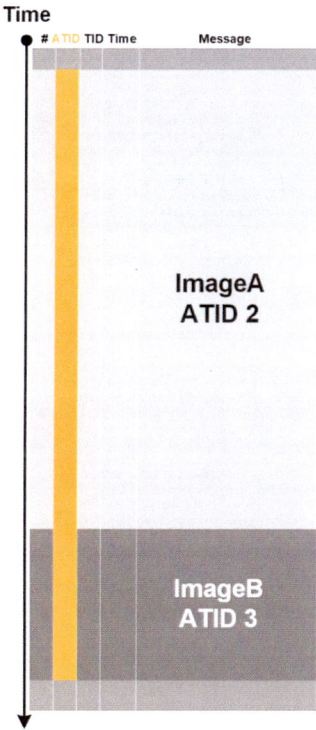

Time

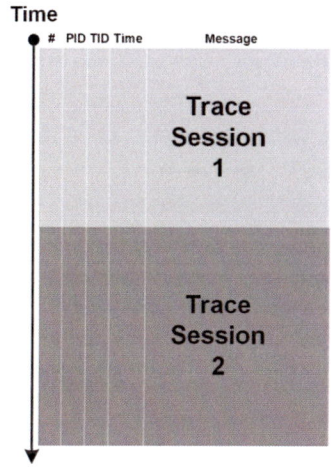

Gossip

This pattern has a funny name **Gossip**. We were thinking originally of calling it *Duplicated Message* but gave it the new name allowing for the possibility of the semantics of the same message to be distorted in subsequent trace messages from different **Adjoint Threads** (page 48). Here is a typical ETW trace example (distortion free) of the same message content seen in different modules (we omitted some columns like Date and Time):

```
#        Module  PID  TID  Message
[...]
26875    ModuleA 2172 5284 LoadImageEvent:
ImageName(\Device\HarddiskVolume2\Windows\System32\notepad.exe)
ProcessId(0x000000000000087C)
26876    ModuleB 2172 5284 LoadImageEvent:
ImageName(\Device\HarddiskVolume2\Windows\System32\notepad.exe),
ProcessId(2172)
26877    ModuleC 2172 5284 ImageLoad: fileName=notepad.exe, pid:
000000000000087C
[...]
```

In such cases, when constructing **Event Sequence Order** (page 126), we recommend choosing messages from one source instead of mixing events from different sources, for example:

```
#        Module   PID  TID Message
[...]
26875    ModuleA 2172 5284 LoadImageEvent:
ImageName(\Device\HarddiskVolume2\Windows\System32\notepad.exe)
ProcessId(0x000000000000087C)
[...]
33132    ModuleA 4180 2130 LoadImageEvent:
ImageName(\Device\HarddiskVolume2\Windows\System32\calc.exe)
ProcessId(0x0000000000001054)
[...]
```

Guest Component

Sometimes, when comparing normal, expected (working) and abnormal (non-working) traces, we can get a clue for further troubleshooting and debugging by looking at module load events. For example, when we see an unexpected module loaded in our non-working trace, its function (and sometimes even module name) can signify some differences to pay attention to:

```
#    PID TID Time        Message
[...]
4492 908 912 11:06:41.953 LoadImageEvent:ImageName(\WINDOWS\system32\3rdPartySso.dll)
[...]
```

We call this pattern **Guest Component**, which differs from **Missing Component** (page 207). Although in the latter pattern, a missing component in one trace may appear in another, the component name is known as apriori and expected. In the former pattern, the component is unexpected. For example, in the trace above, its partial name fragment "Sso" may trigger a suggestion to relate differences in authentication where, in a non-working case, SSO (single sign-on) was configured.

The following diagram illustrates this analysis pattern:

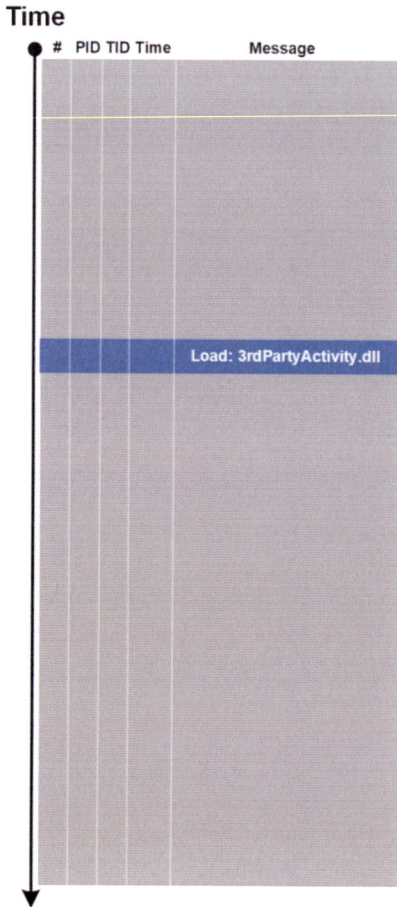

H

Hedges

Sometimes we have variable sequences of **Significant Events** (page 270) when we expect a certain constant number of such events in repeated normal and problem cases. For example, in repeated normal cases, we expect more than ten events, but in repeated abnormal cases - just two events. The latter cases would indicate that something happened inside the processing of the second event. However, if one or more such cases contain 3 or 4 events, that would point to some external influence that aborted the sequence of events. We call such variable event sequences **Hedges** by analogy with hedge or variadic variables[86]. One of the recent examples that we encountered involved multiple abnormal cases with just two events. We were about to investigate the internals of the second event but noticed that one of the cases contained three events. Further analysis indicated that the whole sequence was aborted by some external process after reaching a certain timeout. In the case of 3 events, the first two happened too earlier, and that allowed for the 3rd event to occur before the timeout was triggered:

Time

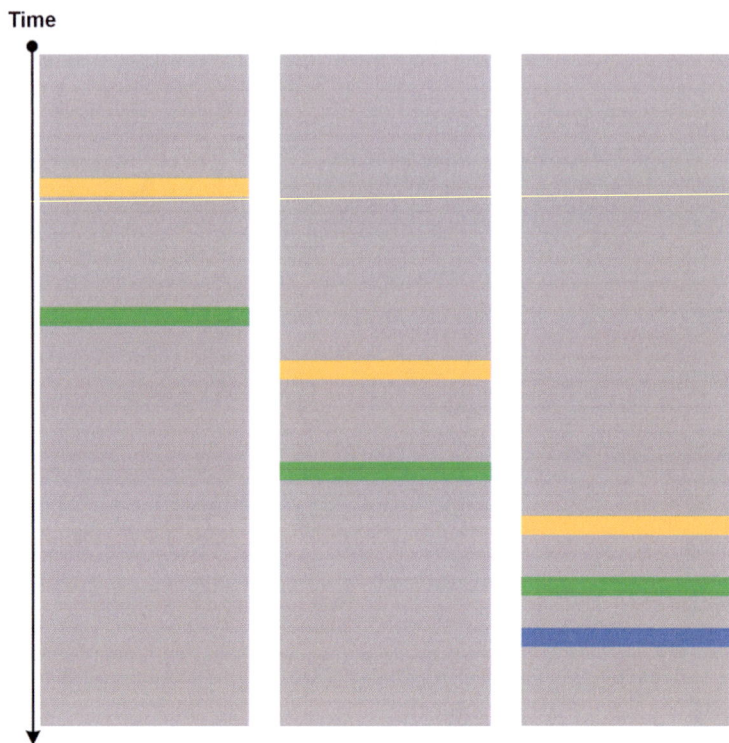

Hidden Error

Sometimes we look at a trace or log, and instead of **Error Messages** (page 123), we only see their "signs," such as a DLL load event for an error or fault reporting module or a module that is related to symbol files such *diasym-reader.dll*. This pattern is called by analogy to **Hidden Exception**[87] in the memory dump analysis pattern catalog, although sometimes we can see such modules in the memory dump **Module Collection**[88]. For example, the presence of *diasymreader* module may signify an unreported .NET exception and suggest a dump collection strategy.

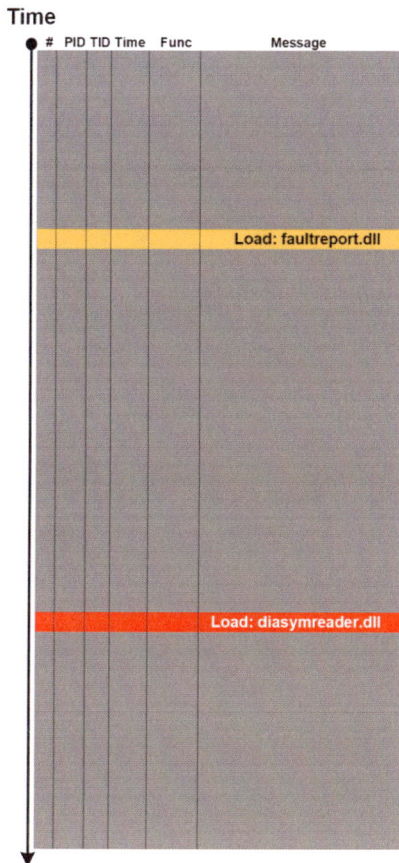

Hidden Facts

The previous patterns, such as **Basic Facts** (page 60) and **Vocabulary Index** (page 362), address the mapping of a problem description to software execution artifacts such as traces and logs. **Indirect Facts** (page 161) analysis pattern addresses the problem of incomplete problem descriptions. However, we need another pattern for completeness that addresses the mapping from a log to troubleshooting and debugging recommendations. We call it **Hidden Facts** that are uncovered by trace and log analysis. Of course, there can be many such hidden facts, and usually, they are uncovered after narrowing down analysis to particular **Threads of Activity** (page 296), **Adjoint Threads** (page 48), **Message Context** (page 191), **Message Set** (page 201), or **Data Flow** (page 95) patterns. The need for that pattern had arisen during the pattern-oriented analysis of the trace case study from Malcolm McCaffery[89] and can be illustrated in the following diagram:

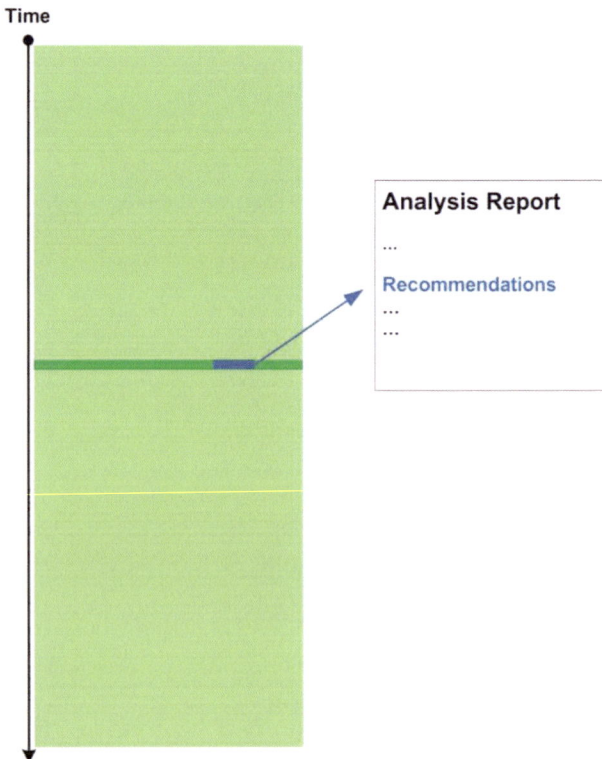

I

Identification Messages

Often, we need to identify the source of messages based on the problem object or subsystem description (*what* question) before we proceed to answer a *"where"* question (where, in a trace, we can find messages related to a problem). Even when we know where messages are, there can be many sources to select from (if we don't know the *where* question, we can use the **Indirect Message** analysis pattern, page 162). To answer the *"what"* question, we propose the **Identification Messages** analysis pattern. **Basic Fact** (page 60) problem description may include properties and behavioral description of the problem object or subsystem. Based on that, we can map them to the log messages that such an object can produce:

Basic Fact **has** properties **and** behaviour

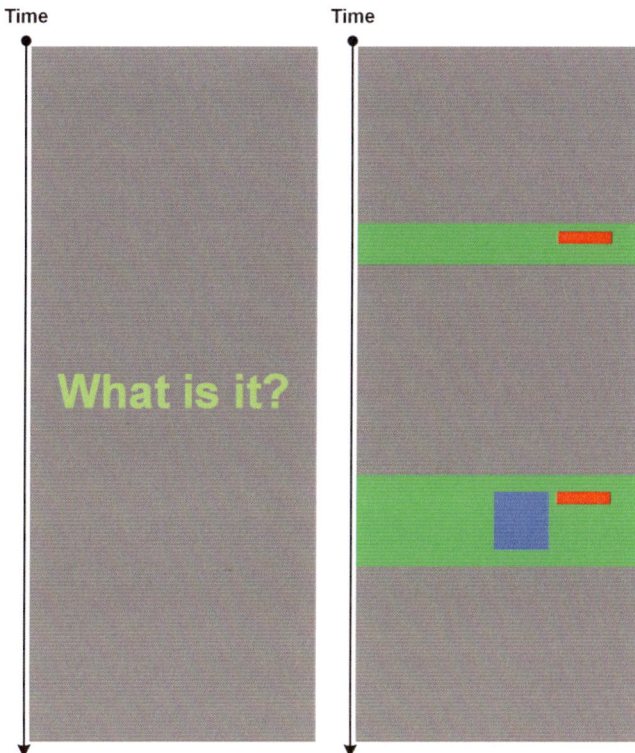

These messages may not be **Error Messages** (page 123) or some other type of messages reflecting abnormal behavior. These messages are only used to identify the software object, module, or subsystem.

For example, there were problems with the custom status bar in one case. However, the window handle for it or its parent wasn't specified in the problem report. In the log file, we had many messages describing the GUI behavior of many windows. To find out the status bar, we thought it should have a small height but long width. Indeed, we found one such child window. Also, the log file contained many messages related to frequent window text changes for this window, possibly reflecting the status bar updates. Having identified the window handle, we proceeded to the analysis of another log with thousands of window messages. Because of the known window handle, we could select only messages related to our problem status bar.

Implementation Discourse

If we look at any non-trivial trace, we see different **Implementation Discourses**. Furthermore, components are written in various languages and adhere to different runtime environments, binary models, and interface frameworks. All these implementation variations influence trace messages' structure, syntax, and semantics. For example, .NET debugging traces differ from file system driver or COM debugging messages. For this reason, we establish the new field of *Software Trace Linguistics* as a science of software trace languages. Some parallels can be drawn here towards software linguistics (the science of software languages), although we came to that conclusion independently while thinking about applying "ethnography of speaking" to software trace narration.

Impossible Trace

Sometimes, we look at a trace and say it is impossible. For example, this fragment shows that the function *foo* had been called:

```
#    Module  PID TID Message
[...]
1001 ModuleA 202 404 foo: start
1002 ModuleA 202 404 foo: end
[...]
```

However, if we look at the corresponding source code (**PLOT**[90]), we see that something is missing: the function *bar* must have been called with its own set of trace messages we don't see in the trace:

```
void foo()
{
   TRACE("foo: start");
   bar();
   TRACE("foo: end");
}

void bar()
{
   TRACE("bar: start");
   // some code ...
   TRACE("bar: end");
}
```

We suspect the runtime code was modified, perhaps by patching. In other cases of missing messages, we can also suspect thrown exceptions or local buffer overflows that lead to wrong return addresses skipping the code with expected tracing statements. The mismatch between the trace and the source code we are looking at is also possible if the old source code did not have the *bar* function called.

Incomplete History

Typical software narrative history consists of requests and responses, for example, function or object method calls and returns:

```
#       Module PID  TID  Time            File      Function Message
[...]
26060 dllA    1604 7108 10:06:21.746 fileA.c foo       Calling bar
[...]
26232 dllA    1604 7108 10:06:22.262 fileA.c foo       bar returns 0x5
[...]
```

The code that generates execution history is *response-complete* if it traces both requests and responses. For such code (except in cases where tracing is stopped before a response), the absence of expected responses could be a sign of blocked threads or quiet exception processing. On the other hand, the code that generates execution history is *exception-complete* if it also traces exception processing. Response-complete and exception-complete code is called *call-complete*. If we do not see response messages for call-complete code, we have **Incomplete History**.

In general, we can talk about the absence of certain messages in a trace as a deviation from the standard trace sequence template corresponding to a use case. The difference there is in a missing request too.

Indexical Trace

This pattern describes **Inter-Correlation** (page 162) pattern variant when we have a trace that has messages of interest pointing to specific **Activity Regions** (page 41) in another trace. The latter trace can be huge, taken from another computer, and split into many parts (**Split Trace**, page 282). This pattern is very helpful when we need to diagnose the problem in the large split trace, but we do not know when it happened. Then an index trace that may have recorded the software execution account (for example, in the case of a broker-like architecture) can point to the right trace fragment from the split trace.

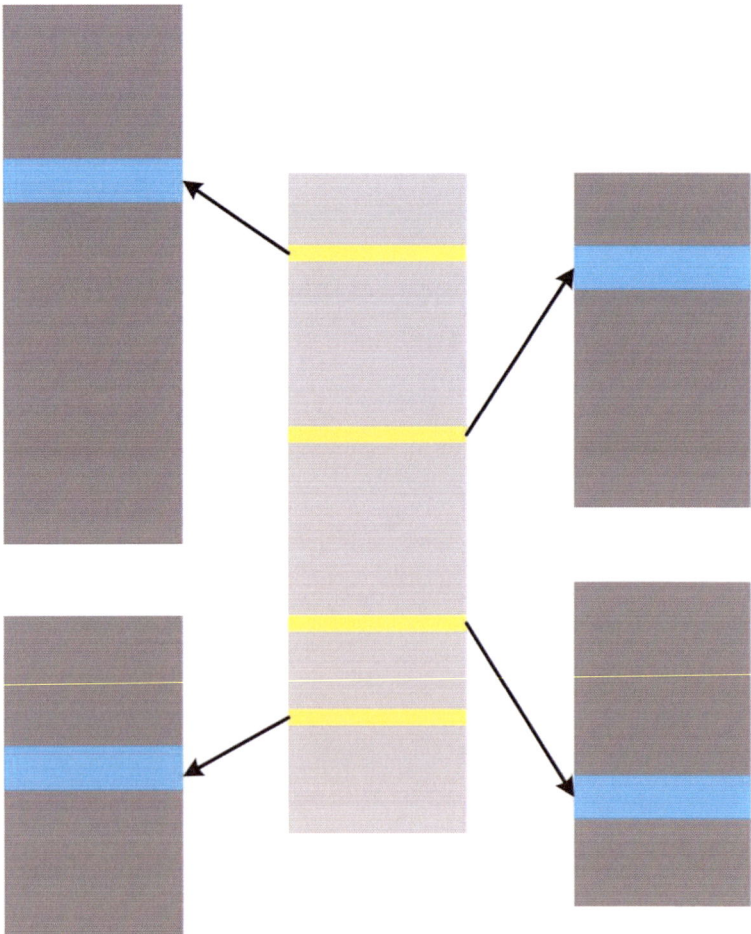

Indirect Facts

Sometimes in the case of missing **Basic Facts** (page 60), we can discern **Indirect Facts** from the message text and even from other patterns. For example, we were interested in all messages from the certain process name in one incident, but its PID was missing from the problem description. Fortunately, we were able to get its PID from one of the individual messages from a completely different source:

Indirect Message

Sometimes we have **Basic Facts** (page 60) in a problem description but can't find messages corresponding to them in a trace or log file, but we are sure the tracing (logging) was done correctly. This may be because we have **Sparse Trace** (page 279), or we are not familiar well with product or system tracing messages (such as with **Implementation Discourse**, page 155).

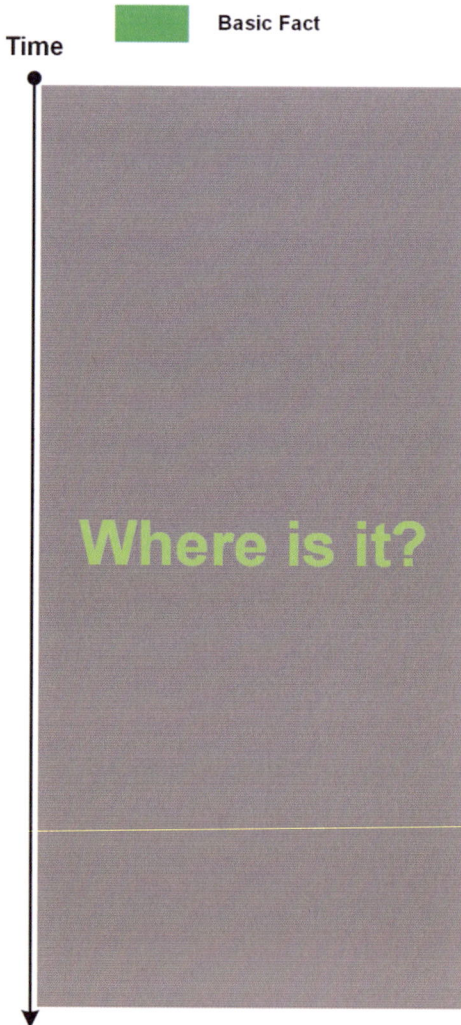

In such a case, we search for an **Indirect Message** of a possible cause:

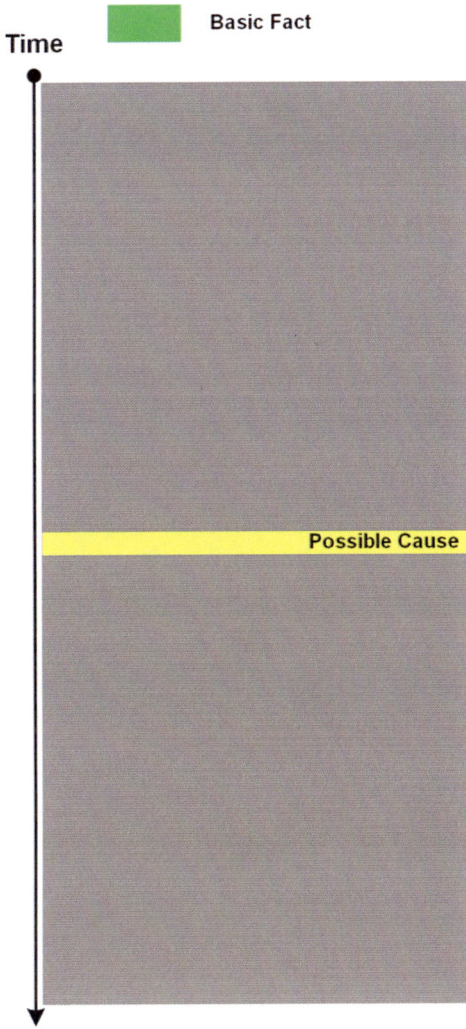

Having found such a message, we may hypothesize that **Missing Message** (page 209) should have been located nearby (this is based on the semantics of both messages), and we then explore the corresponding **Message Context** (page 191):

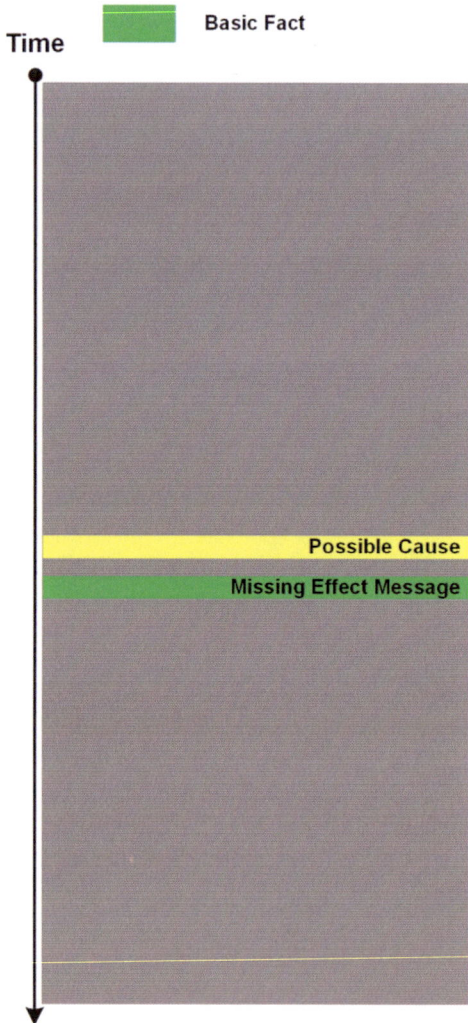

The same analysis strategy is possible for missing causal messages. Here we search for effect or side effect messages:

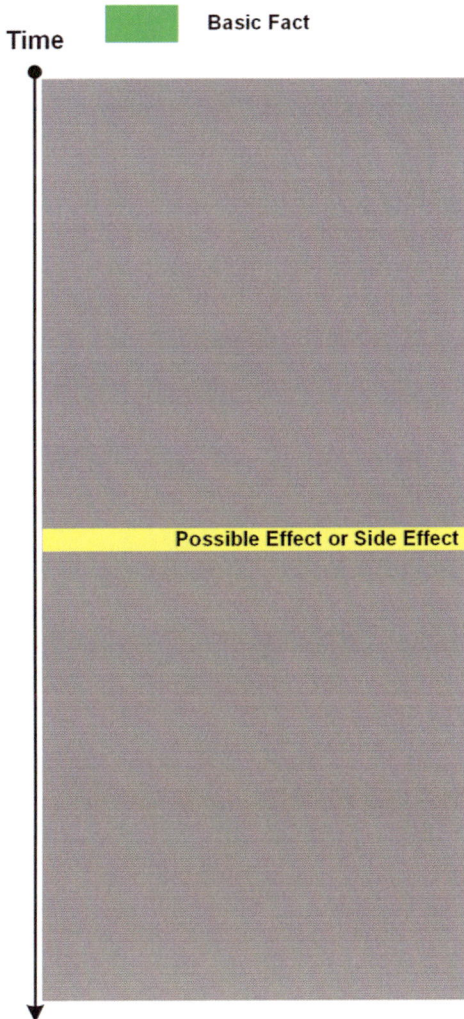

Having found them, we proceed with further analysis:

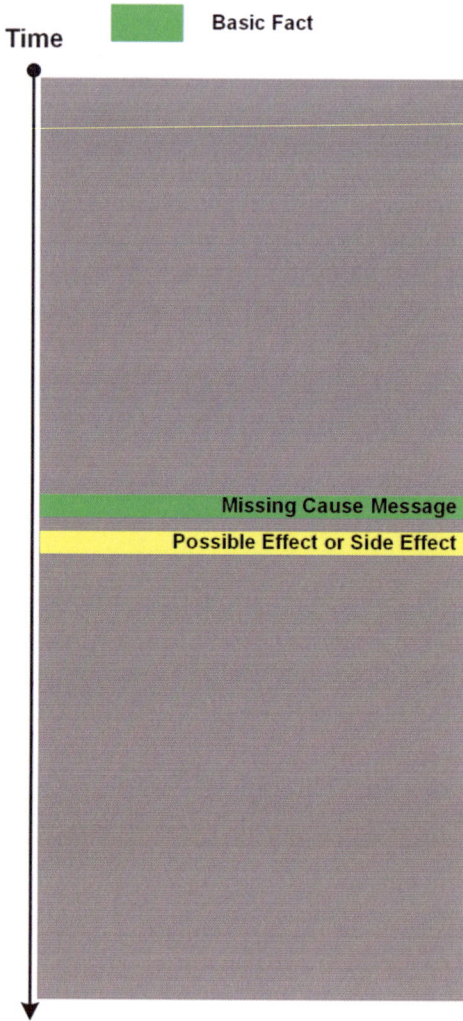

Time

Basic Fact

Missing Cause Message

Possible Effect or Side Effect

Inter-Correlation

This pattern is analogous to the previously described **Intra-Correlation** pattern (page 170), but it involves several traces from possibly different trace agents recorded (most commonly) at the same time or during an overlapping time interval:

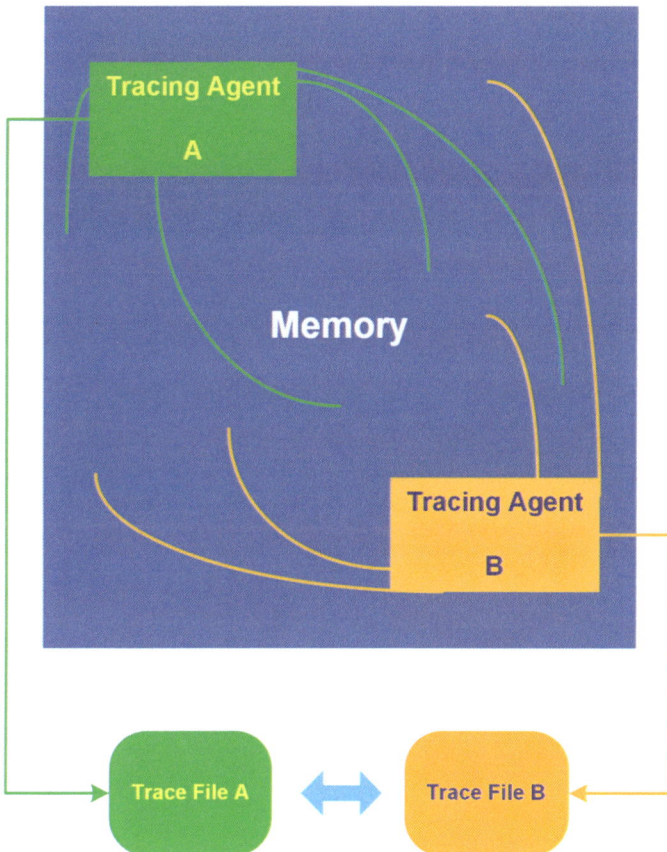

Let's look at a typical example of an application subclassing windows to add an additional look and feel element to its GUI or inject hooks into window messaging. Suppose this application also records important trace data like window parameters before and after subclassing using ETW technology. When we run the application in a terminal services environment, all windows (including other processes) are shown with an incorrect dimension. We, for this reason, request the application trace and, also, the WindowHistory[91] trace to see how the coordinates of all windows change over time. We easily find some **Basic Facts** (page 60) in both traces, such as the window class name or time, but it looks like the window handle is different. In another set of traces recorded for comparison, we have the same window handle values; the class name is absent from the ETW trace, but a process and thread ID for the same window handle are different. We, for this reason, do not see a correlation between these traces and suspect that both traces in two sets were recorded in different terminal sessions, for example:

ETW trace:

```
#     PID  TID  Time           Message
[...]
46750 5890 6960 10:17:18.825  Subclassing, handle=0x100B8, class=MyWindowClass, [...]
[...]
```

WindowHistory trace:

```
Handle: 0001006E Class: "MyWindowClass" Title: ""
   Captured at: 10:17:19:637
   Process ID: 19e0
   Thread ID: 16e4
   Parent: 0
   Screen position (l,t,r,b): (-2,896,1282,1026)
   Client rectangle (l,t,r,b): (0,0,1276,122)
   Visible: true
   Window placement command: SW_SHOWNORMAL
   Foreground: false
   HungApp: false
   Minimized: false
   Maximized: false
[...]
```

Interspace

General traces and logs[92] may have **Message Space** (page 203) regions "surrounded" by the so-called **Interspace**. Such **Interspace** regions may link individual **Message Space** regions like in this diagram generalizing WinDbg **!process 0 3f** command output:

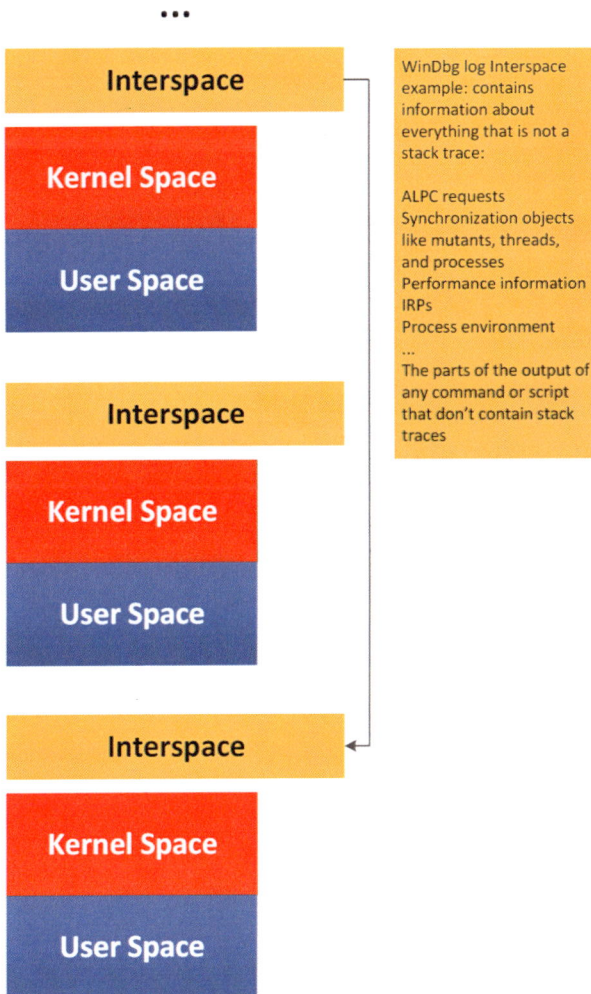

Intra-Correlation

Sometimes we see a functional activity and **Basic Facts** (page 60) in a trace. Then we might want to find a correlation between that activity and facts in another part of the trace. If that intra-correlation fits into our problem description, we may claim a possible explanation or, if we are lucky, we have just found an inference to the best explanation, as philosophers of science like to say. Here is an example, but this time using the WindowHistory tracing tool[93]. A third-party application frequently lost window focus, and the suspicion was on a terminal services client process. We found that the following WindowHistory trace fragment corresponded to that application:

```
Handle: 00050586 Class: "Application A Class" Title: ""
      Title changed at 15:52:4:3 to "Application A"
      Title changed at 15:52:10:212 to "Application A - File1"
[...]
    Process ID: 89c
    Thread ID: d6c
[...]
    Visible: true
    Window placement command: SW_SHOWNORMAL
          Placement changed at 15:54:57:506 to SW_SHOWMINIMIZED
          Placement changed at 15:55:2:139 to SW_SHOWNORMAL
    Foreground: false
        Foreground changed at 15:52:4:3 to true
        Foreground changed at 15:53:4:625 to false
        Foreground changed at 15:53:42:564 to true
        Foreground changed at 15:53:44:498 to false
        Foreground changed at 15:53:44:498 to true
        Foreground changed at 15:53:44:592 to false
        Foreground changed at 15:53:45:887 to true
        Foreground changed at 15:53:47:244 to false
        Foreground changed at 15:53:47:244 to true
        Foreground changed at 15:53:47:353 to false
        Foreground changed at 15:54:26:416 to true
        Foreground changed at 15:54:27:55 to false
        Foreground changed at 15:54:27:55 to true
        Foreground changed at 15:54:27:180 to false
        Foreground changed at 15:54:28:428 to true
        Foreground changed at 15:54:28:771 to false
        Foreground changed at 15:54:28:865 to true
        Foreground changed at 15:54:29:99 to false
        Foreground changed at 15:54:30:877 to true
        Foreground changed at 15:54:57:521 to false
        Foreground changed at 15:55:2:76 to true
        Foreground changed at 15:57:3:378 to false
        Foreground changed at 15:57:11:396 to true
        Foreground changed at 15:57:29:601 to false
        Foreground changed at 15:57:39:803 to true
        Foreground changed at 15:58:54:41 to false
```

```
Foreground changed at 15:59:8:96 to true
Foreground changed at 16:1:19:478 to false
Foreground changed at 16:1:27:527 to true
Foreground changed at 16:1:39:914 to false
Foreground changed at 16:2:0:515 to true
Foreground changed at 16:7:14:628 to false
Foreground changed at 16:7:24:246 to true
Foreground changed at 16:9:53:523 to false
Foreground changed at 16:10:15:919 to true
Foreground changed at 16:10:31:426 to false
Foreground changed at 16:11:12:818 to true
Foreground changed at 16:11:59:538 to false
Foreground changed at 16:12:39:456 to true
Foreground changed at 16:13:6:364 to false
```

Corresponding terminal services client window trace fragment does not show any foreground changes, but another application's main window has lots of them:

```
Handle: 000D0540 Class: "Application B Class" Title: "Application B"
[...]
    Process ID: 3ac
    Thread ID: bd4
[...]
    Foreground: false
        Foreground changed at 15:50:36:972 to true
        Foreground changed at 15:50:53:732 to false
        Foreground changed at 15:50:53:732 to true
        Foreground changed at 15:50:53:826 to false
        Foreground changed at 15:51:51:352 to true
        Foreground changed at 15:51:53:941 to false
        Foreground changed at 15:53:8:135 to true
        Foreground changed at 15:53:8:182 to false
        Foreground changed at 15:53:10:178 to true
        Foreground changed at 15:53:13:938 to false
        Foreground changed at 15:53:30:443 to true
        Foreground changed at 15:53:31:20 to false
        Foreground changed at 15:53:31:20 to true
        Foreground changed at 15:53:31:129 to false
        Foreground changed at 15:53:34:78 to true
        Foreground changed at 15:53:34:795 to false
        Foreground changed at 15:53:34:795 to true
        Foreground changed at 15:53:34:873 to false
        Foreground changed at 15:53:36:901 to true
        Foreground changed at 15:53:42:502 to false
        Foreground changed at 15:53:42:502 to true
        Foreground changed at 15:53:42:564 to false
        Foreground changed at 15:57:3:425 to true
        Foreground changed at 15:57:4:595 to false
        Foreground changed at 15:57:10:507 to true
        Foreground changed at 15:57:11:318 to false
        Foreground changed at 15:57:29:632 to true
        Foreground changed at 15:57:31:67 to false
        Foreground changed at 15:57:32:721 to true
```

```
Foreground changed at 15:57:33:844 to false
Foreground changed at 15:58:54:88 to true
Foreground changed at 15:58:56:178 to false
Foreground changed at 15:59:6:505 to true
Foreground changed at 15:59:7:987 to false
Foreground changed at 16:1:19:525 to true
Foreground changed at 16:1:19:961 to false
Foreground changed at 16:1:26:607 to true
Foreground changed at 16:1:27:434 to false
Foreground changed at 16:1:39:914 to true
Foreground changed at 16:1:39:992 to false
Foreground changed at 16:1:49:798 to true
Foreground changed at 16:2:0:437 to false
Foreground changed at 16:7:14:628 to true
Foreground changed at 16:7:14:847 to false
Foreground changed at 16:7:18:76 to true
Foreground changed at 16:7:24:106 to false
Foreground changed at 16:9:58:790 to true
Foreground changed at 16:10:4:16 to false
Foreground changed at 16:10:4:874 to true
Foreground changed at 16:10:4:890 to false
Foreground changed at 16:10:8:634 to true
Foreground changed at 16:10:15:779 to false
Foreground changed at 16:10:56:766 to true
Foreground changed at 16:10:59:402 to false
Foreground changed at 16:10:59:652 to true
Foreground changed at 16:10:59:667 to false
Foreground changed at 16:12:9:397 to true
Foreground changed at 16:12:39:347 to false
Foreground changed at 16:13:18:375 to true
Foreground changed at 16:14:33:656 to false
```

We can see that most of the time when the *Application A* window loses focus, the *Application B* window gets it.

Intrinsic ID

To perform **Inter-Correlational** (page 167) analysis among traces and logs, especially when we have **Indexical Trace** (page 160), we need a dual operation: an ability to identify traces and **Use Case Trails** (page 359), and, if necessary, find their corresponding **Braids of Activity** (page 65) in an index trace. Some data from the tracing domain or use case description may serve is **Intrinsic ID**. It can be itself some numeric ID, a user, or a computer name.

A typical log analysis case from a distributed environment is illustrated in the following diagram:

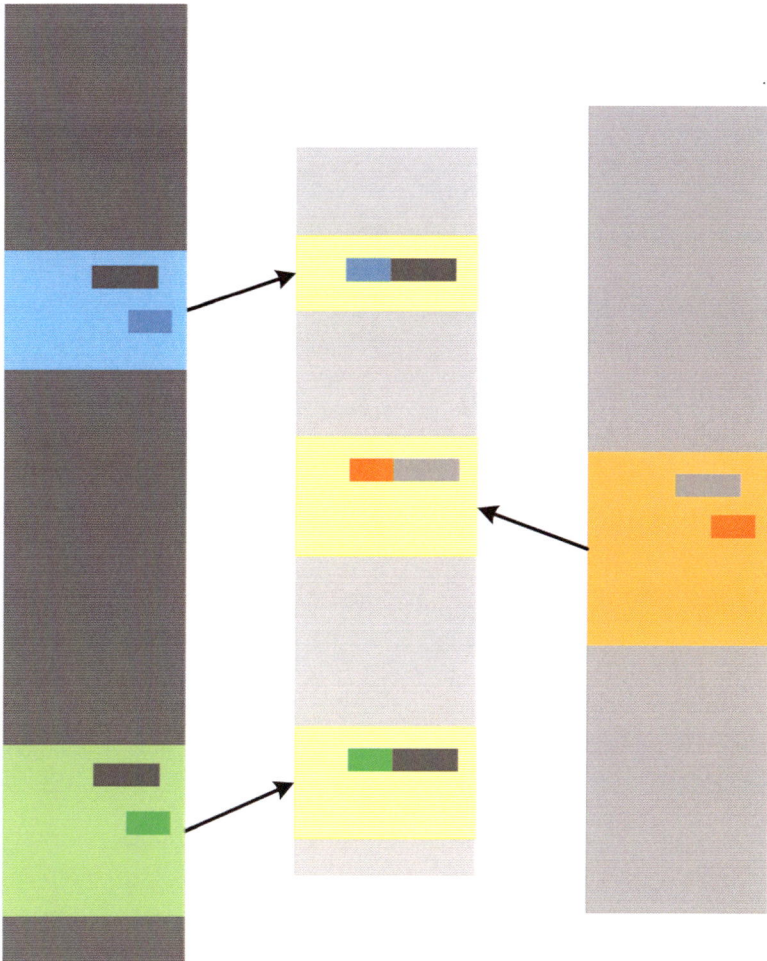

L

Last Activity

Sometimes we need to analyze the last activity before **Significant Event** (page 270) or **Discontinuity** (page 115). By this pattern, we mean a loose semantic collection of messages before the process exit, for example. It may give some clues to further troubleshooting. In one incident, a process was suddenly exiting. Its detailed trace did not have any messages explaining that, probably due to insufficient tracing coverage (**Sparse Trace**, page 279). Fortunately, a different external trace (from Process Monitor) was collected (**Inter-Correlation**, page 167), and it had LDAP network communication messages just before the thread and process exit events.

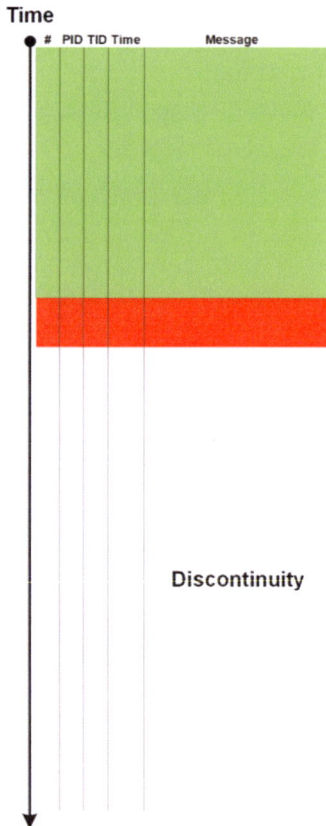

Layered Periodization

We borrowed this pattern name from historiography. This periodization[94] of software trace and log messages includes individual messages, then aggregated messages from threads, then processes as wholes, and finally, individual computers (in a client-server or similar sense). We can better illustrate this graphically.

Message layer:

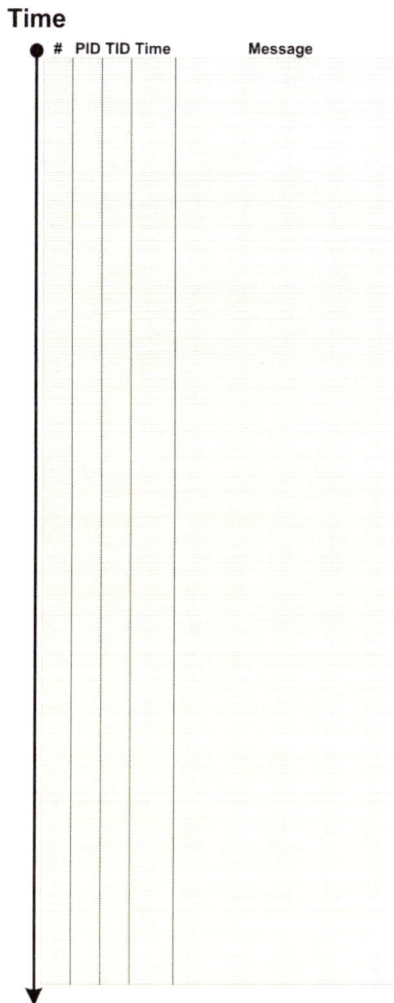

Time

#	PID	TID	Time		Message

Thread layer (different colors correspond to different TID):

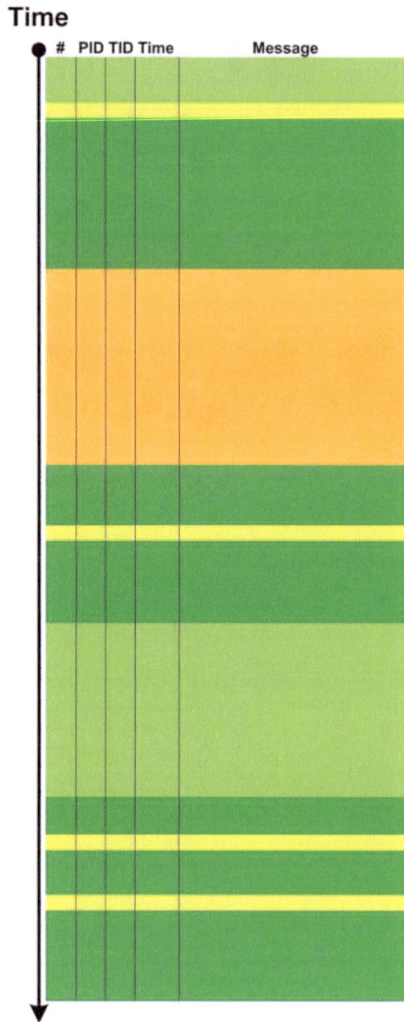

Process layer (different colors correspond to different PID):

Please note that it is also possible to have a periodization based on modules, functions, and individual messages, but it may be complicated because different threads can enter the same module or function. Here other patterns are more appropriate, like **Activity Region** (page 41), **Characteristic Message Block** (page 75), and **Background and Foreground Components** (page 57).

Linked Messages

Sometimes we have **Linked Messages** through some common parameter or attribute. We can find one such example in ETW traces related to kernel process creation notifications. Here we got **Adjoint Thread** (page 48) for module *PIDNotify*:

```
#       Module   PID  TID  Time         Message
[...]
128762 PIDNotify 1260 6208 15:53:15.691 Create: ParentID 0x000004EC PID 0x000018D4
[...]
128785 PIDNotify 6356 6388 15:53:15.693 Load: ImageName
\Device\HarddiskVolume1\Windows\System32\abscript.exe PID 0x000018D4
[...]
131137 PIDNotify 6356 4568 15:53:15.936 Create: ParentID 0x000018D4 PID 0x00001888
[...]
131239 PIDNotify 6280 6376 15:53:15.958 Load: ImageName
\Device\HarddiskVolume1\Windows\System32\wscript.exe PID 0x00001888
[...]
132899 PIDNotify 6356 5704 15:53:16.462 Create: ParentID 0x000018D4 PID 0x00001FD0
[...]
132906 PIDNotify 8144 7900 15:53:16.464 Load: ImageName
\Device\HarddiskVolume1\Windows\System32\cmd.exe PID 0x00001FD0
[...]
```

We see that messages 128762 and 128785 are linked by the PID parameter and linked to messages 131137 and 132899 by PID - ParentID parameter relationship. Similar linkages exist for messages 131137/131239 and 132899/132906.

The following diagram illustrates this analysis pattern:

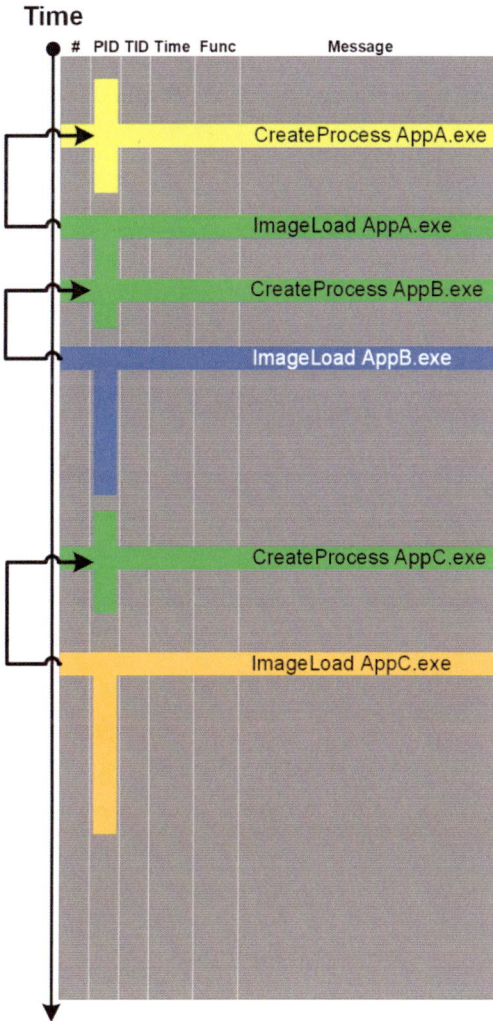

M

Macrofunction

Macrofunction is a single semantic unit of several trace messages where individual messages serve the role of microfunctions. We borrowed this idea and distinction from functionalist linguistics. An example would be a software trace fragment where messages log an attempt to update a database:

```
#      Module    PID  TID   Time          Message
[...]
42582 DBClient 5492 9476  11:04:33.398 Opening connection
[...]
42585 DBClient 5492 9476  11:04:33.398 Sending SQL command
[...]
42589 DBServer 6480 10288 11:04:33.399 Executing SQL command
[...]
42592 DBClient 5492 9476  11:04:33.400 Closing connection
[...]
```

These **Macrofunctions** need not be from the same ATID (**Glued Activity**, page 146) in the traditional sense, like in the example above, unless we form **Adjoint Threads** (page 48) from certain fragments like "DB."

Marked Message

Based on the ideas of Roman Jakobson[95] about "marked" and "unmarked" categories, we propose this pattern that groups trace messages based on having some feature or property. For example, marked messages may point to some domain of software activity related to functional requirements and, for this reason, may help in troubleshooting and debugging. Unmarked messages include all other messages that don't say anything about such activities (although they may include messages pointing to such activities indirectly that we are unaware of) or messages that state explicitly that no such activity has occurred. We can even borrow a notation of distinctive features[96] from phonology[97] and annotate any trace or log after analysis to compare it with **Master Trace** (page 182); for example, compose the following list of software trace distinctive features:

```
session database queries    [+]
session initialization      [-]
socket activity             [+]
process A launched          [+]
process B launched          [-]
process A exited            [-]
[...]
```

Here [+] means the activity is present in the trace, and [-] means the activity is either undetected or definitely not present. Sometimes a non-present activity can be a marked activity corresponding to all-inclusive unmarked present activity (see, for example, **No Activity** pattern, page 219).

Master Trace

When reading and analyzing software traces and logs, we always compare them to **Master Trace**. Other names for this pattern borrowed from narrative theory include *Metatrace, Canonical Trace,* or *Archetype*. When we look at the software trace from a system, we either know the correct sequence of **Activity Regions** (page 41), expect certain **Background and Foreground Components** (page 57), **Event Sequence Order** (page 126), or mentally construct a model based on our experience and **Implementation Discourse** (page 155). For the latter example, software engineers internalize software master narratives when they construct code and write tracing code for supportability. For the former example, it is important to have a repository of traces corresponding to **Master Traces**. Such a repository helps find deviations after **Bifurcation Point** (page 61). Consider such comparisons similar to regression testing when we check the computation output against the expected prerecorded sequence.

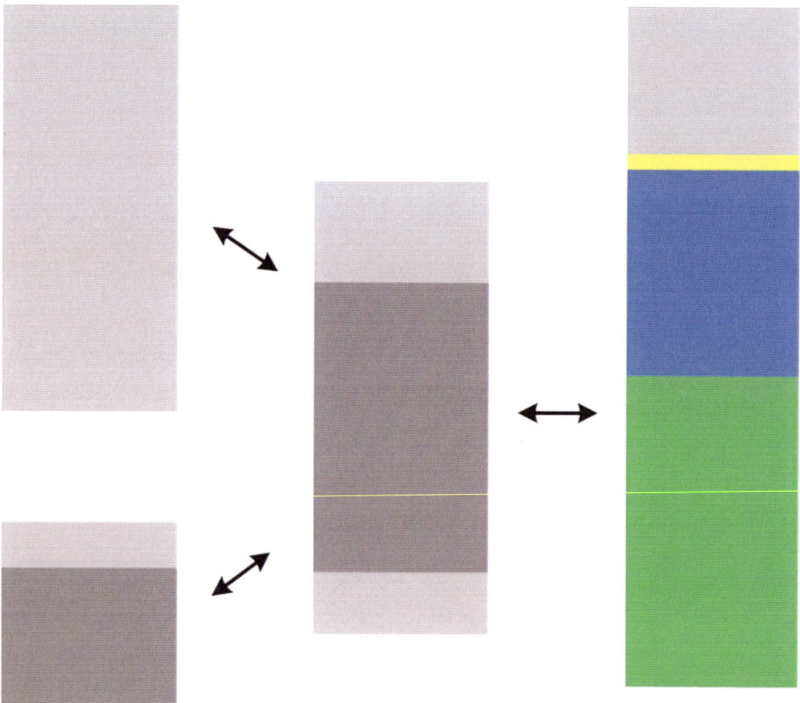

Measurement

Various types of **Measurements** are important in software diagnostics. We consider traces and logs[98] and general software narratives[99] (and even hardware narratives[100]) as a medium for all kinds of possible measurements. Even a small display in a handheld device showing a number is an example of **Singleton Trace** (page 275).

Typical trace and log measurement analysis patterns include **Time Delta** (page 298), **Statement Density and Current** (page 286), and **Trace Acceleration** (page 303). Numeric analysis patterns include **Counter Value** (page 91), **Trace Field** (page 314), **Signal** (page 268) in general, and the possible **Trace Distance** that uses various metrics, for example, the number of messages, **Activity Regions** (page 41), or just hops.

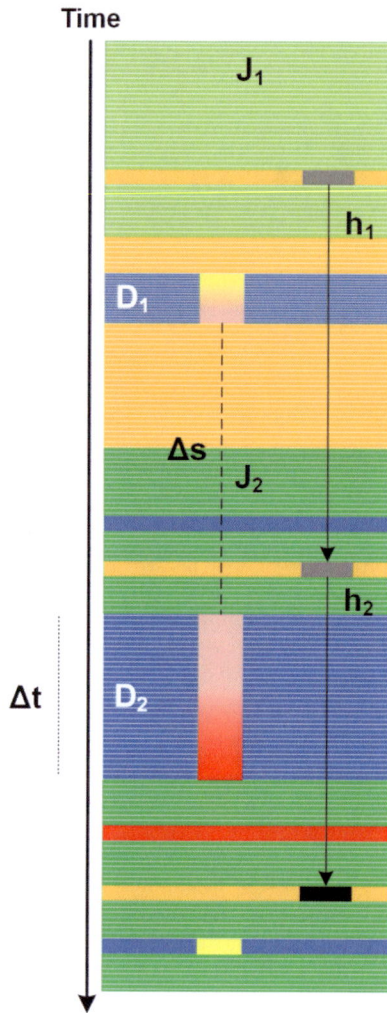

Message Annotations

Message Annotations analysis pattern was on our list for years, so it's time to add it to the trace and log analysis pattern catalog. We also allow several annotations per trace message done at different times and annotating different parts depending on the analysis flow (the topic of the next analysis pattern). When attached to log messages, annotations form their **Adjoint Thread of Activity** (page 48). However, sorted by their annotation time or sequence, we get a different trace called **Annotation Trace** (an example of an analysis narrative[101]). We can apply all relevant analysis patterns to both traces. A sketch of this pattern is depicted in the following diagram:

Message Bond

When constructing **Trace Molecule** (page 324), we may find that some **Message Complex** (page 189) links from different ATIDs point to the same message and **Tracemes** (page 347). In such a case, we have a **Message Bond** by analogy with covalent bonds[102]. One such example is illustrated in the following diagram:

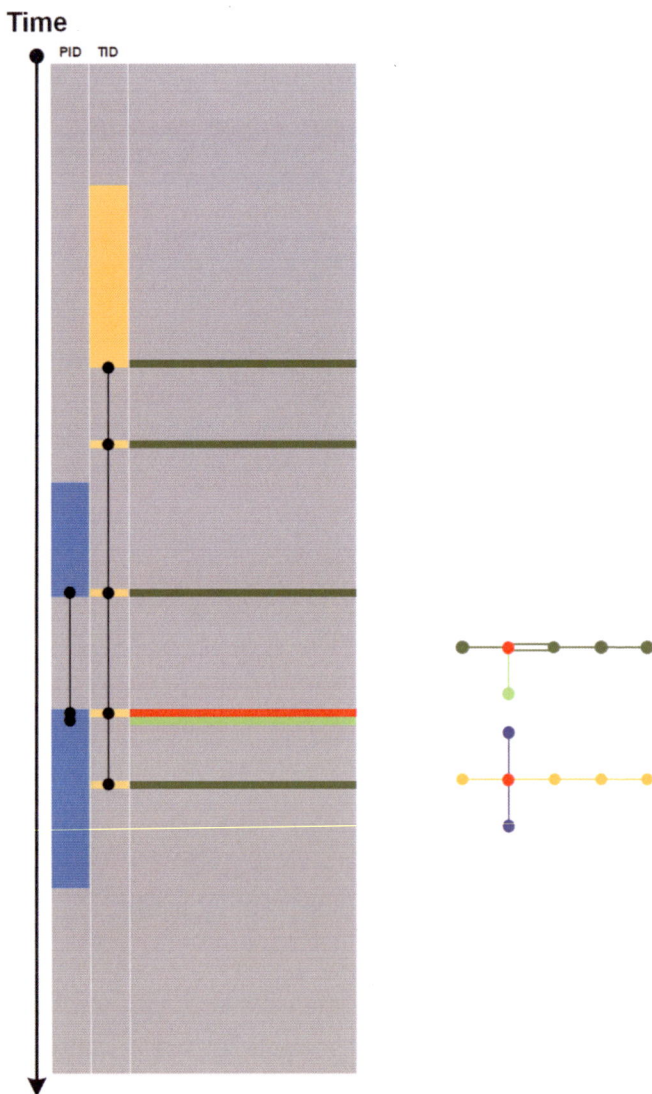

Message Change

Sometimes, when we find **Anchor Message** (page 53) related to our problem description (for example, a COM port error), we are interested in its evolution throughout a software narrative:

```
#        PID    TID    Message
[...]
126303   5768   1272   OpenComPort returns Status = 0x0
[...]
231610   3464   1576   OpenComPort returns Status = 0x0
[...]
336535   5768   4292   OpenComPort returns Status = 0x0
[...]
423508   5252   2544   OpenComPort returns Status = 0xc000000f
[...]
531247   5768   5492   OpenComPort returns Status = 0xc000000f
[...]
639039   772    3404   OpenComPort returns Status = 0xc000000f
[...]
```

Then we can check the activity between changes.

The following diagram illustrates this analysis pattern:

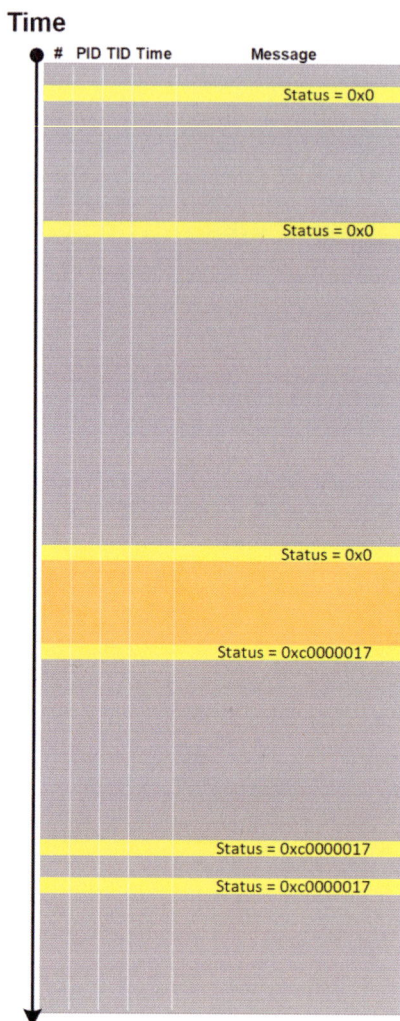

Message Complex

Message Complex takes inspiration from simplicial complexes[103]. First, we select a message, choose TID or ATID, and connect to the nearest messages having the same TID or ATID. This procedure can be repeated for newly connected messages. Then we select another ATID and repeat the process. Three connected messages with the same ATID may form a triangle and may also intersect another triangle with a different ATID if they share the same message. A very simple example is illustrated in the following diagram:

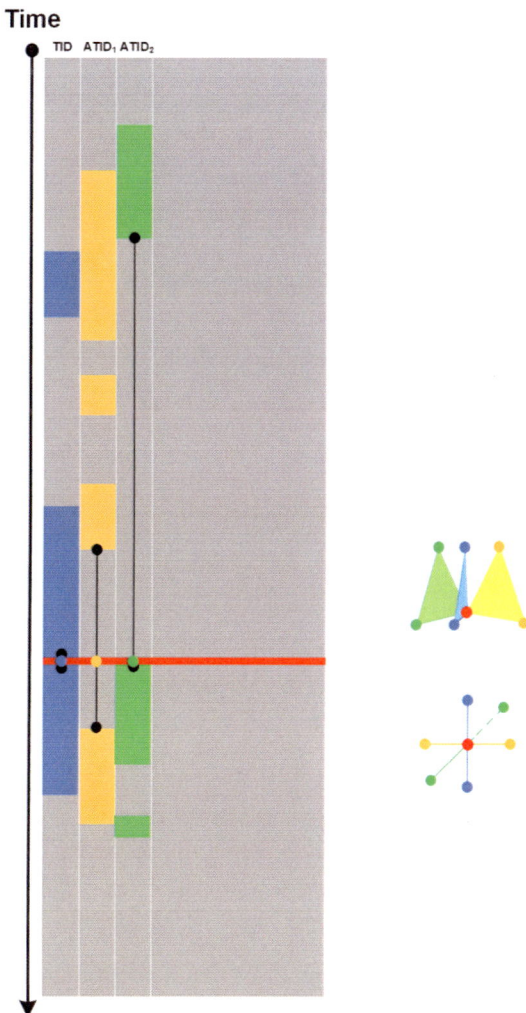

Message Complex is more structural and geometric than **Message Context** (page 191), which is just a set of surrounding messages regardless of their TID or ATID based on some relationship criteria.

Message Context

In some cases, it is useful to consider a message context: a set of surrounding messages having some relation to the chosen message:

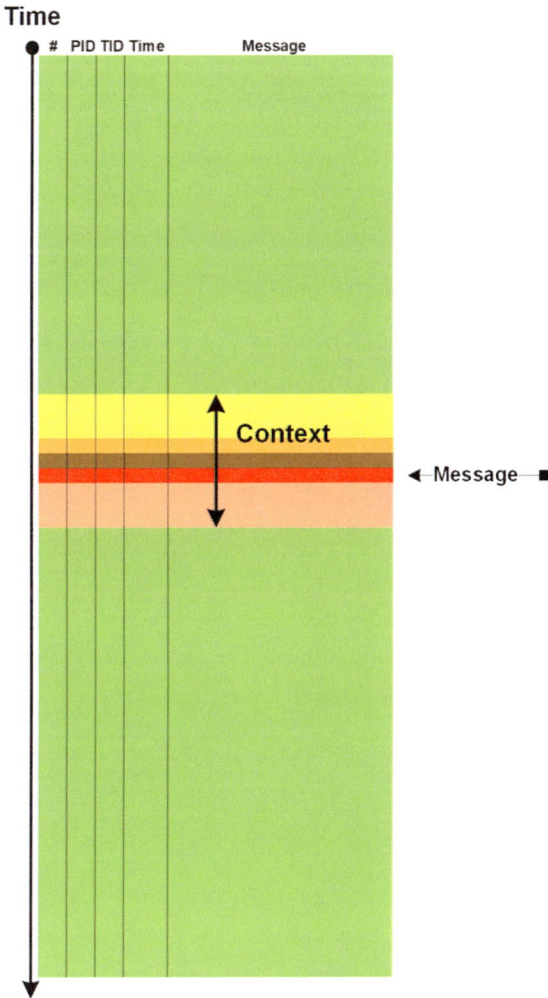

Message Cover

One of the powerful trace analysis techniques is using **Adjoint Threads of Activity** (page 48) to filter various linear message activities (as a generalization of **Thread of Activity**, page 296). Such filtered activities can then be analyzed either separately (**Sheaf of Activities**, page 266) or together, such as a new pattern we introduce here. If we identify parallel ATIDs (ATID is Adjoint TID[104]) and see that one covers the other, we can then make a hypothesis that they are **Intra-Correlated** (page 170). Here is a graphical example of a **Periodic Message Block** (page 233) largely composed of various **Error Messages** (page 123) that cover periodic **Discontinuities** (page 115) from another ATID (we can also consider the latter as **Periodic Message Blocks** consisting of **Silent Messages**, page 271):

This pattern is analogous to a cover[105] in topology.

Message Directory

We can apply **Message Set** (page 202) trace and log analysis pattern to itself
and build a multilevel **Message Directory**. The pattern name comes from the
analogy with memory management page tables, where we can select every
10th message to build a smaller **Message Set**, then select every 10th
message from it to build another **Message Set**, and so on. When looking at
a higher-level **Message Set,** we can choose a trace message and then look
at its **Message Context** (page 191) in the lower-level **Message Sets**:

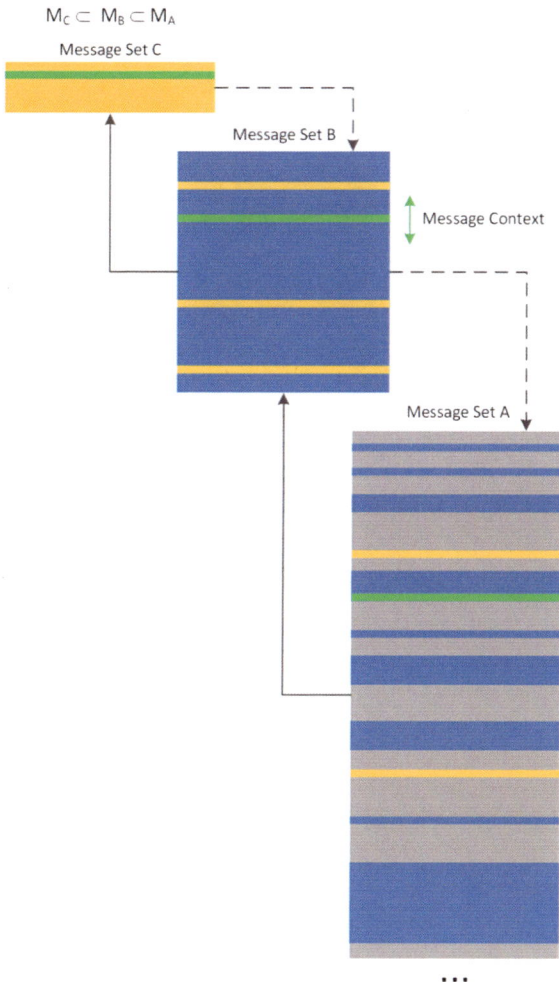

$$M_C \subset M_B \subset M_A$$

Message Set C

Message Set B

Message Context

Message Set A

. . .

Message Directory is similar to **Trace Frames** (page 318) analysis pattern but is fine-grained and more individual message-oriented than the latter analysis pattern. However, the former analysis pattern can be used to implement the latter.

Message Essence

Usually, when we find an interesting message in a log (maybe also a frame from **Exception Stack Trace**, page 129), especially from an unfamiliar component, we also want to search past problem cases either on the Internet or in some internal database. However, if we just put the message as is or some small fragment of it, we may get much noise. So, the problem is to find the optimal **Message Essence**. Often, this is done by omitting variable data (including **Adjoint Thread of Activity** fields, page 48) but leaving **Message Invariants** (page 198) and **Trace Constants** (page 306) usually refine a diagnostic error:

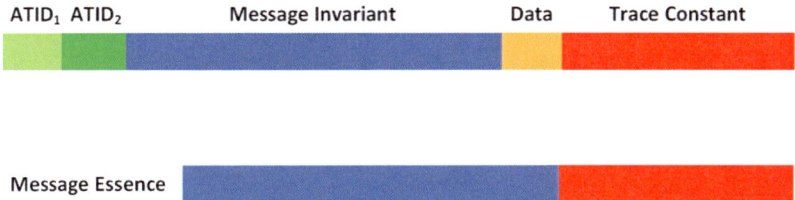

ATID$_1$ ATID$_2$ Message Invariant   Data   Trace Constant

Message Essence

This analysis pattern differs from **Message Invariant**, where the latter is useful when finding its emitter's source code lines (**PLOT**[106]).

Message Flow

Message Flow trace and log analysis pattern generalizes NetFlow[107] to software narratives. We count messages based on the set of **Adjoint Threads of Activity** (page 48), for example, PID.TID. This also subsumes network traces aggregated by Src.Dst. Individual single attributes can also be used, for example, aggregation by **Thread of Activity** (page 296) and also by **Message Sets** (page 202).

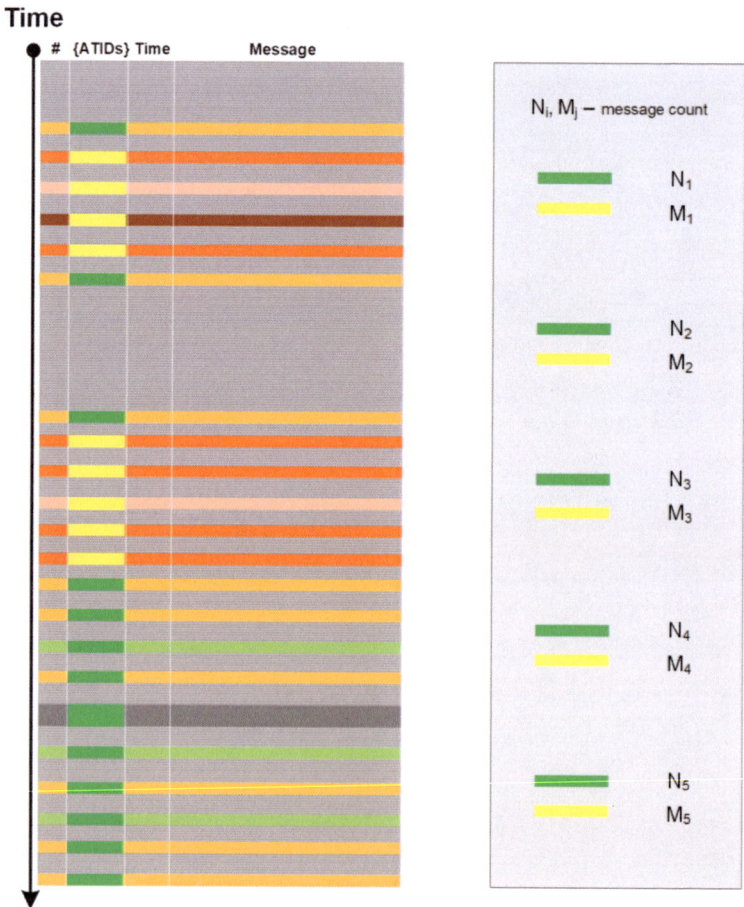

Message Interleave

We factored out **Anchor Messages** (page 53) example of **Message Interleave** into this pattern. It covers the superposition of different **Anchor Messages**, for example, process launch and exit or DLL load and unload:

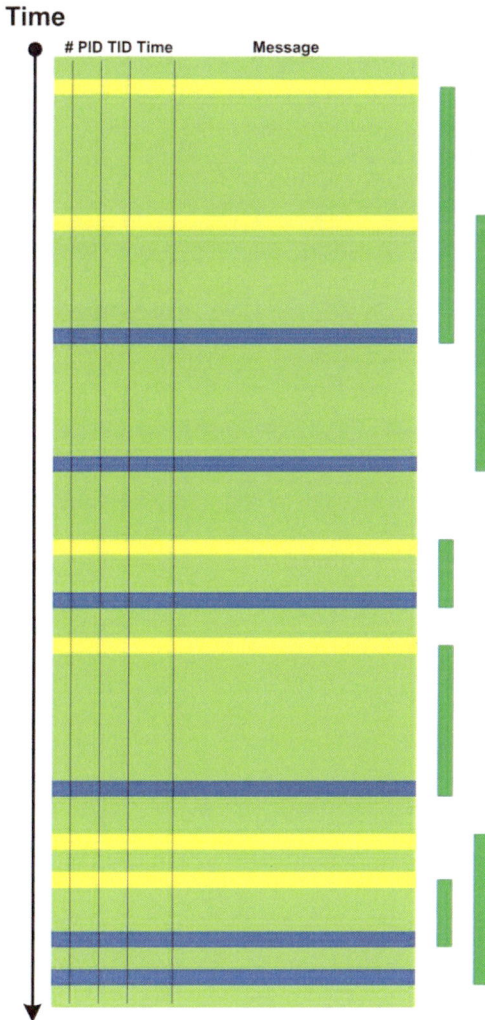

Message Invariant

Most of the time, software trace messages coming from the same source code fragment (**PLOT** [108]) contain invariant parts, such as function and variable names and descriptions, and mutable parts, such as pointer values and error codes. **Message Invariant** is a pattern useful for comparative analysis of several trace files where we are interested in message differences. For example, in one troubleshooting scenario, certain objects were not created correctly for one user. We suspected a different object version was linked to a user profile. So we recorded separate application debug traces for each user, and we could see version 0x4 for a problem user and 0x5 for all other normal users:

```
#     Module  PID   TID   Message
[...]
2782 ModuleA 2124 5648 CreateObject: pObject 0x00A83D30 data ([...]) version 0x4
[...]
```

```
#     Module  PID   TID   Message
[...]
4793 ModuleA 2376 8480 CreateObject: pObject 0x00BA4E20 data ([...]) version 0x5
[...]
```

Message Metadata

Various metrics are covered by **Counter Value** (page 91) trace and log analysis pattern. However, metric labels or metric metadata as implemented by monitoring tools such as **Prometheus**[109] can be mapped directly to **Adjoint Threads of Activity** (page 48) in our trace and log analysis pattern catalog:

```
<Metric Name>{<Label Name>=<Label Value>, ...}=<Metric Value> (from Prometheus data model110)

{<Metric Name ATID>=<ATID Value>, <ATID Name>=<ATID Value>, ..., <Message (Metric Value)>}
```

It allows the application of many trace and log analysis patterns related to threading and adjoint threading (*multibraiding*[111]).

We call this analysis pattern **Message Metadata**. It is illustrated for time series in the following diagram, where we have the same Labels for all metric names (in general, labels may be different):

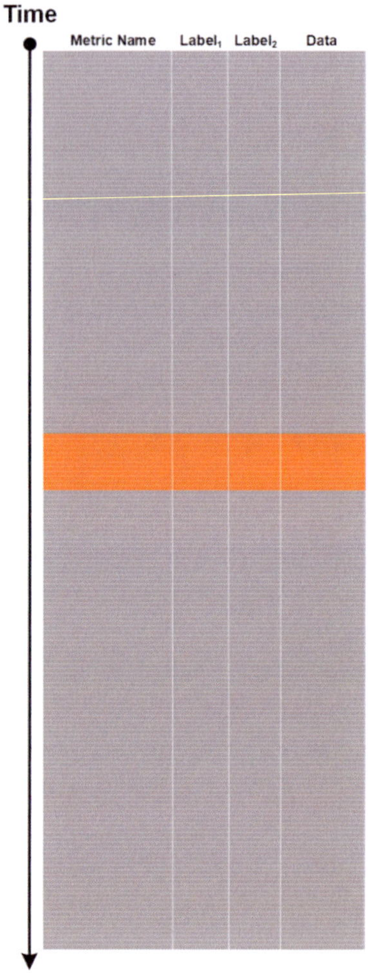

Time

Metric Name	Label$_1$	Label$_2$	Data

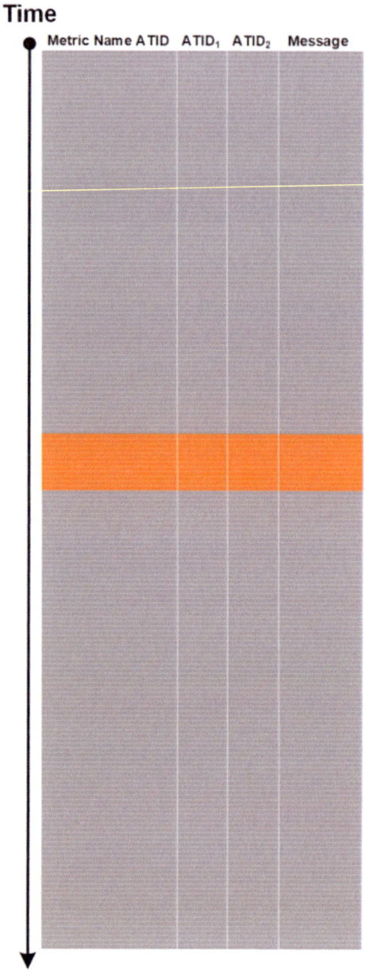

Time

Metric Name	A TID	A TID$_1$	A TID$_2$	Message

Message Pattern

Message Pattern trace and log analysis pattern is an ordered set of messages from a **Thread of Activity** (page 296) or **Adjoint Thread of Activity** (page 48) having **Message Invariants** (page 198) that can be used for matching another ordered set of messages in another (**Inter-Correlation**, page 167) or the same trace or log (**Intra-Correlation**, page 170). For example, a typical **Message Pattern** from one of our trace and log analysis sessions is depicted in the following diagram:

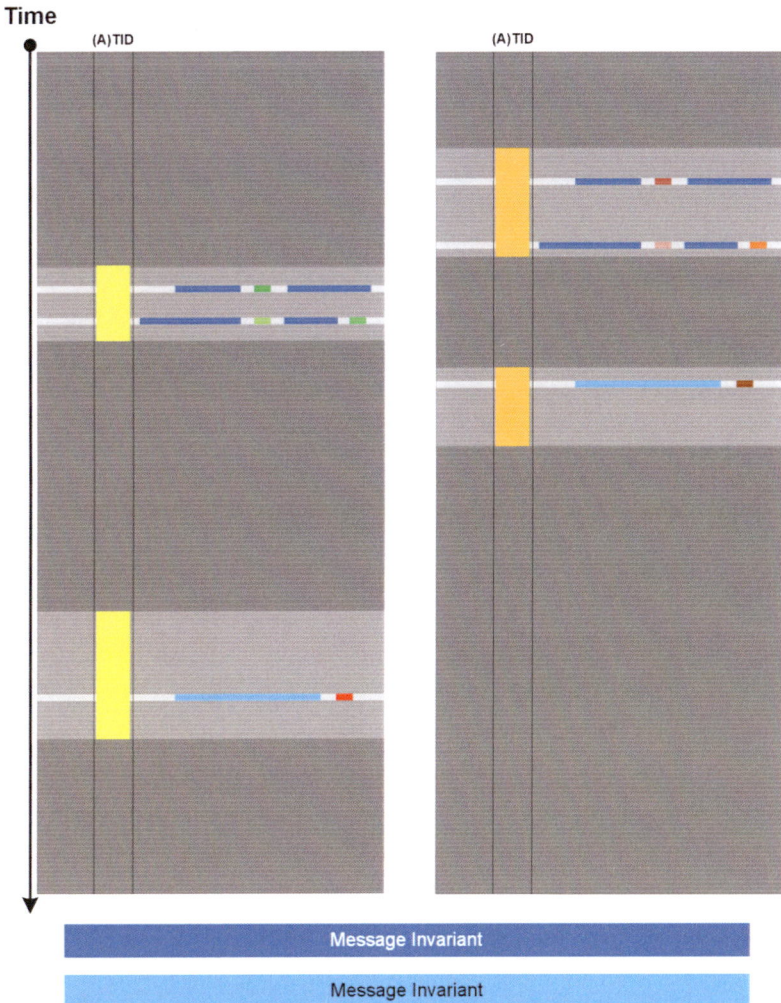

Message Set

Often, especially for large software logs, we need to select messages based on some criteria, be it a set of **Error Messages** (page 123), a set of messages containing **Basic Facts** (page 60), or some other predicate. Then we can use selected messages from that message set as **Anchor Messages** (page 53) or reverse **Pivot Messages** (page 240) as an aid in further analysis.

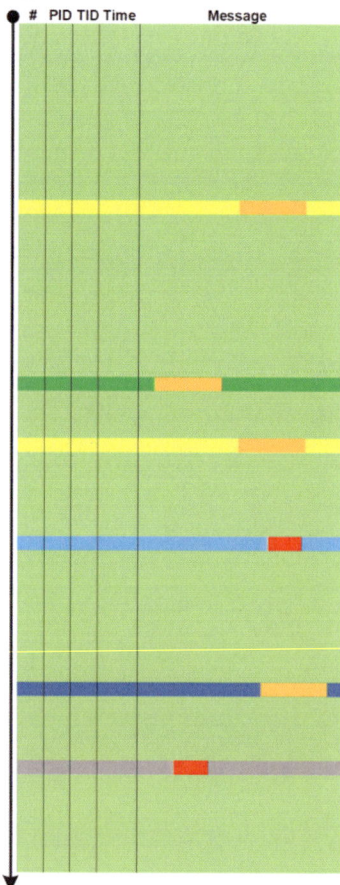

{ $m_\#$ | Fact A or Fact B }

Message Space

The message stream can be considered as a union of **Message Spaces**. A message space is an ordered set of messages preserving the structure of the overall trace. Such messages may be selected based on the memory space they came from or can be selected by some other general attribute or a combination of attributes and facts. The difference from **Message Set** (page 201) is that **Message Space** is usually much larger (with large scale structure), with various **Message Sets** extracted from it later for fine-grained analysis. This pattern also fits nicely with **Adjoint Spaces** (page 45). Here's an example of the kernel and managed spaces in the same ETW trace from the Windows platform, where we see that kernel space messages came not only from the System process but also from other process contexts:

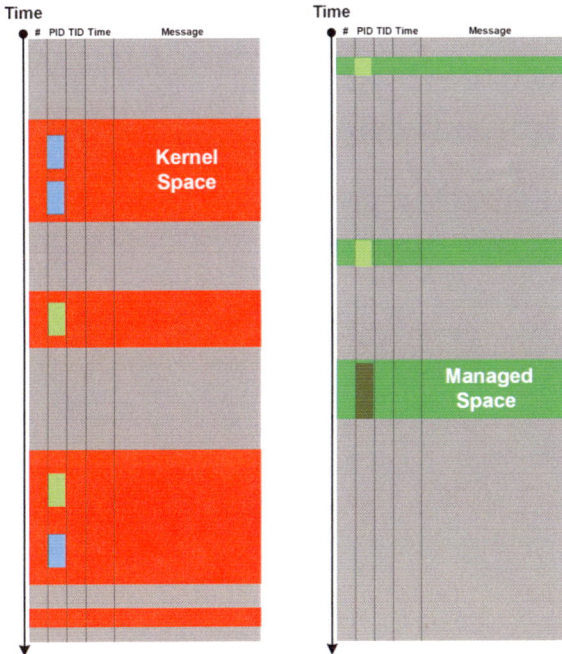

In the context of general traces and logs[112] such as debugger logs, separate **Message Space** regions may be linked (or "surrounded") by **Interspace** (page 169).

Meta Trace

So far, we have been discussing trace analysis patterns related to the execution of a particular software version. However, software code changes, and also its tracing and logging output: from large-scale changes where components are replaced to small-scale code refactoring affecting message structure and format. On a software narratological level, this corresponds to a narrative about a software trace or log and its evolution. Such an analysis pattern is different from **Master Trace** (page 182) pattern, where the latter is similar to what Metanarrative [113] is usually meant in narratology: a master or grand idea, an expected trace if all functional requirements were correctly identified and implemented during software construction, and non-functional ones met during software execution.

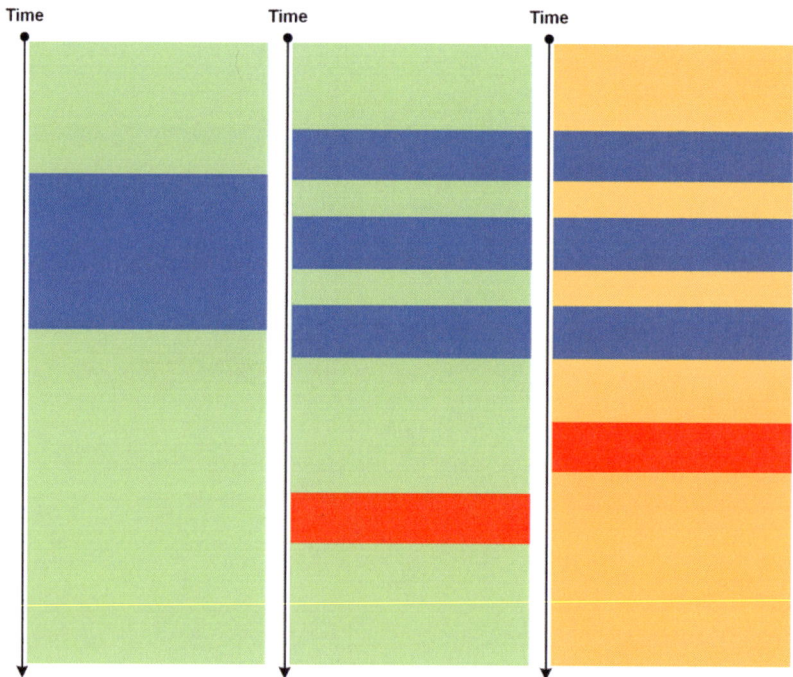

Milestones

Trace messages may correspond to specific implementation code, such as recording the status of an operation, dumping data values, or printing errors, or they may correspond to higher levels of software design and architecture and even to use case stories. We call such messages **Milestones** by analogy with project management[114]. Alternative names can be *Chapter Messages*, *Summary Messages*, *Checkpoints*, or *Use Case Messages*. These differ from **Macrofunctions** (page 180), which are collections of messages grouped by some higher function. **Milestone** messages are specifically designed for distinct trace statements:

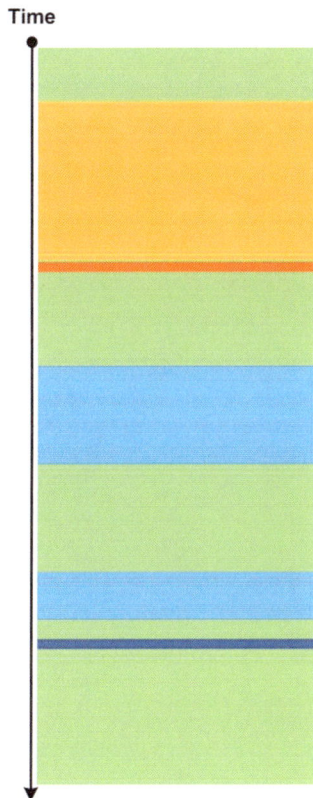

They can also be a part of **Significant Events** (page 270), serve the role of **Anchor Messages** (page 53), and be a part of **Basic Facts** (page 60) and **Vocabulary Index** (page 362).

Minimal Trace

If we run software with its default configuration and no interaction (input data), we get its **Minimal Trace**:

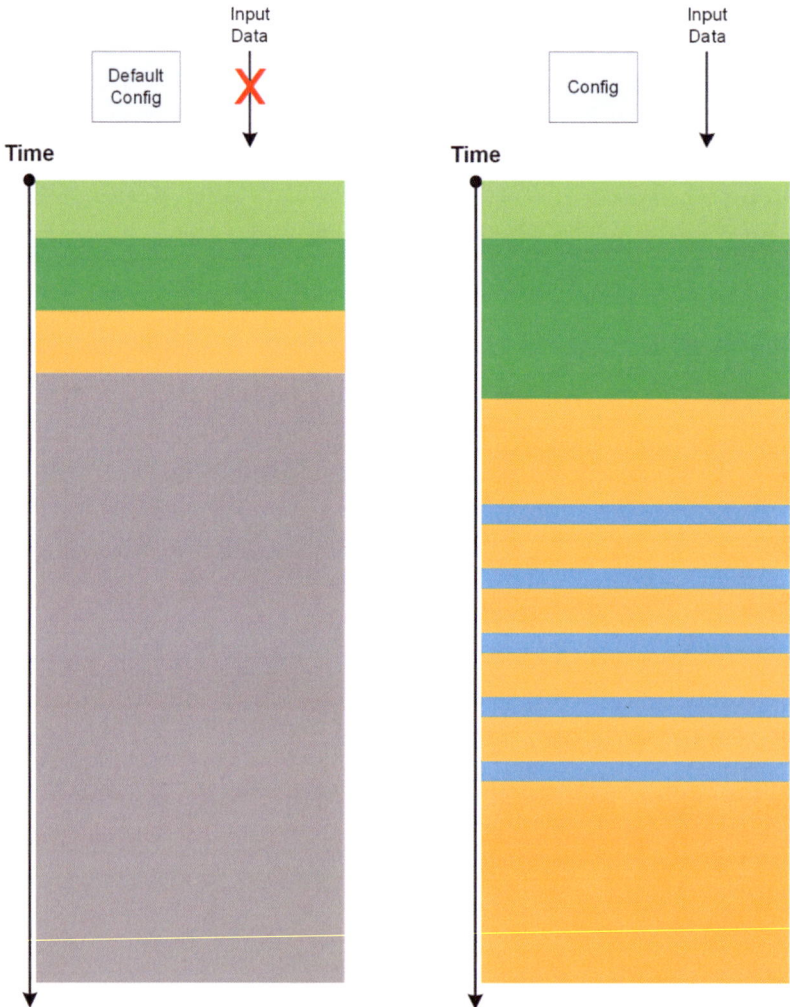

Such traces may have their own **Master Trace** (page 182). Also, **Minimal Trace** is a specific **Use Case Trail** (page 359). Metaphorically, they can be considered minimal surfaces[115].

Missing Component

When we do not see expected trace statements, we wonder whether the component was not loaded, its container ceased to exist, or simply it was not selected for tracing. In many support cases, there is a trade-off between tracing everything and the size of trace files. Customers and engineers usually prefer smaller files to analyze. However, in the case of predictable and reproducible issues with short duration, we can always select all components or deselect a few (instead of choosing a few).

In **Discontinuity** (page 115) pattern, the possibility of a sudden and silent gap in trace statements could happen because not all necessary components were selected for tracing.

Sometimes, in cases when the missing component was selected for tracing, but we do not see any trace output from it, other module traces can give us an indication, perhaps showing the load failure message. For example, Process Monitor tracing done in parallel can reveal load failures.

The following diagram illustrates this analysis pattern:

Missing Data

Some tracing architectures, especially the ones that intercept API calls by filtering or hooking, may log synchronous requests by remembering to write done return result in the same trace message later on when the response is available after the wait. If such data is still not available in the log or trace, it may point to some blocked request for which another software execution artifact analysis (such as memory dump analysis) is necessary. In some cases, the analysis of the corresponding **Fiber Bundle** (page 136) stack trace may point to the **Blocking Module**[116] or the involvement of file system filters (**Stack Trace**[117]). This analysis pattern, which we call **Missing Data**, is illustrated in the following diagram:

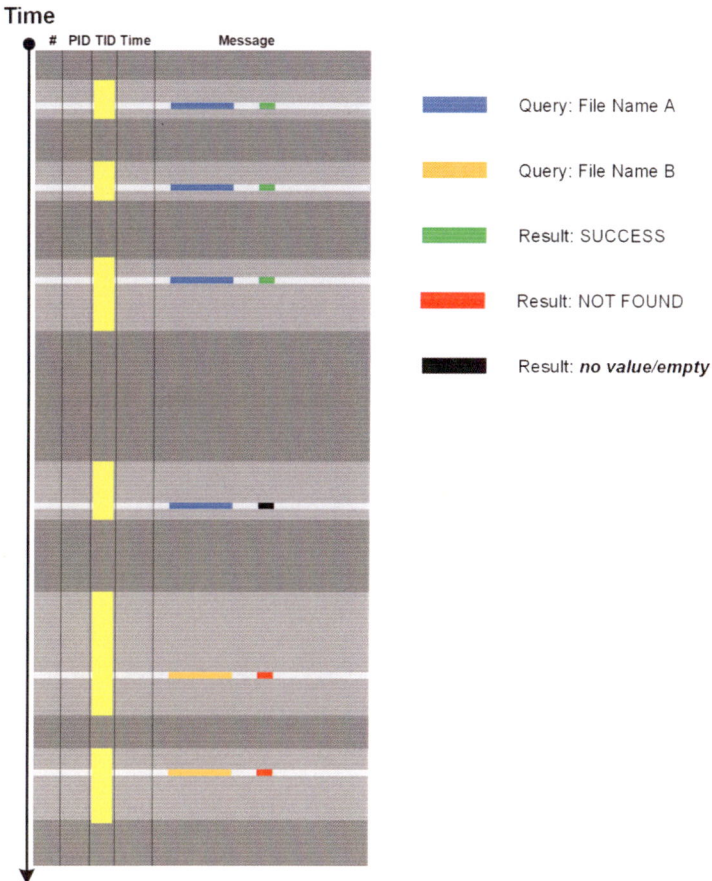

Missing Message

Sometimes the absence of messages, for example, errors and exceptions, may save time during troubleshooting and debugging by pointing to what was not happening and providing additional insight. For example, in the picture below, we see the same exceptions in the new and old incidents. However, in the old incident, we see another exception that was linked to one unavailable server in distributed broker architecture. For this reason, we can assume provisionally that all servers were operational when the new incident happened.

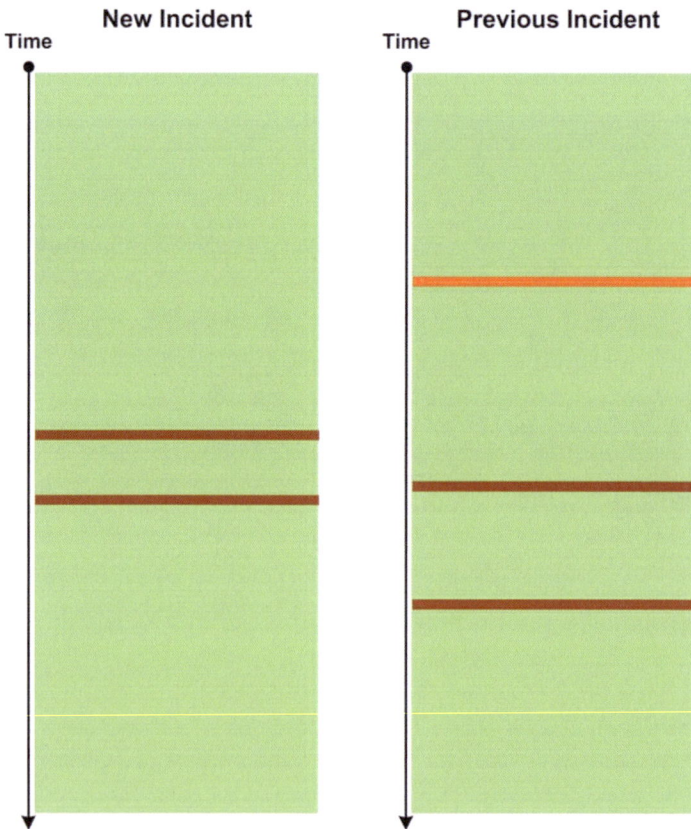

The **Missing Message** pattern is different from **Missing Component** (page 207) pattern, where the latter may point to the component that was not loaded or executed or simply that it was not selected for tracing.

Moduli Trace

In addition to **Declarative Trace** (page 102), we have code statements that may be intercepted by external API tracing tools (*CreateFile*, *CloseHandle*):

```
void myThread ()
{
   while (true)
   {
      DebugLog(…);

      // ...

      HFILE hFile = CreateFile(…);

      // ...
      if (failure)
         OutputDebugString("…");

      CloseHandle(hFile);
   }
}
```

In the sample code above, we have different logs resulting from **Declarative Trace** (*DebugLog*, *OutputDebugString*):

Debug.log

DebugView

Also, we have a log saved by an external tracing tool (for example, Process Monitor) that includes our API calls:

All such trace-generating source code statements form **Moduli Trace** as soon as they are executed:

```
DebugLog(…);
CreateFile(…);
CloseHandle(…);
DebugLog(…);
CreateFile(…);
CloseHandle(…);
DebugLog(…);
CreateFile(…);
CloseHandle(…);
OutputDebugString(…);
DebugLog(…);
CreateFile(…);
CloseHandle(…);
DebugLog(…);
CreateFile(…);
CloseHandle(…);
DebugLog(…);
CreateFile(…);
CloseHandle(…);
DebugLog(…);
CreateFile(…);
CloseHandle(…);
DebugLog(…);
CreateFile(…);
CloseHandle(…);
DebugLog(…);
CreateFile(…);
CloseHandle(…);
OutputDebugString(…);
DebugLog(…);
CreateFile(…);
CloseHandle(…);
DebugLog(…);
CreateFile(…);
CloseHandle(…);
DebugLog(…);
```

Such a trace can also be analyzed using trace and log analysis patterns like other trace types. We take the idea of this analysis pattern from moduli spaces[118] in mathematics that parametrize other spaces.

Motif

Often, when we look at software trace fragments, we recognize certain motifs such as client-server interaction, publisher-subscriber notifications, database queries, plugin sequence initialization, and others. The idea of this pattern name comes from *motives*[119] in mathematics. It differs from **Master Trace** (page 182) analysis pattern, which corresponds to a normal use-case or working software scenario and may contain several **Motifs**, as it usually happens in complex software environments. On the other side of the spectrum, there are software narremes (basic narrative units [120]) and **Macrofunctions** (single semantic units, page 180). **Motifs** help to further bridge the great divide between software construction and software diagnostics with software narremes corresponding to implementation patterns, **Macrofunctions** to design patterns, and **Motifs** to architectural patterns, although the overlap between these categories is possible.

Motivic Trace

We can "integrate" the trace message stream into another, smaller trace. By analogy with motivic integration[121] in contemporary mathematics, we call this analysis pattern **Motivic Trace**. There can be border cases where the whole trace is reduced to one message, or every message is associated with a different message (perhaps shorter or a number). **Message Sets** (page 202) that are integrated into **Motivic Trace** can be completely different (for example, based on **Motives**, page 214) in comparison with **Quotient Trace** (page 250), where we reduce **Message Sets** that have the same common attribute.

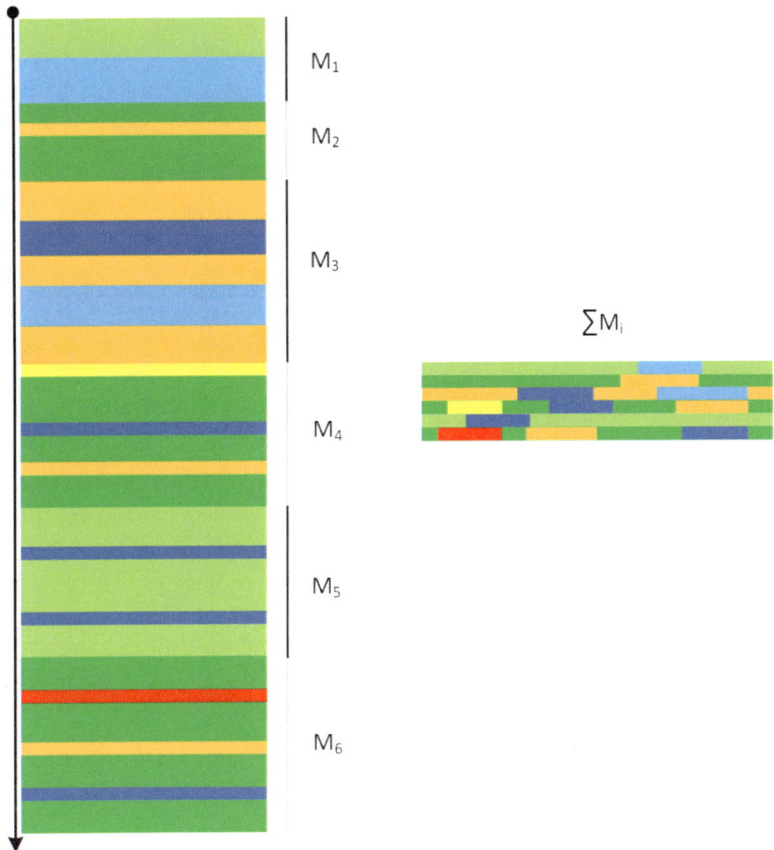

Multidimensional Message

Ideally, a trace or log message should contain only one piece of information, including associated data. However, some **Multidimensional Messages** may contain unrelated information, including several **Message Invariants** (page 198) and variable data places, for example:

```
Entry GetData. Error opening file: 0x5" or "Window handle: 0xa60834 pHandler:
0x456210F0
```

Such messages may be split into several independent messages and, if necessary, additional ATIDs (new **Adjoint Threads of Activity**, page 48) may be added as depicted in this diagram of **Combed Trace** (page 82):

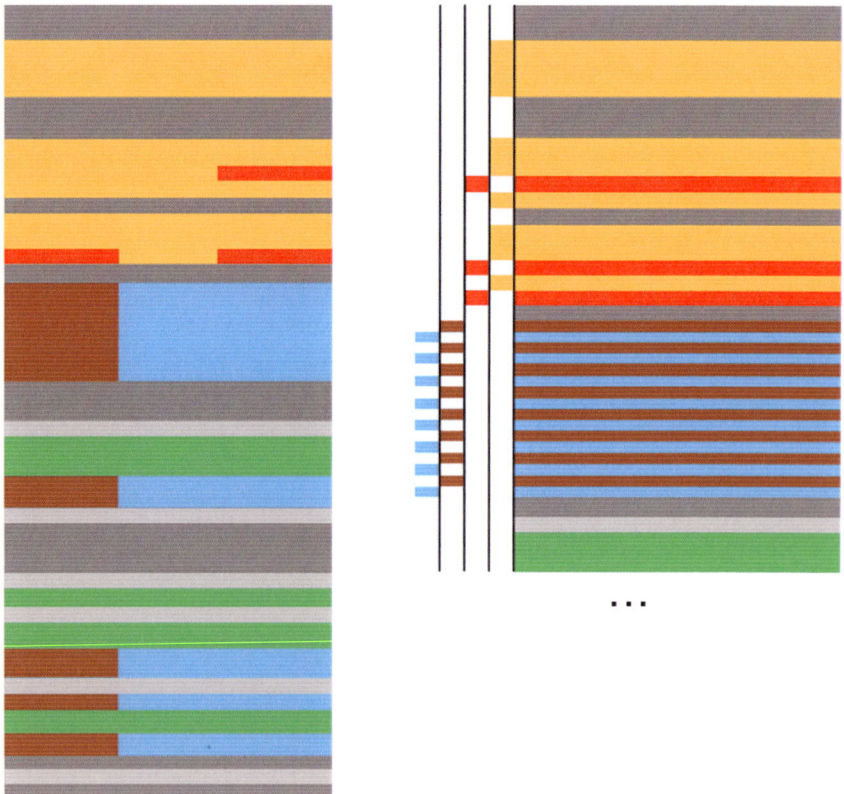

Another example is **Exception Stack Trace** (page 129) messages in some logging implementations.

N

News Value

News Value is a pattern that assigns relative importance to software traces for problem-solving purposes, especially when it is related to a problem description, recent incidents, and timestamps of other supporting artifacts (memory dumps, other traces). For example, in one scenario, an ETW trace was provided with three additional log files:

```
#       Source PID  TID  Date       Time         Message
0       Header 1260 1728 12/14/2010 06:48:56.289 ?????
[...]
215301 Unknown 640  808  12/14/2010 07:22:57.508 ????? Unknown( 16): GUID=[...]
(No Format Information found).


// LogA
05/11/10 18:28:15.1562 : Service() - entry
[...]
14/12/10 10:31:58.0381 : Notification: sleep
* Start of new log *
14/12/10 10:34:38.4687 : Service() - entry
[...]
14/12/10 11:53:35.2729 : Service.CleanUp complete
* Start of new log *
14/12/10 11:56:11.7031 : Service() - entry
[...]
14/12/10 15:25:23.3004 : Notification: sleep


// LogB
[ 1] 12/14 10:34:29:890 Entry: ctor
[...]
[ 2] 12/14 11:53:30:866 Exit: COMServer.Server.DeleteObject


// LogC
[ 1] 12/14 11:56:03:359 Entry: ctor
[...]
[20] 12/14 15:30:20:110 Exit: Kernel32.Buffer.Release
```

From the problem description, we expected *LogB* and *LogC* to be logs from two subsequent process executions where the first launch fails (*LogB*) and the second launch succeeds (*LogC*). Looking at their start and end times, we see that they make sense from the problem description perspective, but we have to dismiss the ETW trace and most of *LogA* as recorded earlier and having no value for **Inter-Correlation** (page 167) analysis of more recent logs. We also see that portions of *LogA* overlap with *LogB* and *LogC* and, for this reason, have analysis value for us.

In the following diagram that illustrates this analysis pattern, in relation to a trace on the left (1st), only the 3rd trace has some value as the other two were recorded either earlier or later:

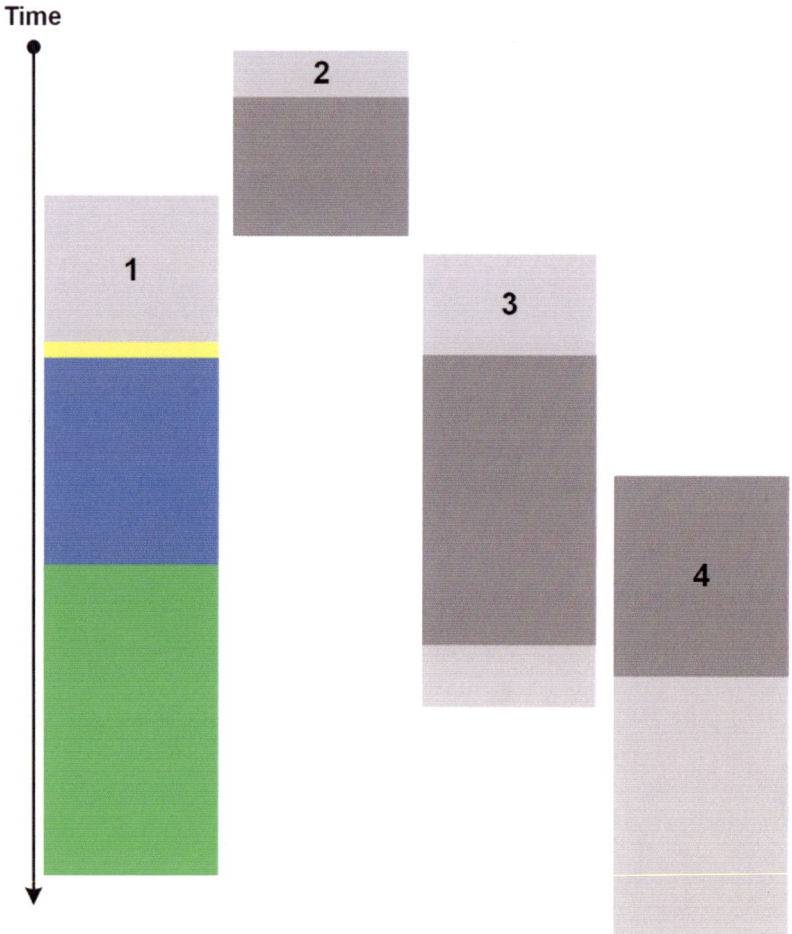

No Activity

No Activity is the limit of the **Discontinuity** pattern (page 115). The absence of activity can be seen at a thread level or at a process level, where it is similar to the **Missing Component** pattern (page 207). The difference from the latter pattern is that we know for certain that we selected our process modules for tracing but do not see any trace messages. Consider this example:

```
#  Source        PID  TID  Time          Function      Message
1  TraceSettings 1480 8692 08:04:20.682                **** Start Trace Session
[... TraceSettings messages 2-11 show that we selected AppA for tracing ...]
12 ModuleB       3124 4816 08:04:37.049 WorkerThread  Worker thread running
13 TraceSettings 1480 8692 08:04:41.966                **** Trace Session was stopped
```

Only modules from the *AppA* process and modules from a coupled process (for example, *ModuleB*) were selected. However, we only see a reminder message from the coupled process (3124.4816: *ModuleB! WorkerThread*) and no messages for 21 seconds. Fortunately, the *AppA* process memory dump was saved during the tracing session:

```
Debug session time: Fri May 21 08:04:31.000 2010 (GMT+0)
```

We see two threads waiting for a critical section:

```
0:000> ~*kL

  14  Id: 640.8b8 Suspend: 1 Teb: 7ffa7000 Unfrozen
ChildEBP RetAddr
0248f8c0 7c827d29 ntdll!KiFastSystemCallRet
0248f8c4 7c83d266 ntdll!ZwWaitForSingleObject+0xc
0248f900 7c83d2b1 ntdll!RtlpWaitOnCriticalSection+0x1a3
0248f920 0040dea8 ntdll!RtlEnterCriticalSection+0xa8
[...]
0248f9a4 77ce78aa rpcrt4!Invoke+0x30
0248f9c0 77ce7a94 rpcrt4!NdrCallServerManager+0x17
0248fcb8 77ce7b7c rpcrt4!NdrStubCall+0x1d6
0248fcd0 77c7ff7a rpcrt4!NdrServerCall+0x15
0248fd04 77c8042d rpcrt4!DispatchToStubInCNoAvrf+0x38
0248fd58 77c80353 rpcrt4!RPC_INTERFACE::DispatchToStubWorker+0x11f
0248fd7c 77c7e0d4 rpcrt4!RPC_INTERFACE::DispatchToStub+0xa3
0248fdbc 77c7e080 rpcrt4!RPC_INTERFACE::DispatchToStubWithObject+0xc0
0248fdfc 77c812f0 rpcrt4!LRPC_SCALL::DealWithRequestMessage+0x41e
0248fe20 77c88678 rpcrt4!LRPC_ADDRESS::DealWithLRPCRequest+0x127
0248ff84 77c88792 rpcrt4!LRPC_ADDRESS::ReceiveLotsaCalls+0x430
```

```
0248ff8c 77c8872d rpcrt4!RecvLotsaCallsWrapper+0xd
0248ffac 77c7b110 rpcrt4!BaseCachedThreadRoutine+0x9d


  15  Id: 640.18c0 Suspend: 1 Teb: 7ffdb000 Unfrozen
ChildEBP RetAddr
01b8ff40 7c827d29 ntdll!KiFastSystemCallRet
01b8ff44 7c83d266 ntdll!ZwWaitForSingleObject+0xc
01b8ff80 7c83d2b1 ntdll!RtlpWaitOnCriticalSection+0x1a3
01b8ffa0 0040dba7 ntdll!RtlEnterCriticalSection+0xa8
[...]
01b8ffec 00000000 kernel32!BaseThreadStart+0x34
```

Unfortunately, it belongs to a missing thread and blocked threads wait forever:

```
0:000> !cs -l -o -s
-------------------------------------------
DebugInfo        = 0x01facdd0
Critical section = 0x01da19c0 (+0x1DA19C0)
LOCKED
LockCount        = 0x2
WaiterWoken      = No
OwningThread     = 0x00001384
RecursionCount   = 0x1
LockSemaphore    = 0x578
SpinCount        = 0x00000000
ntdll!RtlpStackTraceDataBase is NULL. Probably the stack traces are not enabled

0:000> ~~[1384]
            ^ Illegal thread error in '~~[1384]'
```

AppA process was hanging, explaining why we do not see any activity in the trace.

The following diagram illustrates this analysis pattern:

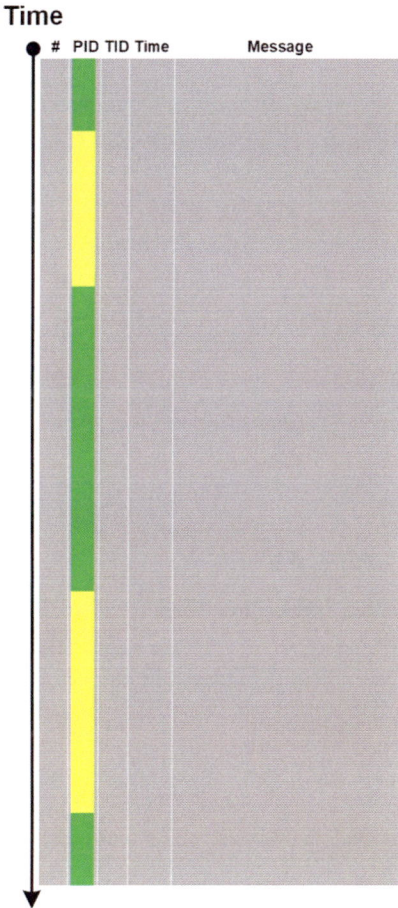

No Trace Metafile

This pattern is similar to the **No Component Symbols**[122] memory analysis pattern:

```
#      Module   PID  TID  Time         Message
21372 \src\dllA 2968 5476 3:55:10.004 Calling foo()
21373 Unknown   2968 5476 3:55:10.004 ????? Unknown( 27): GUID=1EF56EBD-A7FC-
4892-8DBA-00AD813F8A24 (No Format Information found).
21374 Unknown   2968 5476 3:55:10.004 ????? Unknown( 27): GUID=1EF56EBD-A7FC-
4892-8DBA-00AD813F8A24 (No Format Information found).
21375 Unknown   2968 5476 3:55:10.004 ????? Unknown( 27): GUID=1EF56EBD-A7FC-
4892-8DBA-00AD813F8A24 (No Format Information found).
21376 Unknown   2968 5476 3:55:10.004 ????? Unknown( 28): GUID=1EF56EBD-A7FC-
4892-8DBA-00AD813F8A24 (No Format Information found).
21377 Unknown   2968 5476 3:55:10.004 ????? Unknown( 23): GUID=1EF56EBD-A7FC-
4892-8DBA-00AD813F8A24 (No Format Information found).
21378 \src\dllA 2968 5476 3:55:10.004 Calling bar()
```

In some cases, when we don't have TMF files (Trace Meta Files), it is possible to detect broad behavioral patterns such as:

- **Circular Trace** (page 78)
- **Statement Density and Current** (page 286)
- **Discontinuity** (page 115)
- **Time Delta** (page 298)
- **Trace Acceleration** (page 303)

Looking at **Thread of Activity** (page 296), we can sometimes also infer the possible component name based on surrounding trace messages with present TMF files, especially when we have source code access. For example, in the trace shown above, it can be *dllA* or any other module that the *foo* function calls.

Null Reference

Message data may point to other messages in the same trace (see the example of **Linked Messages**, page 178) or the other trace (see the **Data Selector** example, page 99). But similar data in other messages may not point to any other messages in the same or different, perhaps **Truncated** (page 352), traces and logs collected at the same time - similar to invalid pointers, for example, kernel addresses in process memory dumps, or user space addresses in kernel memory dumps. We call this analysis pattern **Null Reference** (also notice the analogy with foreign key values in data tables where Null is not a value). Another analogy here is a referential failure[123]. This analysis pattern is illustrated in the following diagram adapted from the **Linked Messages** analysis pattern diagram.

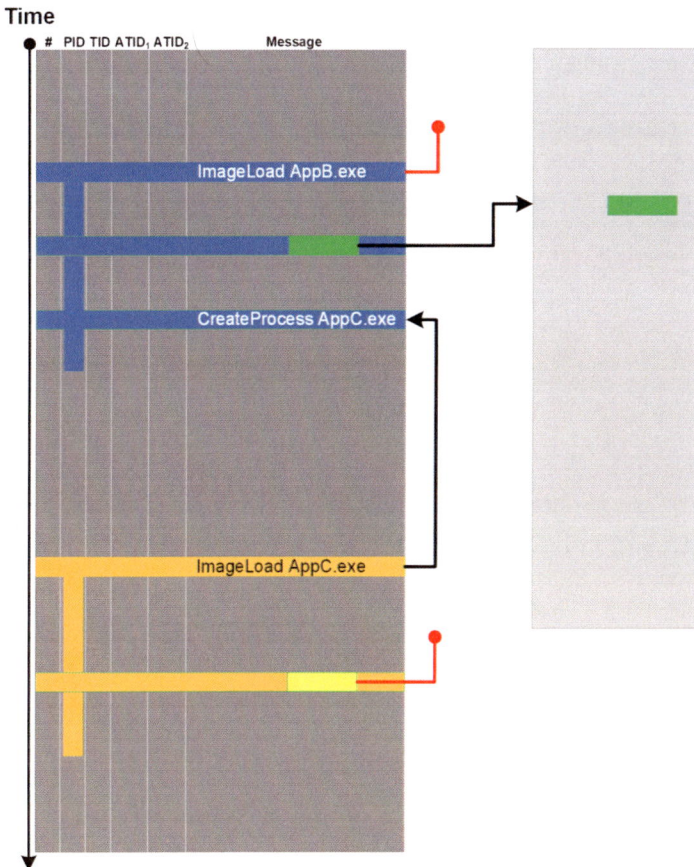

This analysis pattern is different from **Missing Data** (page 209), where the reference is itself missing.

These **Null References** can be remediated by longer supplemental traces, **Fiber Bundle** (page 136), and **Adjoint Spaces** (page 45).

O

Opposition Messages

We borrowed this pattern name from the binary opposition[124] originating in Saussure's structuralism[125]). It covers the following pairs of messages usually found in software traces and logs such as:

- open/close
- create/destroy
- allocate/free (deallocate)
- call/return
- enter/exit (leave)
- load/unload
- save/load
- lock/unlock
- map/unmap

The absence of an opposite may point to some problems, such as synchronization and leaks or **Incomplete History** (page 159, for example, wait chains). Of course, there can always be a possibility that a second term is missing due to **Sparse Trace** (page 279), but this is a poor implementation choice that leads to confusion during troubleshooting and debugging.

Original Message

This pattern deals with software trace messages where a certain activity is repeated several times, but only the first message occurrence or specific message vocabulary has significance for the analysis activity. A typical example from ETW tracing is module load events:

```
#       Module PID   TID   Time         Message
[...]
35835 ModuleA 11000 11640 17:27:28.720 LoadImageEvent:
\Device\HarddiskVolume2\Windows\System32\userinit.exe PId 5208
[...]
37684 ModuleA 12332 9576 17:27:29.063 LoadImageEvent:
\Windows\System32\userinit.exe PId 573C
[...]
37687 ModuleA 12332 9576 17:27:29.064 LoadImageEvent:
\Windows\System32\userinit.exe PId 573C
[...]
```

What we are looking for here is **Message Invariant** (page 198) like ".exe," but we are interested in the occurrence of specific path structures like \Device\HarddiskVolume because, in our troubleshooting context, they signify process launch sequence during terminal session initialization.

Ornament

There are messages in traces and logs that alone do not have useful information. These are adornments or ornamentation messages that we initially called *Delineator* or *Separator* messages that structure message stream or *Figural Events* (where we borrowed the name *figural* from Lyotard[126]), such as formatting the next message with { }. Such messages only make meaning with other meaningful messages. We call this pattern **Ornament**. It helps in using trace analysis patterns and trace pattern identification.

For example, the **Ornament** can also be present in individual messages as a character prefix. It can be a part of **Message Invariant** (page 198) or the variable itself. Some ornamentation can play a rhetorical[127] function.

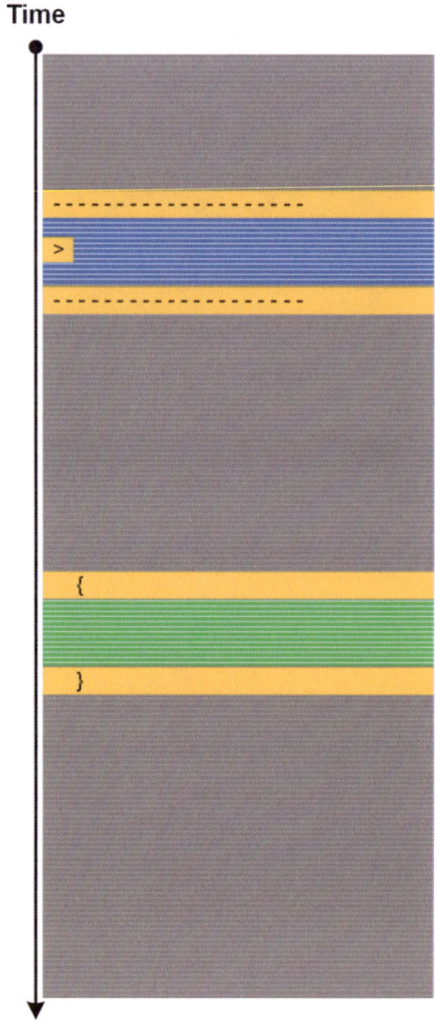

Although ornament is present in non-software architecture, this concept has never been explored in the pattern–oriented software architecture and construction. We propose a similar concept for source code (software construction) in addition to the ornamentation of its **Declarative Trace** (page 100). For software post-construction, we also add an ornament part to the software structure and behavior parts.

P

Palimpsest Messages

Palimpsest Messages are messages where some part or all of their content was erased or overwritten.

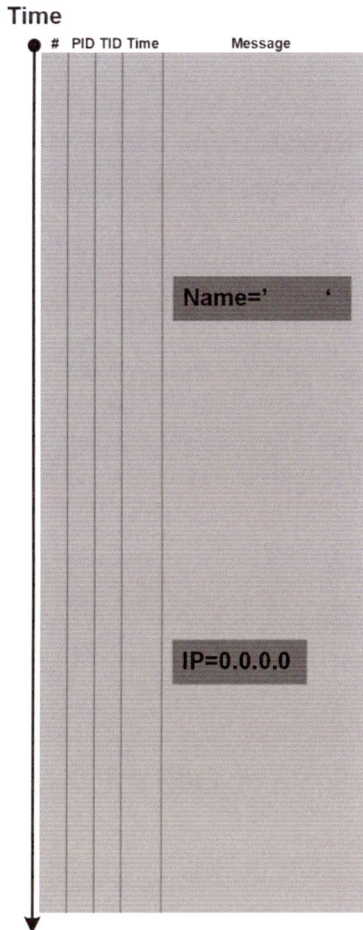

Time

#	PID TID Time	Message

Name='   '

IP=0.0.0.0

The name of this pattern comes from palimpsest [128] manuscript scrolls. Such messages may be a part of malnarratives [129] or result from **Circular Tracing** (page 78) or trace buffer corruption. Sometimes, not all relevant data is erased, and by using **Intra-** (page 169) and **Inter-Correlation** (page 167) and via the analysis of **Message Invariants** (page 198), it is possible to recover the original data. Also, as in **Recovered Messages** (page 251) pattern, it may be possible to use **Message Context** (page 191) to infer some partial content.

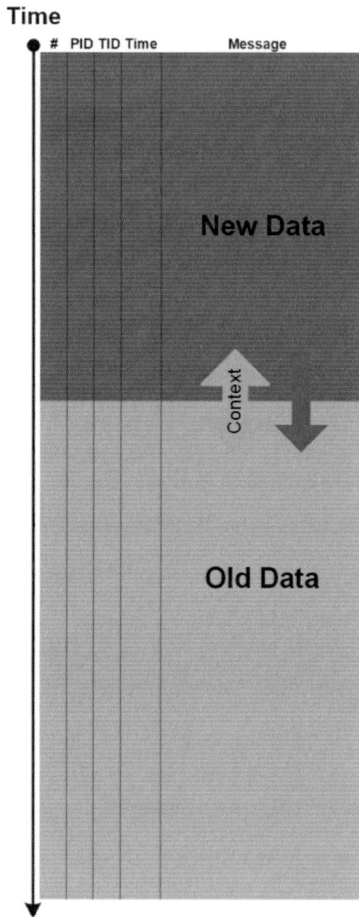

Periodic Error

Periodic Error is the obvious and, to some extent, the trivial pattern. It is an error or status value that is observed periodically many times:

```
No     PID  TID   Date      Time         Message
[...]
664957 1788 22504 4/23/2009 17:59:14.600 MyClass::Initialize: Cannot open connection
"Client ID: 310", status=5
[...]
668834 1788 19868 4/23/2009 19:11:52.979 MyClass::Initialize: Cannot open connection
"Client ID: 612", status=5
[...]
```

or

```
No     PID  TID   Date      Time         Message
[...]
202314 1788 19128 4/21/2009 16:03:46.861 HandleDataLevel: Error 12005 Getting Mask
[...]
347653 1788 17812 4/22/2009 13:26:00.735 HandleDataLevel: Error 12005 Getting Mask
[...]
```

Here single trace entries can be isolated from the trace and studied in detail. We should be aware, though, that some modules might report **Periodic Errors** that are false positive, in a sense that they are expected as a part of implementation details, for example, when a function returns an error to indicate that the bigger buffer is required or to estimate its size for a subsequent call.

The following diagram illustrates this pattern:

Time

#	PID	TID	Time	Message

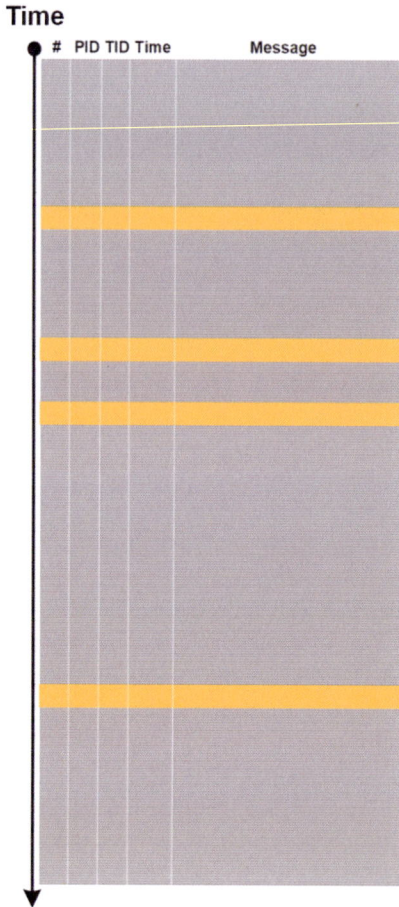

Periodic Message Block

This pattern is similar to **Periodic Error** (page 231) but not limited to errors or failure reports. One such example we recently encountered is when some adjoint activity (such as messages from specific PID, **Adjoint Thread**, page 48) stops appearing after the middle of the trace, and, after that, there are repeated blocks of similar messages (**Message Invariant**, page 198) from different PIDs with their threads checking some condition (for example, waiting for an event and reporting timeouts):

Phantom Activity

Sometimes we put trace statements to track responses to certain environmental actions and conditions but are surprised to see them in logs when nothing happened outside that could have triggered them:

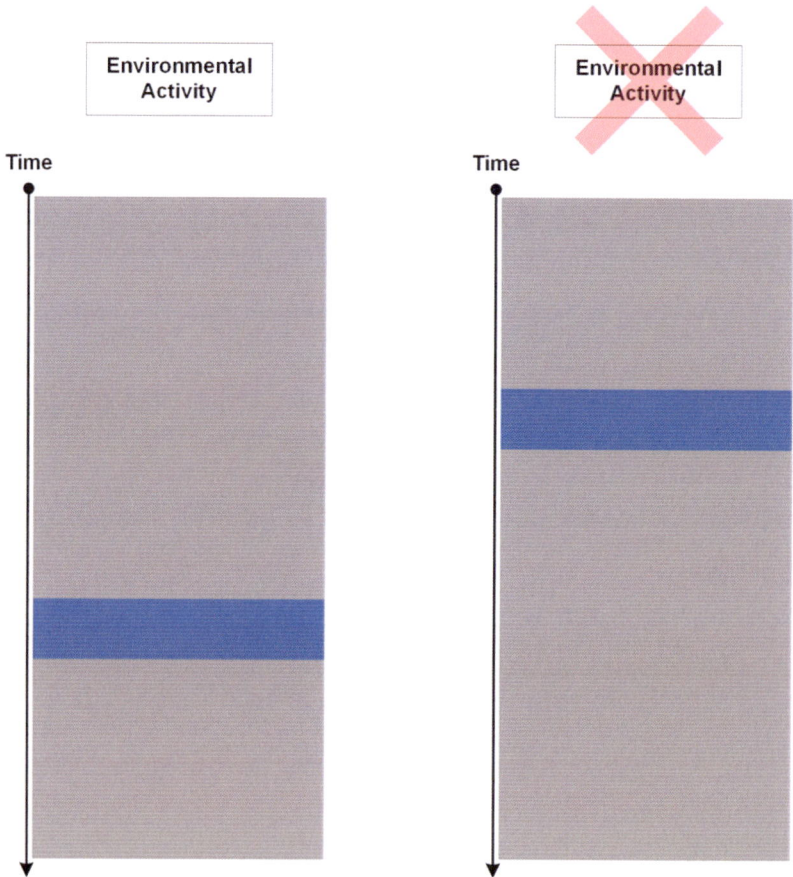

We call such an analysis pattern **Phantom Activity**. It is an indicator that the internal program state was not updated correctly. The difference between such activities and **Defamiliarizing Effect** (page 103) is that the former messages are expected but not in their current **Message Context** (page 191).

Phase Transition

Traces and logs may show drastic qualitative and quantitative pattern changes. We call this analysis pattern **Phase Transition** by analogy with phase transition [130] in physical, biological, and other complex systems. Usually, the goal of the analysis is to find a parameter that caused such a transition. Here are a few self-explanatory examples.

Change in **Statement Density and Current** (page 286):

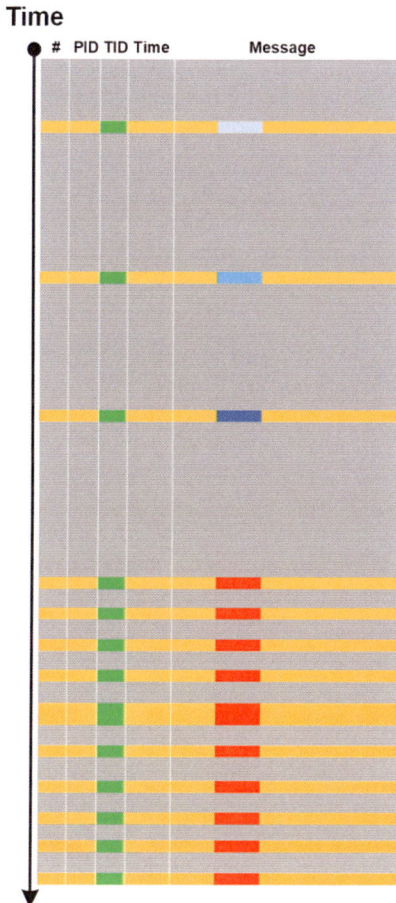

The sudden proliferation of (**Adjoint,** page 48) **Threads of Activity** (page 296):

Discontinuity (page 115) of **Activity Region** (page 41) with only **Drone Messages** (page 118) left:

Piecewise Activity

Activity Regions (page 41) or blocks of messages having the same TID or PID usually follow each other in a typical complex software trace. Such the following can be completely random and independent, or it may be linear based on IPC or some inter-thread communication mechanism. For example, after filtering out **Background Components** (page 57), we may find that an RPC client call setup is followed by messages from an RPC server:

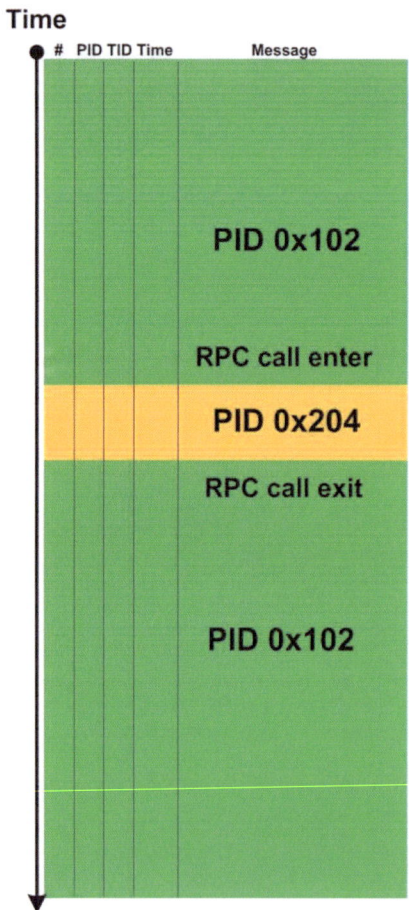

Using a coordinate approach with the message number and PID axes, we can reformat this minimal trace diagram:

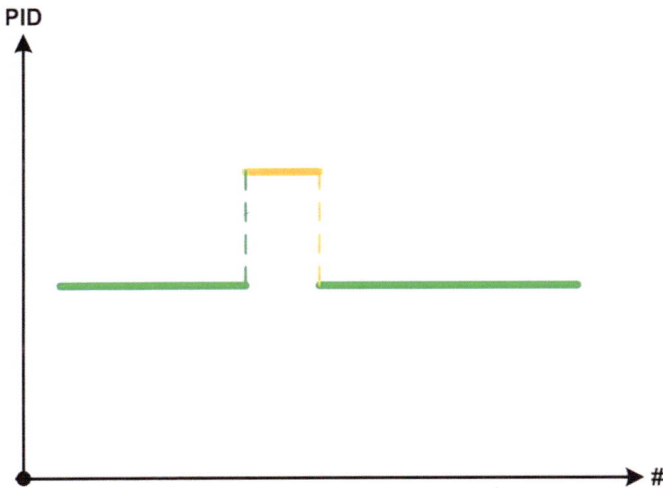

We borrowed the name for this pattern from the concept of a piecewise linear function[131] in mathematics (and piecewise continuity). In some problem software behavior scenarios where we encountered such an analysis pattern, it was complemented by **Discontinuity** (page 115) pattern. For example, an RPC call may be blocked, and we do not see client messages after that break until the end of the trace. In such cases, we always recommend forcing a complete memory dump to check for the wait chain memory analysis patterns[132].

Pivot Message

Suppose we form **Adjoint Thread** (page 48) based on some message or operation type or some other attribute:

However, we do not know where to start to look backward for any anomalies relevant to our problem:

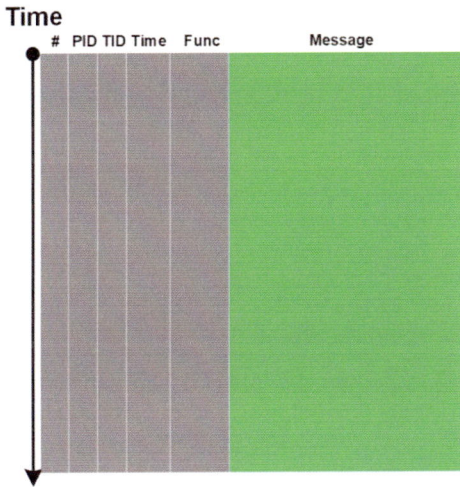

We go back to our full trace and find a problem message:

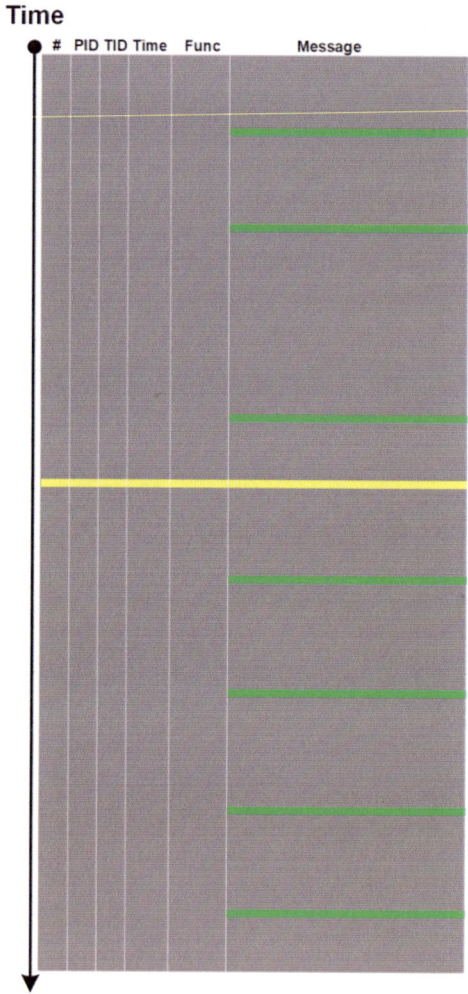

Although not in our **Adjoint Thread** that we formed previously, we consider it as **Pivot Message** that helps us to go back there:

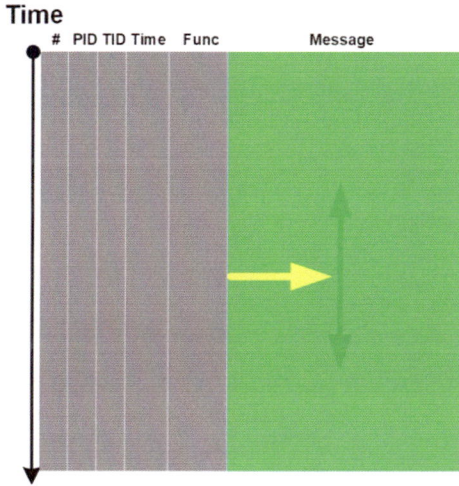

Poincaré Trace

Considering and extending **Trace Dimension** (page 309) to TID, ATID, and Time, we use the Poincaré section[133] and Poincaré map[134] analogies to introduce the **Poincaré Trace** analysis pattern. We choose a value of one "coordinate," for example, Time, and then form the new trace that consists of messages from different (A)TIDs that have the same timestamp as the Time value or the last message(s) from other different ATIDs if they happened before section Time:

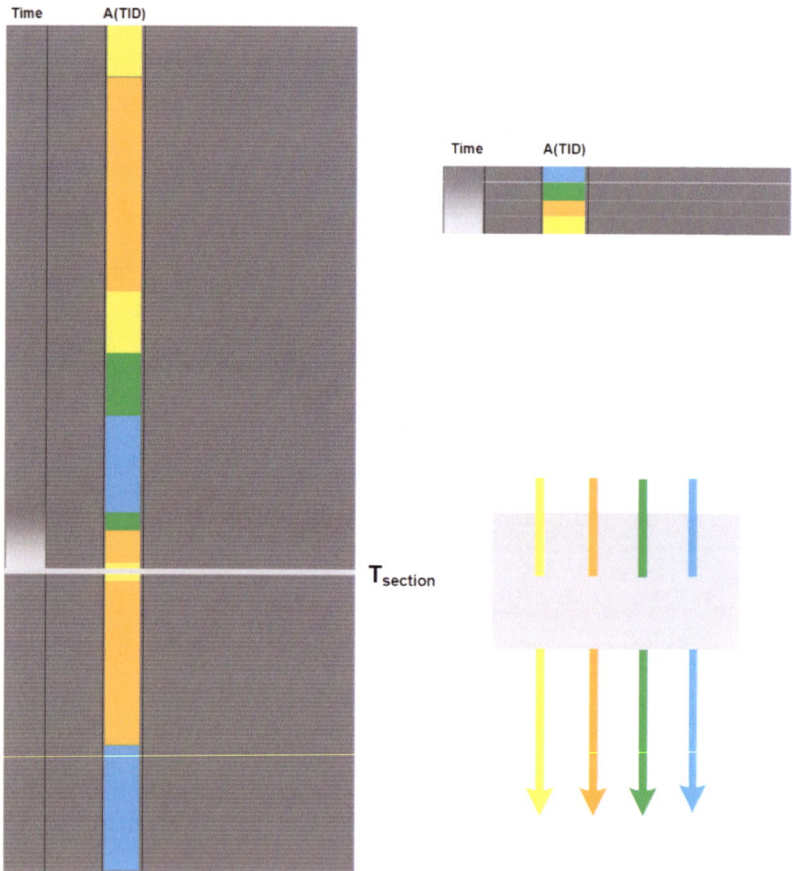

If we choose a different ATID than Time and TID, then **Poincaré Trace** is equivalent to the **Adjoint Thread of Activity** (page 48). If ATID is TID, we have **Thread of Activity** (page 296) as a trivial case. If we have **Thread of**

Activity, we can choose some ATID and get **Poincaré Trace** as illustrated in the following diagram where the thick black line in the right **Poincaré Trace** represents **Discontinuity** (page 115) and its **Time Delta** (page 298):

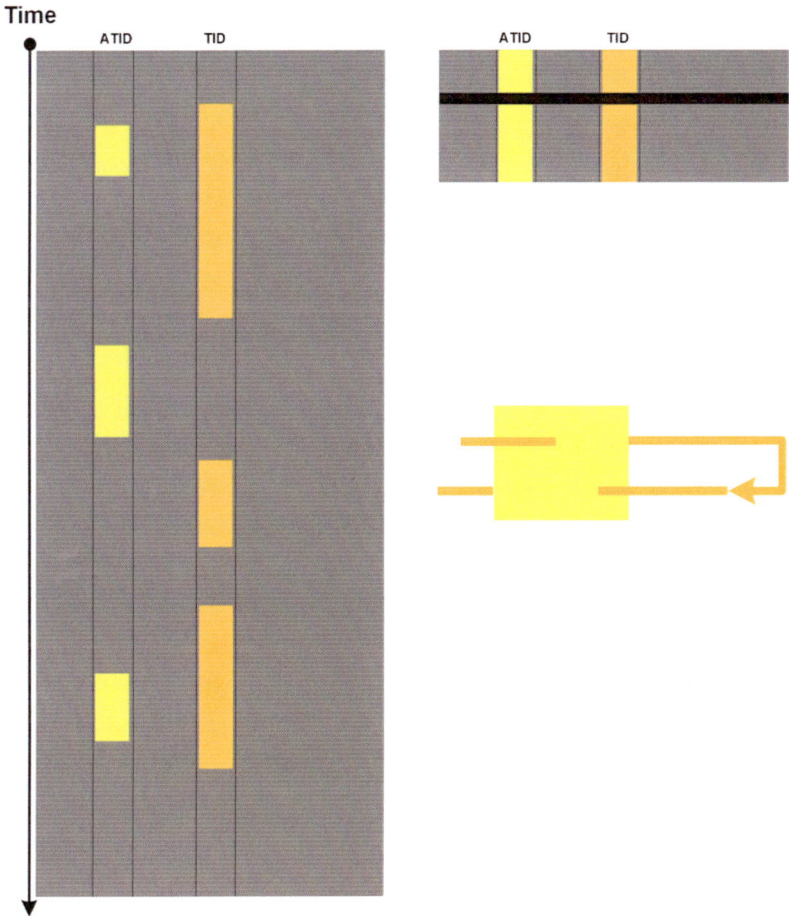

Polytrace

The advent of virtualization simplified the debugging of complex issues by allowing one to save the snapshot of the execution environment and then resume it from the save point of execution. Moreover, it allows continuing tracing using a different set of environmental conditions and input data. New tracing continuations constitute a network that we call **Polytrace**:

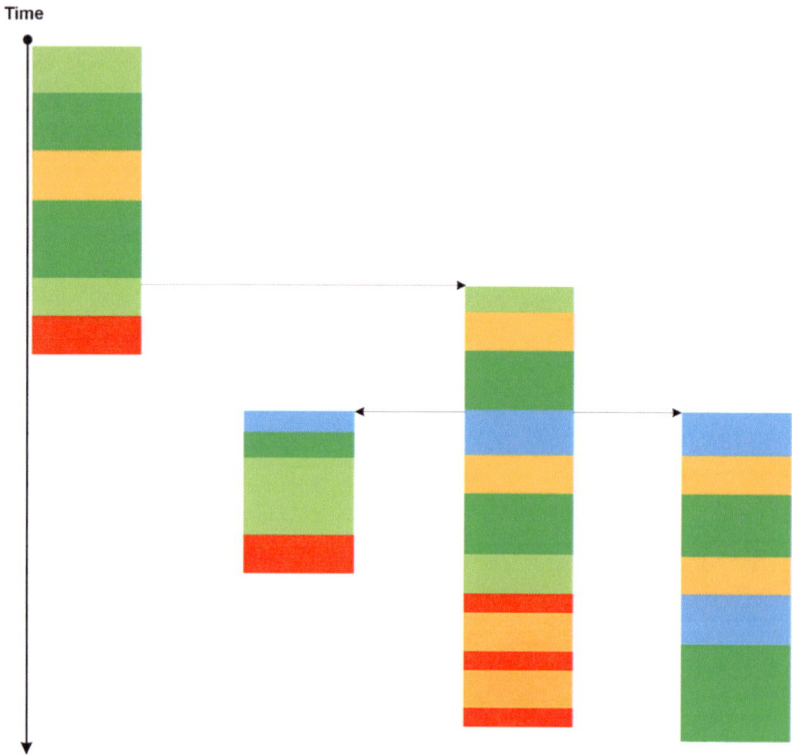

The **Bifurcation Point** (page 61) for two identical trace beginnings may be considered an example of a simple **Polytrace**.

Projective Space

When we have hundreds of separate trace files from **Split Trace** (page 282) and a smaller **Split Trace** with fewer files or just a single trace file that was recorded simultaneously (for example, a client from some client-server environment), we can "project" the smaller **Message Space** (page 203) into the larger **Message Space** as depicted in the following diagram:

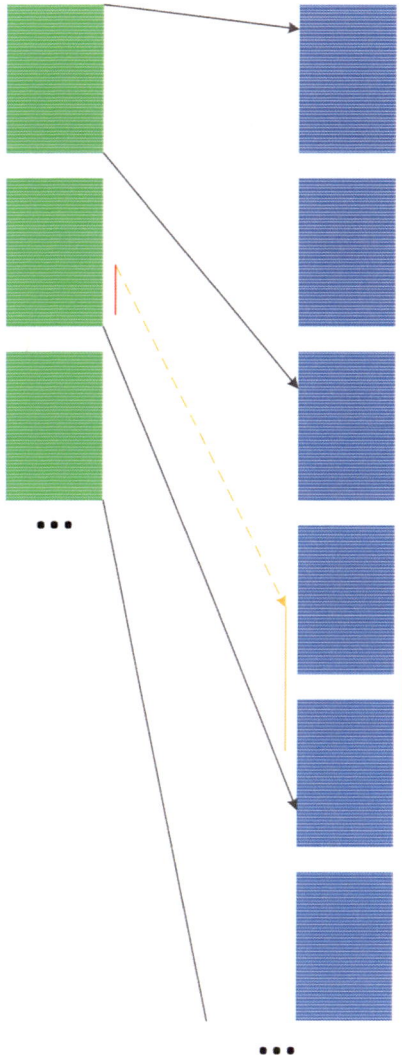

This **Projective Space** analysis pattern can be used in conjunction with **Indexical Trace** (page 160), where time interval can be used as an index into the larger **Split Trace.** Such a projection may not be accurate, but assuming that the target trace **Statement Current** (page 286) is uniform on average, it can still be a very good heuristic instead of a binary search. For example, recently, we had 4 sequential trace files for the client and 36 sequential files for the server. The software problem interval was specified in **Basic Facts** (page 60). We found it in the second path of the 4th client trace. We, therefore, only inspected the last 4 traces of the 36 in the server sequential trace set and found it contained in the 35th server trace.

This pattern uses a projective space[135] metaphor from mathematics.

Punctuated Activity

Sometimes we have a uniform stream of messages that belong to some **Activity Region** (page 41), **Thread of Activity** (page 296), or **Adjoint Thread of Activity** (page 48). We can use micro-**Discontinuities** (page 115) to structure that message stream, especially if the semantics of trace messages is not yet fully clear to us. It may also help us to recognize **Visitor Trace** (page 361). Originally we wanted to call this pattern *Micro Delays*, but after recognizing that such delays only make sense for one activity (since there can be too many of them in the overall log), we named this pattern **Punctuated Activity**. Usually, such delays are small compared to **Timeouts** (page 300) and belong to **Silent Messages** (page 271).

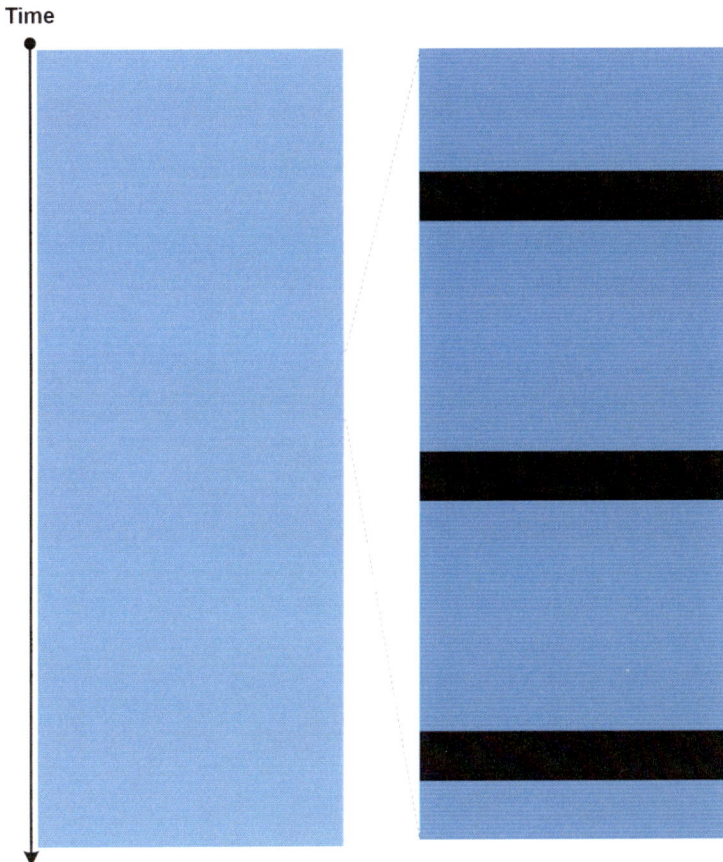

Time

Q

Quotient Trace

In **Adjoint Message** (page 43) analysis pattern description, we mentioned compressing message sequences having the same message attribute into one message. Considering the trace as a "topological" space and message attribute as an "equivalence" relation, we introduce the **Quotient Trace** analysis pattern by analogy with quotient space[136] in topology. By endowing message sequences having the same attribute with some "metric," such as cardinality of **Message Set** (page 202), we can also visually distinguish quotient messages if they have the same attribute but from different sequences at different times. All this is illustrated in the following diagram:

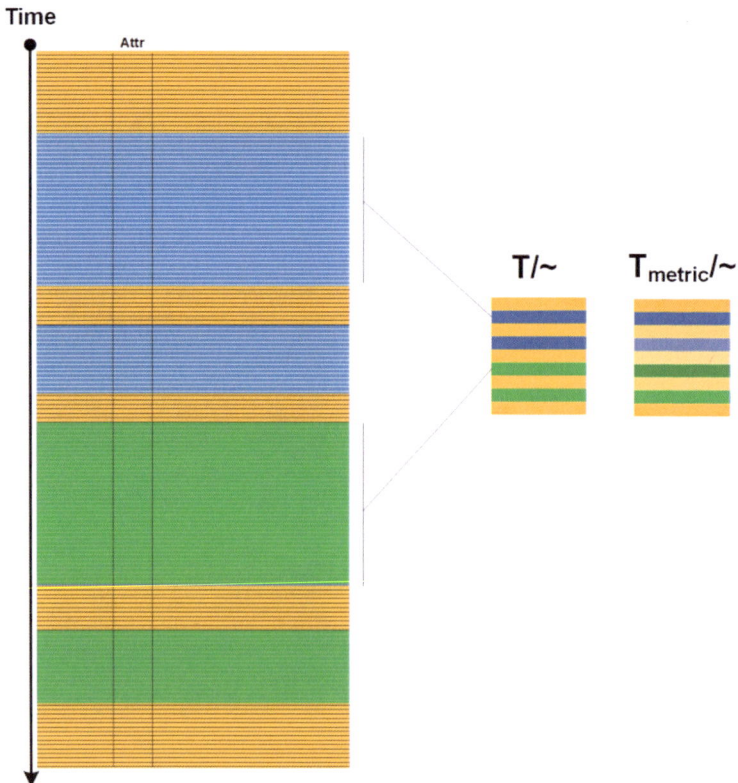

R

Random Data

Trace and log message text consists of constant, unchanging **Message Invariants** (page 198) and some varying data. The latter can be classified into **Random Data,** such as memory addresses, especially when ASLR [137] is enabled, **Counter Values** (page 91), and variable data but constants, such as error values and NULL pointers. Individual values from **Signals** (page 268) are not considered random, but their sequence can be. This analysis pattern is depicted in the following diagram (adapted from **Data Association** analysis pattern, page 94):

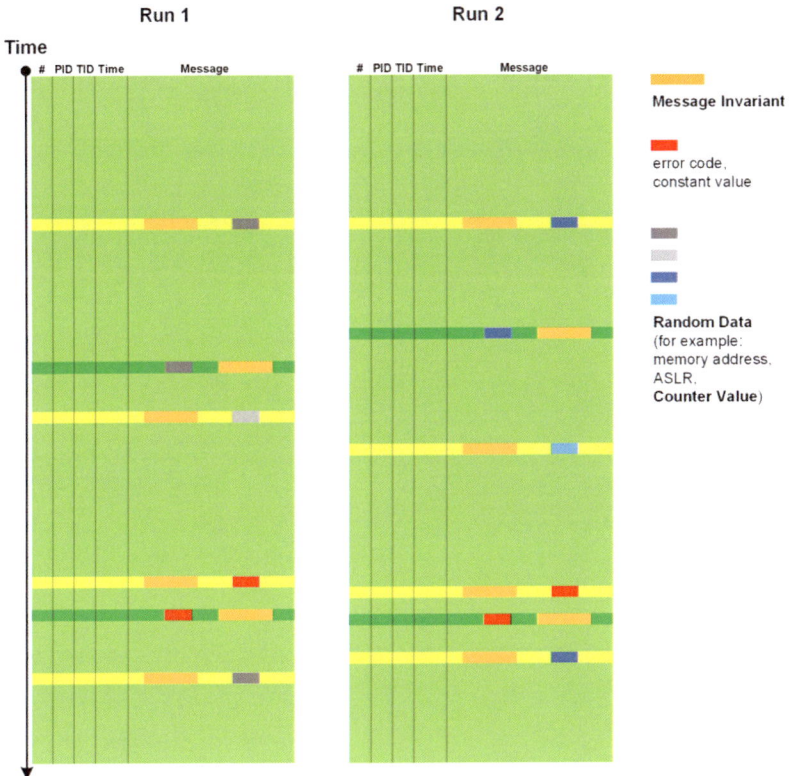

Recovered Messages

If we analyze ETW-based traces, we may frequently encounter the **No Trace Metafile** (page 222) pattern, especially after product updates and fixes. This complicates pattern analysis because we may not be able to see **Significant Events** (page 270), **Anchor Messages** (page 53), and **Error Messages** (page 123). In some cases, we can recover messages by comparing **Message Context** (page 191) for unknown messages. If we have source code access, this may also help. Both approaches are illustrated in the following diagram:

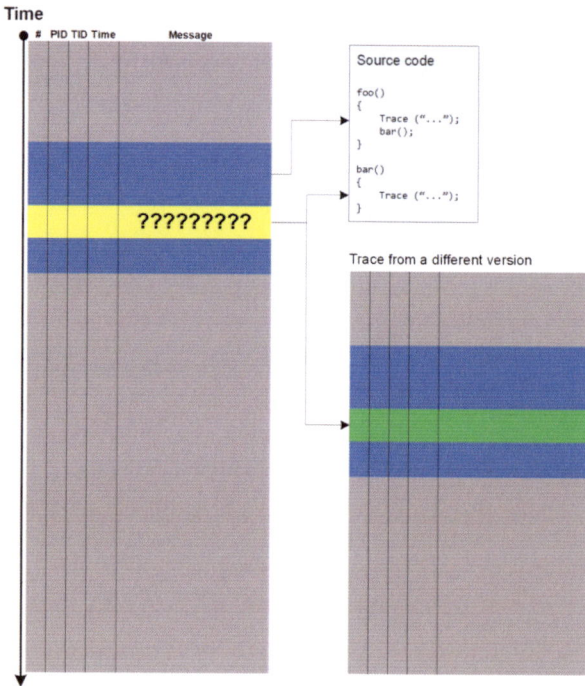

The same approach may also be applied to different kind of trace artifacts when some messages are corrupt. In such cases, it is possible to recover diagnostic evidence and, therefore, we call this pattern **Recovered Messages**.

Relative Density

This pattern describes anomalies in semantically related pairs of trace messages, for example, "data arrival" and "data display." Their **Statement Densities** (page 286) can be put in a ratio (also called specific gravity[138]) and compared between working and non-working scenarios. Because the total numbers of trace messages cancel each other, we have just the mutual ratio of two message types. In our hypothetical "data" example, the increased ratio of "data arrival" to "data display" messages accounts for reported visual data loss and sluggish GUI.

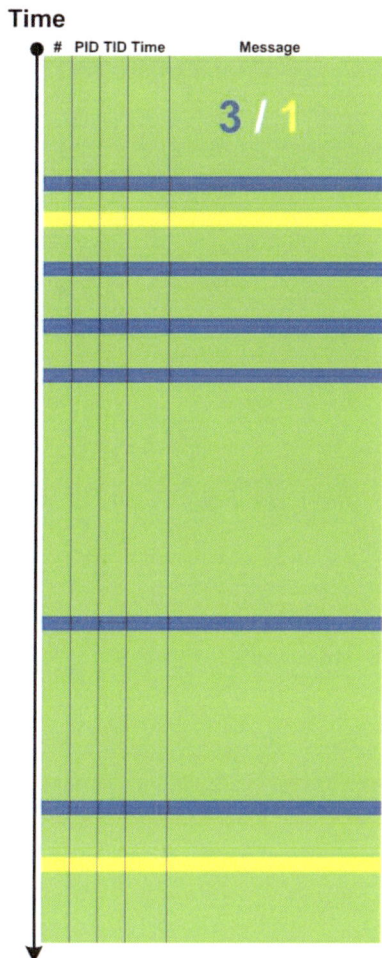

Renormalization

Using the metaphor **of renormalization**[139] from physics, we introduce the **Renormalization** trace and log analysis pattern where a selected message and its **Message Context** (page 191) are replaced by a single message:

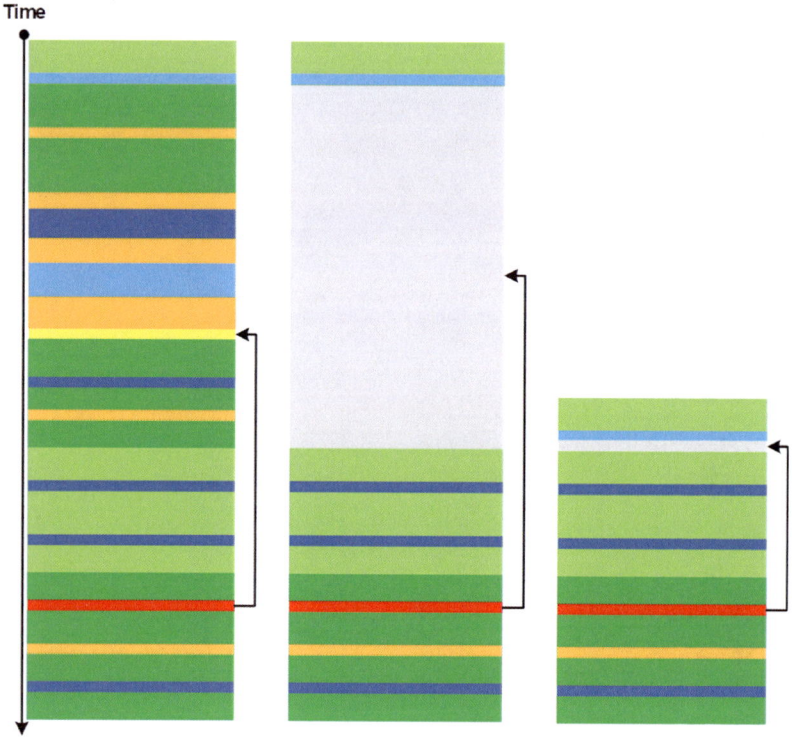

Resume Activity

If **Break-in Activity** (page 67) is usually unrelated to a thread or an **Adjoint Thread** that has a discontinuity, then the **Resume Activity** pattern highlights messages from that thread:

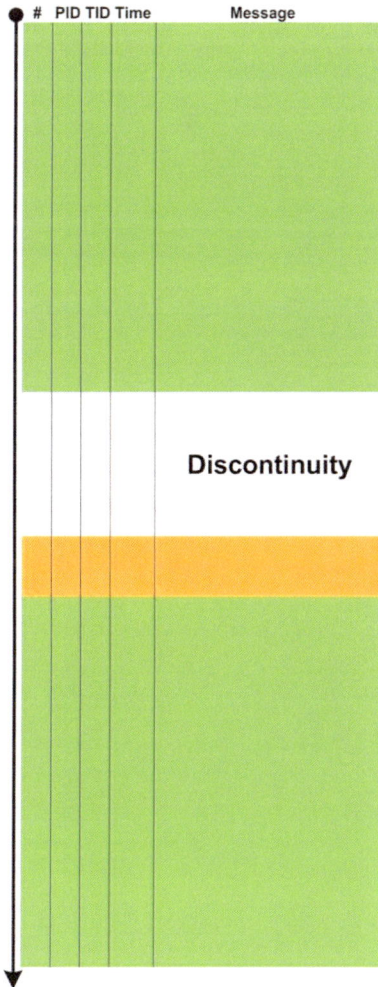

We can see the difference in the following graphical representation of the two traces where, in a working trace, a break-in preceded resume activity, but in a non-working trace, both patterns were absent:

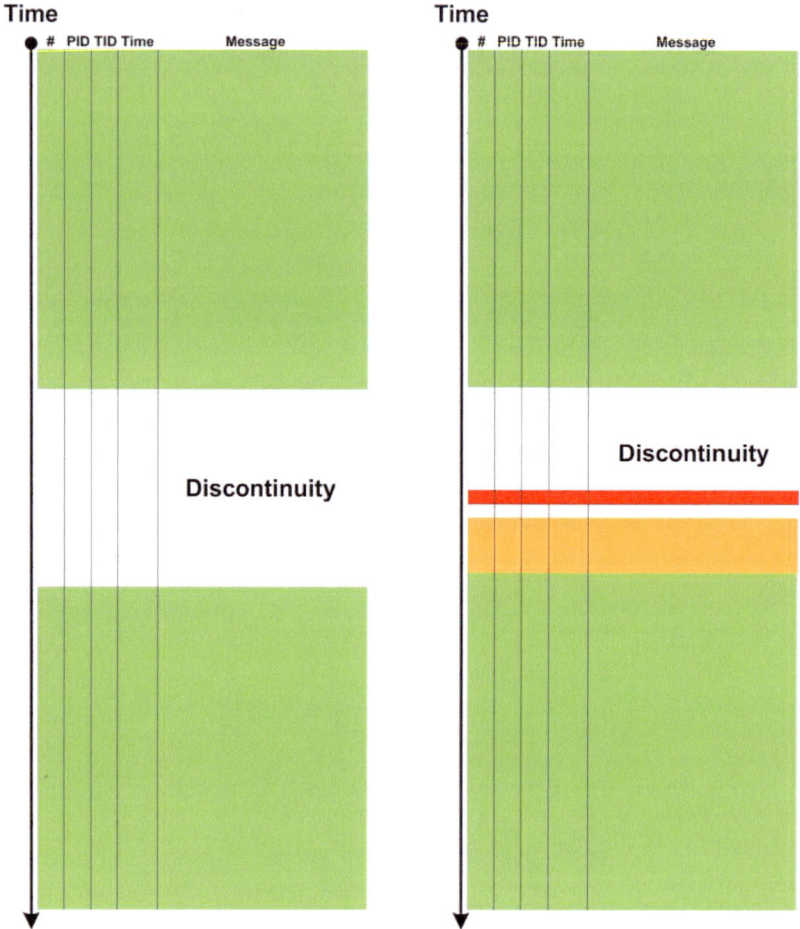

Ruptured Trace

Recently we analyzed a few logs that ended with a specialized **Activity Region** (page 41) from a subsystem that sets operational parameters. The problem description stated that the system became unresponsive after changing parameters in a certain sequence. Usually, for that system, when we stop logging (even after setting parameters), we end up with messages from some **Background Components** (page 57) since some time passes between the end of setting parameters activity and the time the operator sends stop logging request:

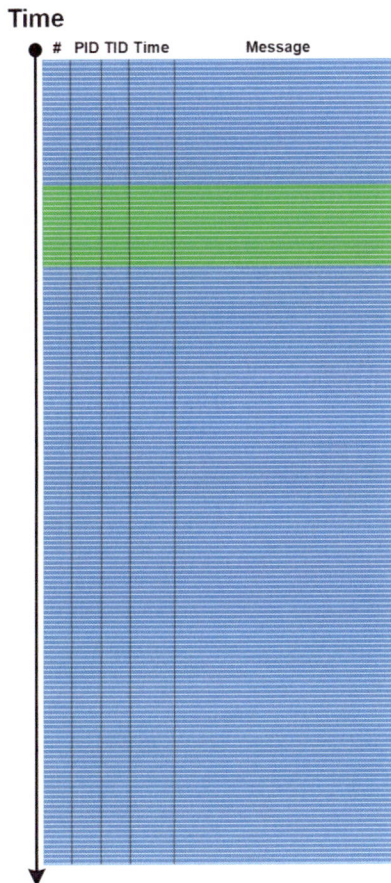

However, in the problem case, we see that message flow stops right in the middle of a parameter setting activity:

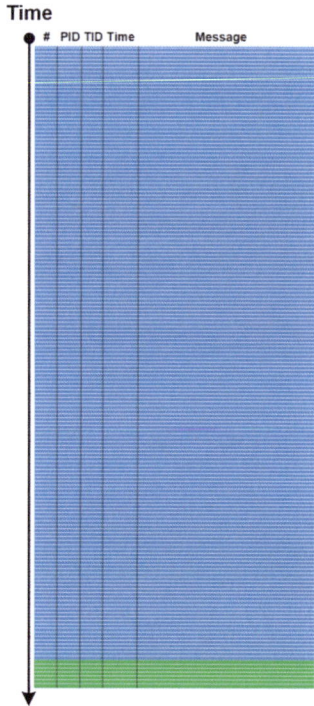

So we advised to check for any crashes or hangs, and, indeed, it was found that the system was experiencing system crashes, and we got memory dumps for analysis where we found **Top Module**[140] from a 3rd-party vendor related to parameter setting activity.

Please also note an analogy here between normal thread stack traces from threads that are waiting for most of the time and **Spiking Thread**[141] stack trace caught up in the middle of some function.

We call this pattern **Ruptured Trace** after a ruptured computation[142].

Note that if it is possible to restart the system and resume the same tracing, we may get an instance of the **Blackout** (page 63) analysis pattern.

S

Script Messages

Messages that contain scripting statements can be signs of malnarratives[143] that result from log injection during attempts to exploit possible cross-channel scripting[144] (XCS) and cross-site scripting[145] (XSS) vulnerabilities. Such **Script Messages** may be spread across a log, as illustrated in the following diagram:

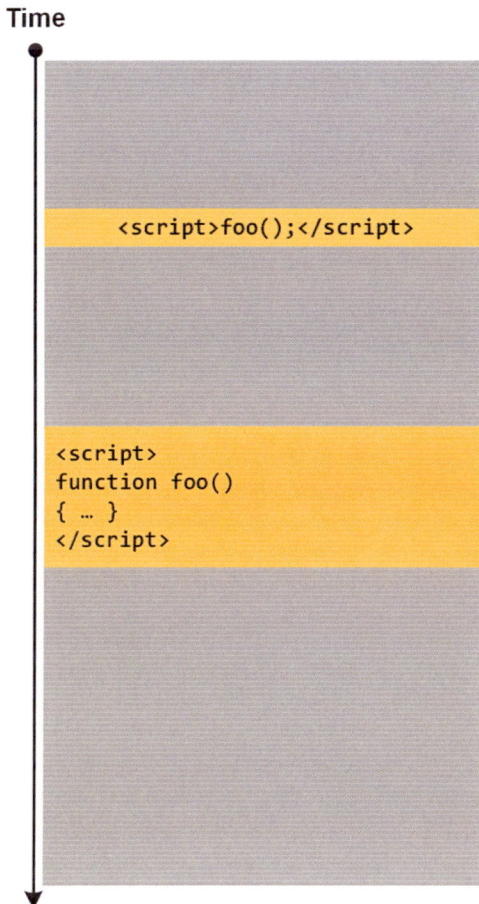

Time

```
<script>foo();</script>
```

```
<script>
function foo()
{ … }
</script>
```

Semantic Field

Semantic Field is a set of messages that belong to a particular category or subject:

Time

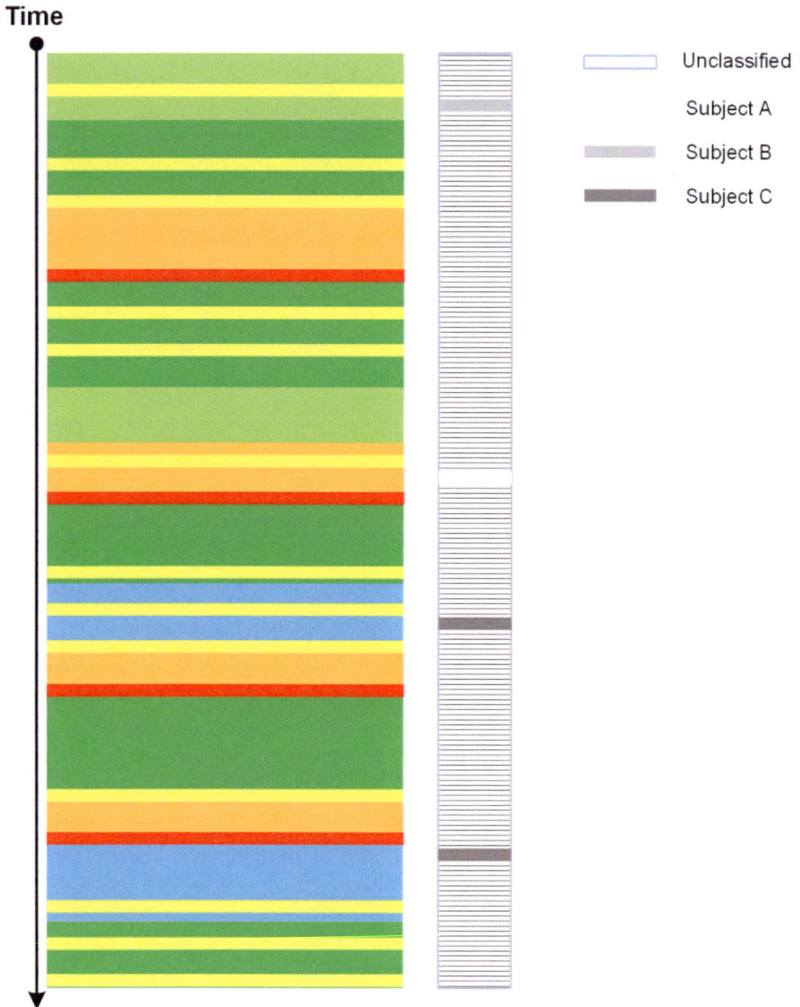

It differs from the **Trace Field** (page 314), which is a function, not an already prepared codomain of mapping.

Semantic Fields may be formed by the analysis of **Implementation Discourse** (page 157), for example, using machine learning techniques.

The pattern name was inspired by the semantic field[146] in linguistics and came to our attention when reading the "German Loanwords in English: An Historical Dictionary" book.

Sequence Repeat Anomaly

Sometimes we have **Periodic Message Blocks** (page 233) of a few adjacent messages, for example, when flags are translated into separate messages per bit. Then we may have a pattern of **Sequence Repeat Anomaly** when one of several message blocks has missing or added messages compared to more numerous expected identical message blocks. Then **Missing Message** (page 209) **Message Context** (page 191) may be explored further. The following diagram illustrates the pattern:

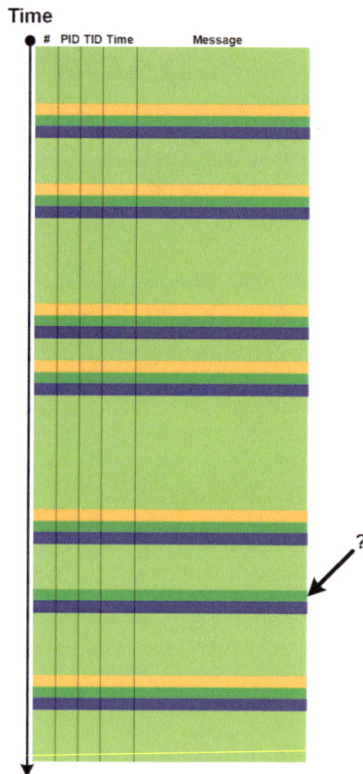

The name of the pattern comes from the notion of repeated DNA sequences[147].

Serial Trace

Most of the time, tracing and logging is done sequentially, for example, when a service or application is restarted after the crash, bugfix, or the host is rebooted. Then we can glue all resulting traces together (similar to **Glued Stack Trace**[148]) into one larger **Serial Trace**. Here we assume the same **Trace Schema** (page 333) for all individual traces and logs. It can also be considered as flattening a 2-dimensional **Tensor Trace** (page 292):

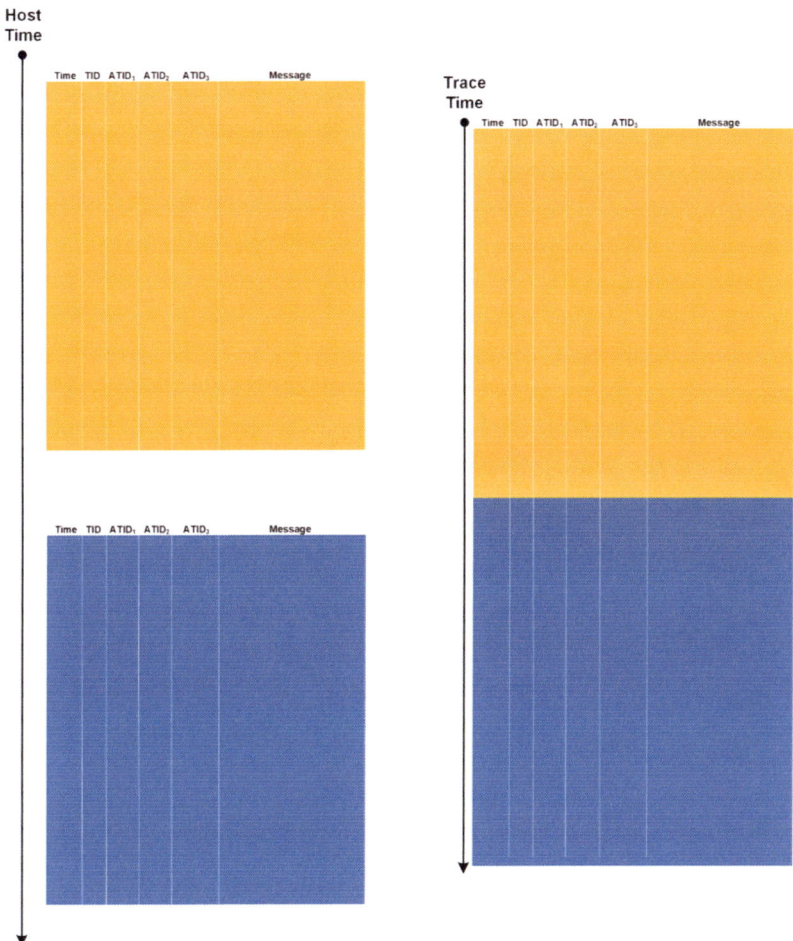

It allows us to apply various trace and log analysis patterns to the unified **Serial Trace** instead of doing **Inter-Correlation**, page 167 (vs. **Intra-Correlation**, page 170).

Serial Trace analysis pattern differs from **Meta Trace** (page 204), a trace about trace, and **Master Trace** (page 182), which we compare all other traces to. On the other hand, it is similar to **Trace Mask** (page 322) when there is no overlap in time. Also, **Serial Trace** is not a reverse of **Split Trace** (page 282) in a general case due to **Visibility Limits** (page 360) between individual traces.

When gluing traces together, **Ornament** (page 227) messages may be added to serve as a boundary between fragments.

Shared Point

Sometimes we know from **Basic Facts** (page 60) some data or activity we seek to identify in different traces collected together to perform **Inter-Correlational** analysis (page 167). It can be a shared file name, a named synchronization object, a locked file with sharing violations, a common virtual address in kernel space, or just some activity notification. We call this pattern by analogy with intersecting curves in some abstract space.

It is similar to **Linked Messages** (page 178) pattern but is more high-level and not confined to a common parameter (which can be an action description).

Sheaf of Activities

Inter-Correlation (page 167) analysis between a normal and problem logs to find **Bifurcation Point** (page 61, and a possible root cause) becomes a difficult task when both traces come from separate environments with different **Background Components** (page 57). Here a new analysis pattern with a name borrowed from sheaves[149] from mathematics can help. This pattern is also a tool for tracking the properties of trace message subsets. First, we find out important message types around some **Activity Region** (page 41) where we hope to find a difference between two traces:

Time

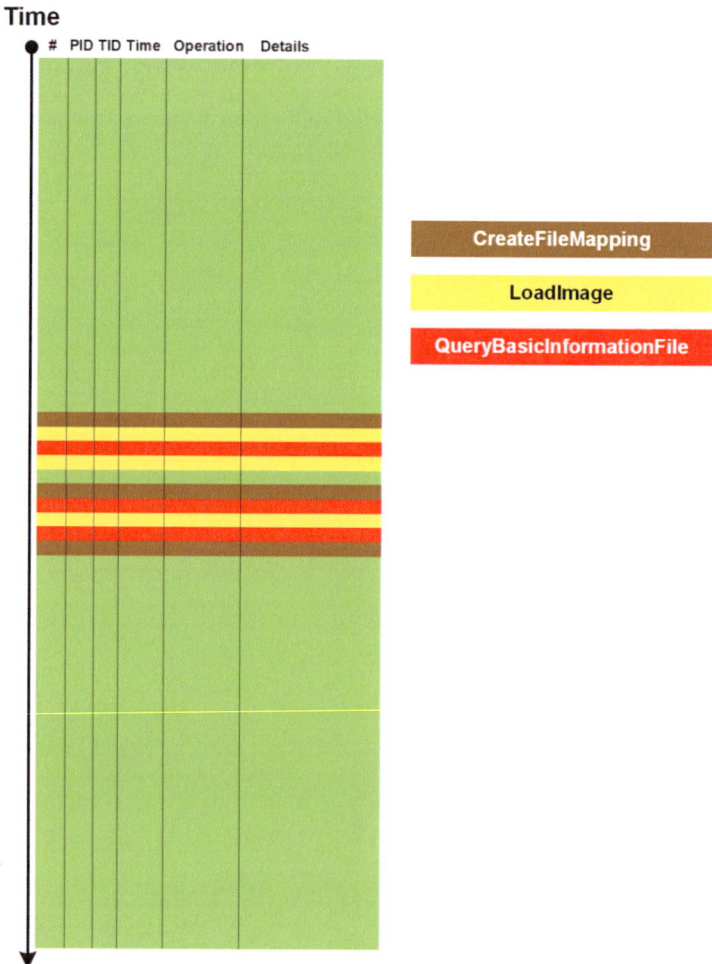

Then we create several **Adjoint Threads** (page 48) from different message types, for example, based on the operation type or function name:

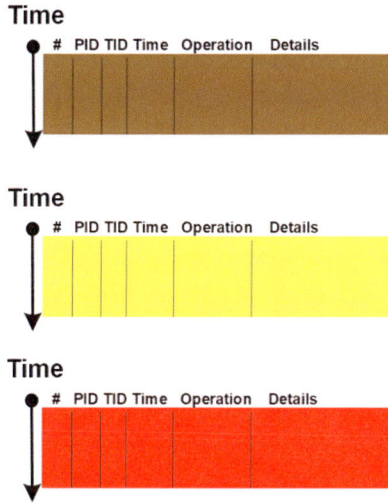

Then we analyze subtraces separately to find out a bifurcation point in each of them and then use this knowledge to find out differences between the original full traces.

Signal

According to the definition by Michael Robinson,[150] "a signal consists of a collection of related measurements." For traces and logs, we can apply a similar definition and consider a **Signal** as a collection of *local* messages having the same **Message Invariant** (page 198) and corresponding variable data values. Signals are examples of **Message Sets** (page 202). The typical example is sets of related **Counter Value** (page 91) messages. Signals can be obtained by obtaining the **Adjoint Thread of Activity** (page 48) of a specific message (to filter out **Background Components** "noise," page 57) as illustrated in the following diagram:

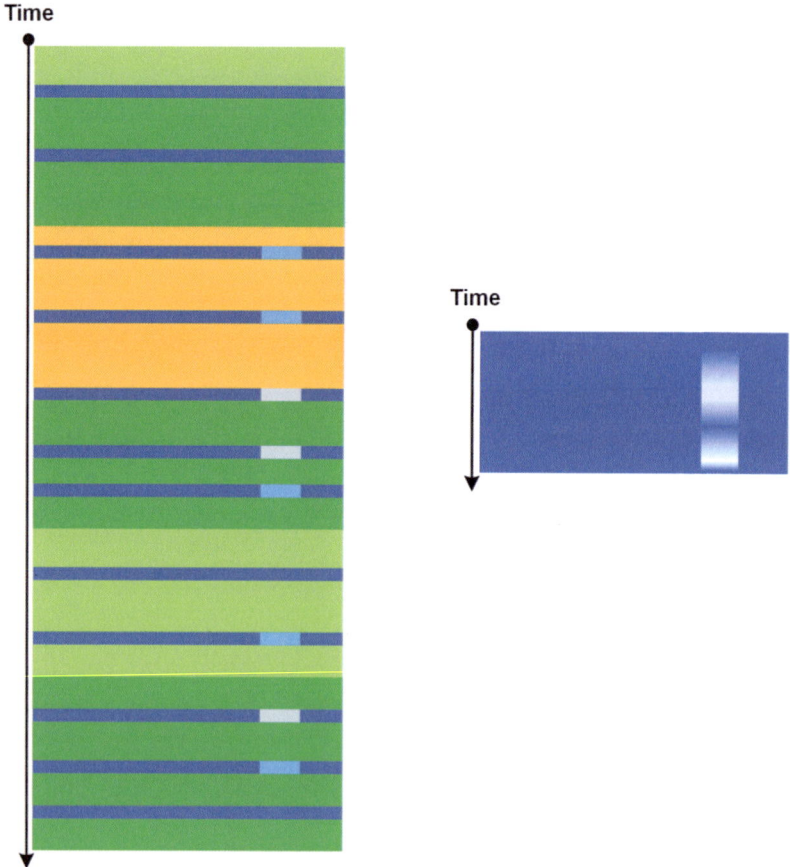

Generally, the variable "measurement" part can form **Braid of Activity** (page 65).

We introduce the **Signal** analysis pattern to bridge the gap between Software Narratology[151] and Hardware Narratology[152].

Significant Event

When looking at software traces and doing either a search for or just scrolling, certain messages grab attention immediately. We call them **Significant Events**. It could be a recorded exception (**Exception Stack Trace**, page 129) or an error, **Basic Fact** (page 60), a trace message from **Vocabulary Index** (page 362), or just any trace statement that marks the start of some activity we want to explore in-depth, for example, a certain DLL is attached to the process, a coupled process is started, or a function is called. The start of a trace and the end of it are trivial **Significant Events** and are used in deciding whether the trace is **Circular** (page 78), in determining the trace recording interval or its average **Statement Current** (page 286).

Significant Interval

Sometimes, we ask for a log file to see **State and Event** pattern (page 283), and see it there, only to find that we cannot do a **Back Trace** (page 56) of **State Dumps** (page 285) from some **Significant Event** (page 270) for **Inter-Correlation** (page 167) analysis because our **Data Interval** (page 96) is truncated (**Truncated Trace**, page 352). This highlights the importance of proper tracing intervals that we call **Significant Interval** analysis pattern by analogy with significant digits[153] in scientific measurements. The following diagram illustrates the pattern:

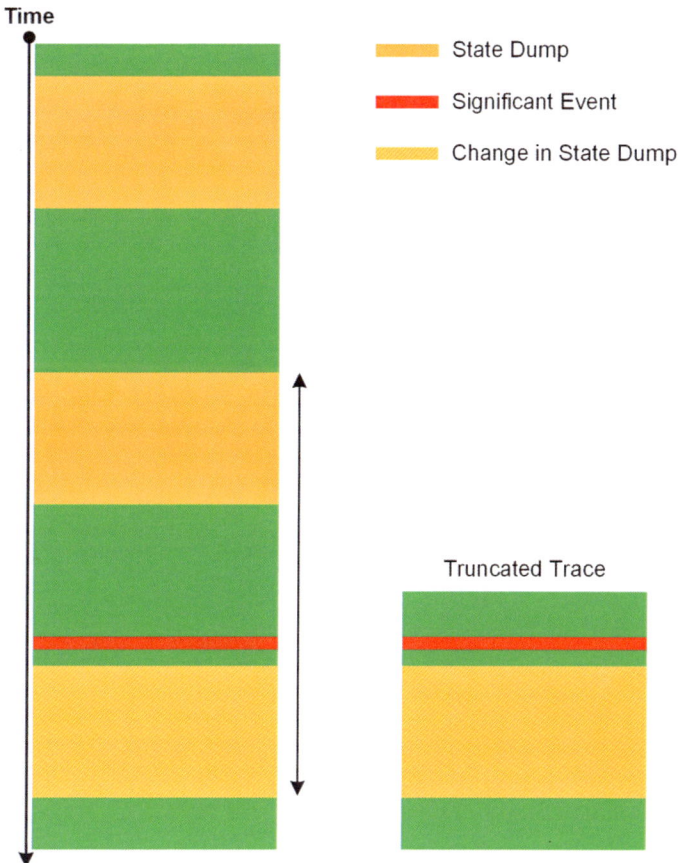

If you find out you get truncated traces and logs often, you may want to increase **Statement Current** (page 286) for state logging.

Silent Messages

We mostly analyze real messages in software traces and logs. In such message streams, we may easily see detectable **Discontinuity** (page 115) patterns. However, in some cases, it is beneficial to analyze the absence of messages. The message stream is not uniform; there may be different **Statement Currents** (page 286). If the time resolution is 1 ms, for example, then we may have current N msg/ms, or in the case of lesser current, such as 0.5 msg/ms, we have the so-called **Silent Messages** (----):

```
[...]
11 ms: message
12 ms: ----
13 ms: message
14 ms: ----
15 ms: message
16 ms: message
17 ms: ----
18 ms: ----
19 ms: message
[...]
```

So, by a silent message, we understand the possible message that would occupy the minimal time resolution gap. If we look at the following illustration, we see that the whole pattern analysis apparatus can be applied to analyze the distribution of silent messages.

This pattern differs from the **Discontinuity** pattern because the latter is about large unexpected silences and differs from **Sparse Trace** (page 279), which is about missing trace statements from source code.

Singleton Event

There are events that, by design or system configuration, should be seen in a log only once or not seen at all if the code responsible for them was executed before the tracing session. For example, the launch of certain services during system initialization should not be seen again when we trace system activity long after that. It can also be just messages from singleton[154] objects in the application log. The appearance of extra **Singleton Events** may point to design violations or some abnormal system events such as process restart. The latter may **Intra-Correlate** (page 170) with the start of the fault handling process, such as *WerFault.exe* in Windows Process Monitor logs (**Guest Component**, page 149).

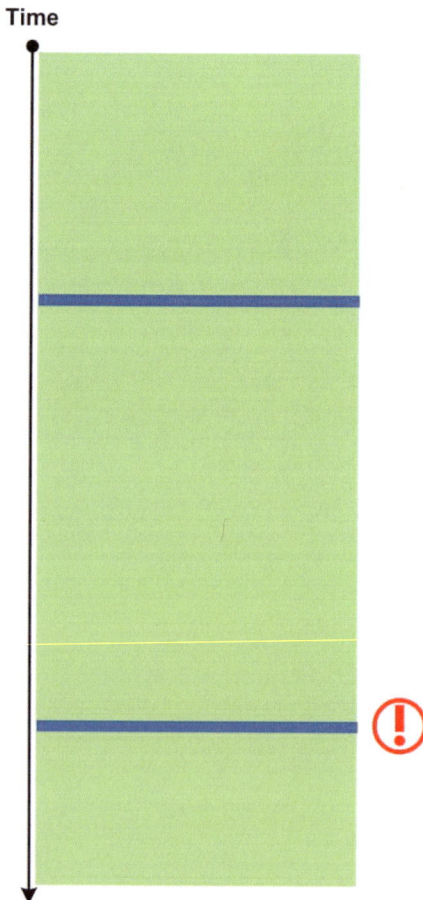

Singleton Trace

Status updates, error message boxes and even abort errors can all be considered as examples of software traces and logs. We call such a log with one message only **Singleton Trace**. Please don't confuse it with **Singleton Event** (page 268) analysis pattern, which is trivial for **Singleton Traces**. We illustrate this pattern with this picture of the error message (in Russian, it means "The machine doesn't work. Code: SB") from a lemonade-dispensing machine:

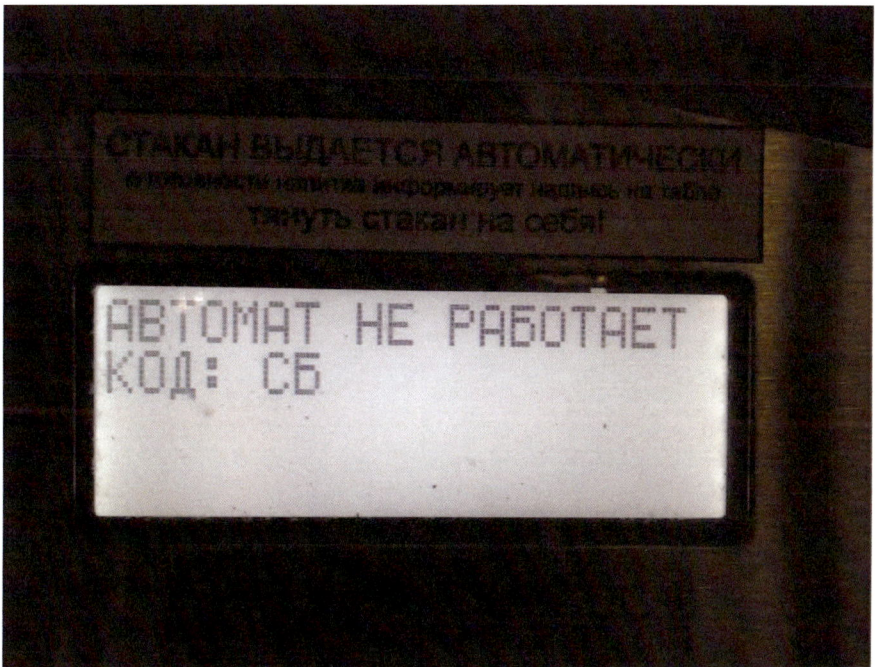

The message in such a trace may contain the associated stack trace as a trivial example of a **Fiber Bundle** (page 136).

Small DA+TA

Recently we performed the diagnostic analysis of a software incident where certain functionality was not available to users and provided the report based on analysis patterns such as **Focus of Tracing** (page 141) and **Opposition Messages** (page 225). We also conjectured some hypotheses explaining the observed abnormal behavior. However, in the end, the problem was solved not by the analysis of a lengthy software execution log but by looking at the small configuration INI file where not working functionality was simply disabled in one line:

```
EnableFunctionality = 0
```

Even before that analysis, we were thinking about the importance of **Small DA+TA**, such as configuration files and registry details that can be considered as general software traces[155]. Here DA+TA means Dump Artifact + Trace Artifact, and Big DA+TA refers to software execution memory dump artifacts and trace artifacts that can be huge. The analysis pattern is illustrated in the following diagram, where we see no difference between working and non-working scenarios due to insufficient trace coverage (**Sparse Trace**, page 279):

configuration file A

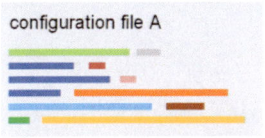

configuration file B

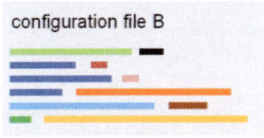

Time

Time

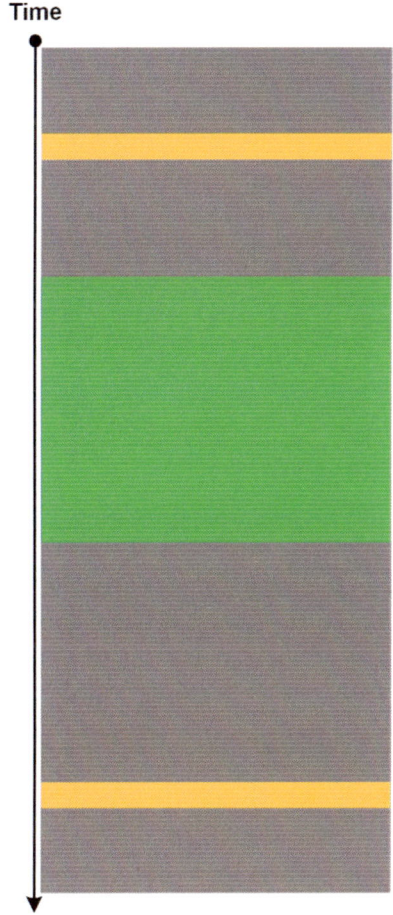

Sorted Trace

If we have an attribute, we can sort messages based on that attribute values and get **Sorted Trace**. If that attribute is TID or ATID, we get the sequence of **Threads of Activity** (page 296) or **Adjoint Threads of Activity** (page 48):

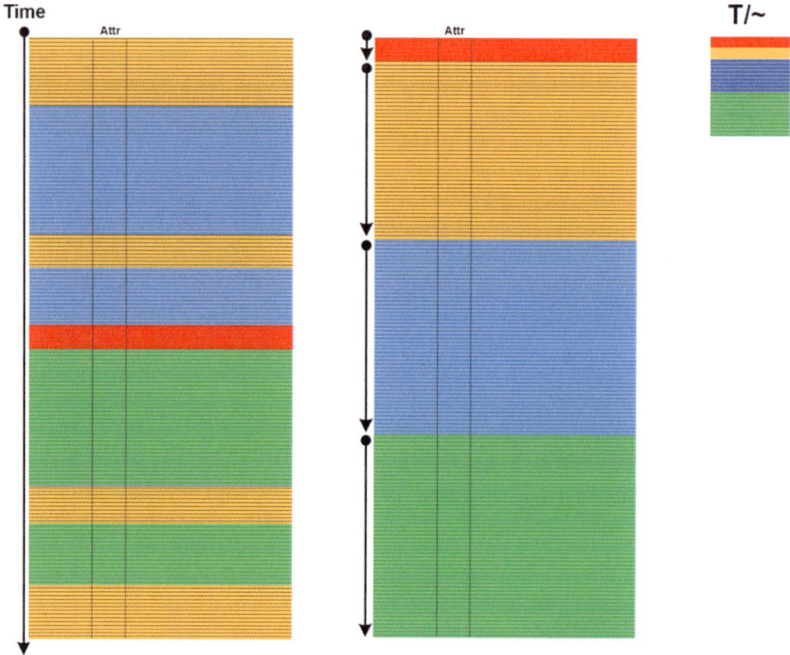

If we sort by message types or **Message Invariants** (page 198) or some message data, we get a sequence of **Fibers of Activity** (page 138).

The diagram above also shows on the right **Quotient Trace** (page 250) by message type equivalence after additional sorting inside each **Adjoint Thread of Activity**.

Sparse Trace

Sometimes we do not see anything in the trace or see very little because trace statements did not cover particular source code fragments (see also **PLOTs**[156]):

Time

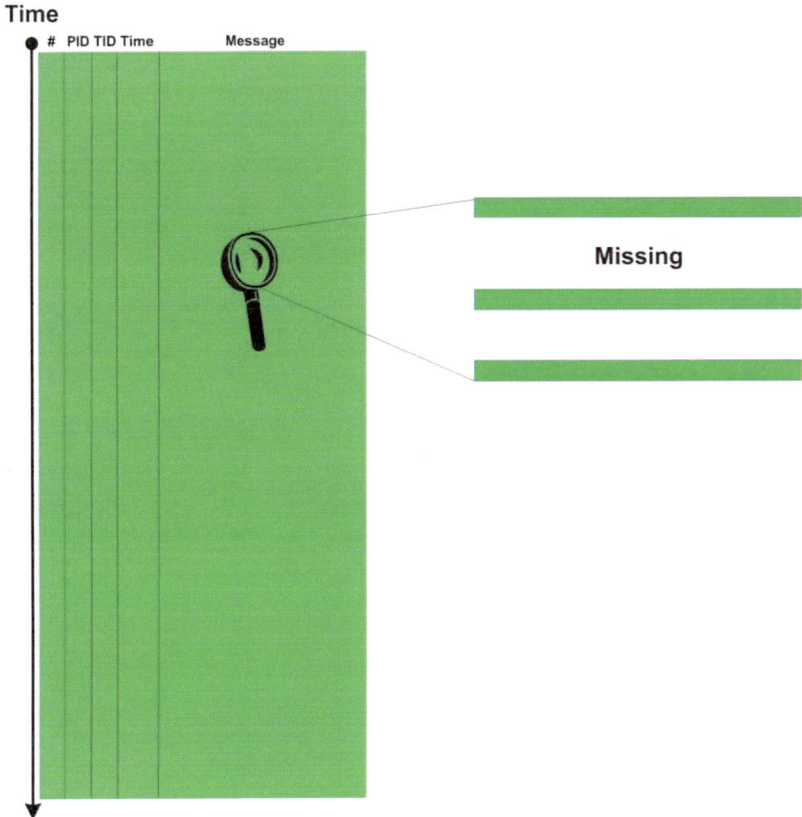

The **Sparse Trace** pattern is different from **Missing Component** (page 207) pattern, where some modules are not included for logging explicitly, although there is a logging code there, or **Visibility Limit** (page 360) pattern, where tracing is intrinsically impossible. Often technical support and escalation engineers request to add more trace statements, and software engineers extend tracing coverage iteratively as needed:

Split Message

Depending on tracing architecture, we may have trace or log messages split into several statements. For example, some API and library tracing tools may log a function call after it returns with a result, but some tools or tracing libraries may log calls in the context of corresponding threads and, therefore, be preempted by other tracing and logging threads and even interrupted. In the latter cases, we may have **Split Message** like depicted in the following diagram:

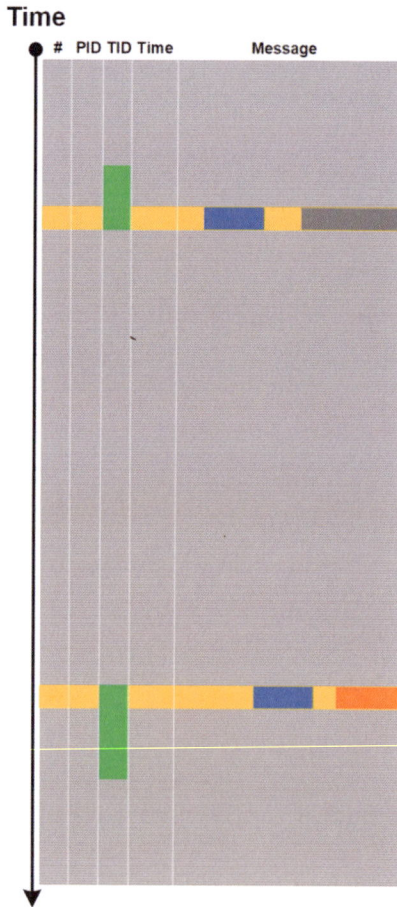

A typical example here is Linux *strace*[157] tool. We can recognize such messages by their **Message Invariant** (page 198) and **Ornament** (page 227).

Split Message is different from **Opposition Messages** (page 225) analysis pattern, where messages are logged from different source code tracing statements when, for example, a function call result is logged separately. But, in the same vein, when we see an unfinished **Split Message,** we may assume some sort of **Discontinuity** (page 115).

Split Trace

Some tracing tools, such as CDFControl,[158] have the option to split software traces and logs into several files during long recording. Although this should be done judiciously, it is necessary sometimes. What to do if we get several trace files and we want to use some other analysis tools? If we know that the problem happened just before the tracing was stopped, we can look at the last few such files from the file sequence (although we recommend **Circular Trace** here, page 78). Otherwise, we can convert them into CSV files and import them into Excel, which also supports adjoint threading[159].

The following diagram illustrates this pattern:

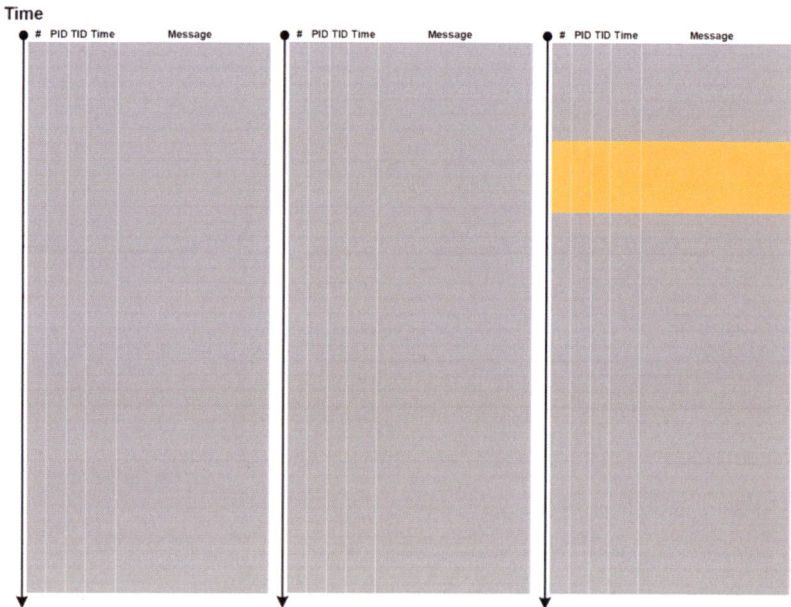

State and Event

For the event- or message-driven architectures, it is important to differentiate between event and state messages (including state transition). For example, a system may be doing some work while being in some particular state with much tracing and responding to various external events, each having a corresponding trace message. Upon such an event, the system transitions to some other state with its own set of possible trace messages. We call such a pattern **State and Event**. A typical example here is a windowing terminal services system and WM_ENDSESSION event illustrated in the following abstract trace diagram with a corresponding state transition diagram below it:

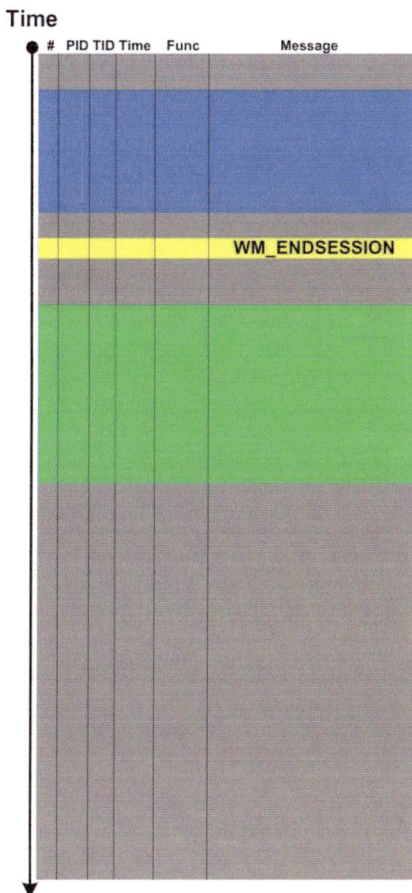

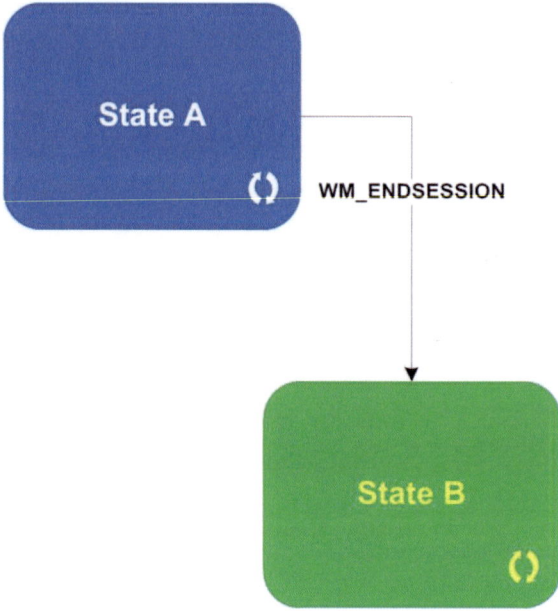

State A

( )

WM_ENDSESSION

State B

( )

State Dump

Introduced in Debugging TV[160] Frames episode 0x32 about Android/Java debugging, this pattern solves the problem of program state analysis when memory dump generation is not available or does not help or is complicated as in the case of interpreted code. A developer identifies a set of state variables and periodically prints their values to the output logging stream. Such output may also include but is not limited to **Counter Values** (page 91).

Statement Density and Current

Sometimes we have several disjoint **Periodic Errors** (page 231) and possible **False Positives** (page 134). We wonder where we should start or assign relative priorities for troubleshooting suggestions. Here **Statement Density and Current** pattern can help. The statement (message) density is simply the ratio of the number of occurrences of the specific trace statement (message) in the trace to the total number of all different recorded messages.

Consider this software trace with two frequent messages:

```
N      PID  TID
21     5928 8092 LookupAccountSid failed. Result = -2146238462
[...]
1013   5928 1340 SQL execution needs a retry. Result = 0
```

We have approx. 7,500 statements for the former and approx. 1,250 statements for the latter. The total number of trace statements is 185,700, so we have the corresponding approx. trace densities: 0.04 and 0.0067. Their relative ratio of 7,500/1,250 is 6.

We collected another trace of the same problem at a different time with the same errors. It has 71,100 statements, and only 160 and 27 statements are counted for the messages above. We have approx. the same ratio of 160/27 (5.93) that suggests messages are correlated. However, statement density is much lower, 0,002 and 0.00038 approx., and this suggests a closer look at the second trace to see whether these problems started sometime later after the start of the recording.

We can also check **Statement Current** as the number of statements (messages) per unit of time. We recorded the first trace over 195 seconds and the second over 650 seconds. For this reason, we have 952 msg/s and 109 msg/s, respectively. It suggests that the problem might have started at some time during the second trace, or there were more modules selected for the first trace. To make sure, we adjust the total number of messages for these two traces. We find the first occurrence of the error and subtract its message number from the total number of messages. For our first trace, we see that messages start from the very beginning, and in our second trace, they also almost start from the beginning. So such adjustment should not give much better results here. Also, these statements continue to be recorded until the very end of these traces.

To avoid being lost in this discussion, we repeat the main results:

```
              Density          Relative Density   Current,
                                                  all msg/s
Trace 1    0.04 / 0.0067       6                  952
Trace 2    0.002 / 0.00038     5.93               109
```

The possibility that much more was traced that resulted in lower density for the second trace should be discarded because we have a much lower current. Perhaps the environment was not quite the same for the second tracing. However, the same relative density for two different errors suggests that they are correlated, and the higher density of the first error suggests that we should start our investigation from it.

The reason we came up with this statistical trace analysis pattern is that two different engineers analyzed the same trace, and both suggested different troubleshooting paths based on selected **Error Messages** (page 123) from software traces. So, ultimately, we did a statistical analysis to prioritize their suggestions.

Density part is illustrated in the following diagram:

$$D_1 > D_2$$

Current part is illustrated in the following diagram:

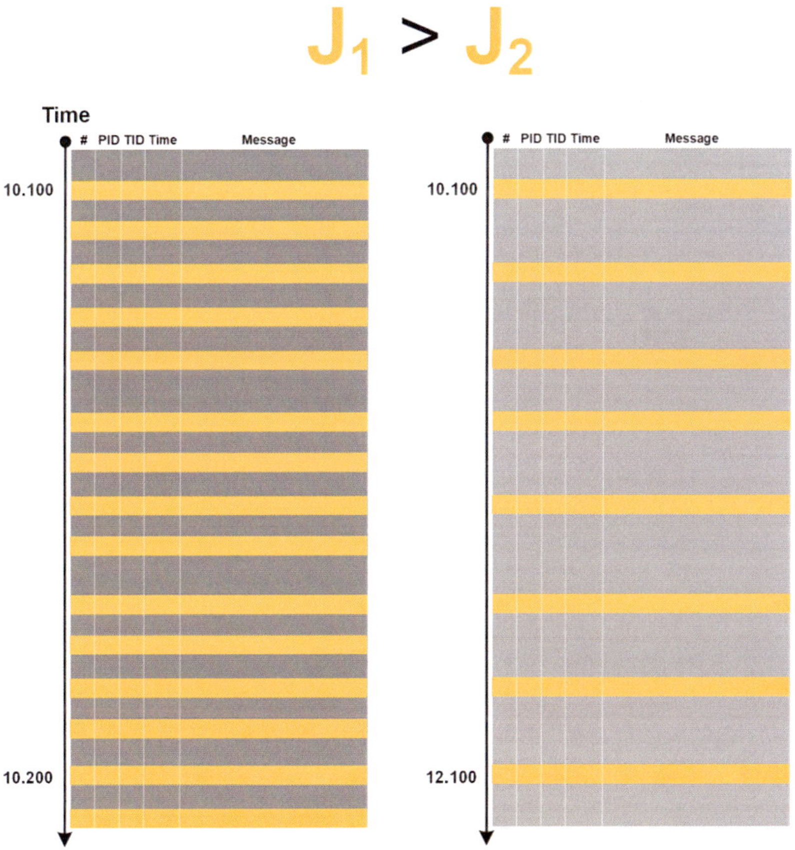

$$J_1 > J_2$$

Strand of Activity

Strand of Activity combines different **Threads of Activity** (page 296) or **Adjoint Threads of Activity** (page 48) of the same type.

Time

Strands extend cable and rope composition metaphors that start with **Fibers of Activity** (page 138) and continue with threads and **Braids of Activity** (page 66).

Surveyor

Sometimes, the presence of some messages in a trace or log shows that some other tracing or logging tool was running or that some process was also doing tracing. We call this analysis pattern **Surveyor**. Such discovered tracing may not be related to the trace we are looking at (compare to **Trace Extension**, page 311) but may help with finding additional traces in the system, as illustrated in the following diagram:

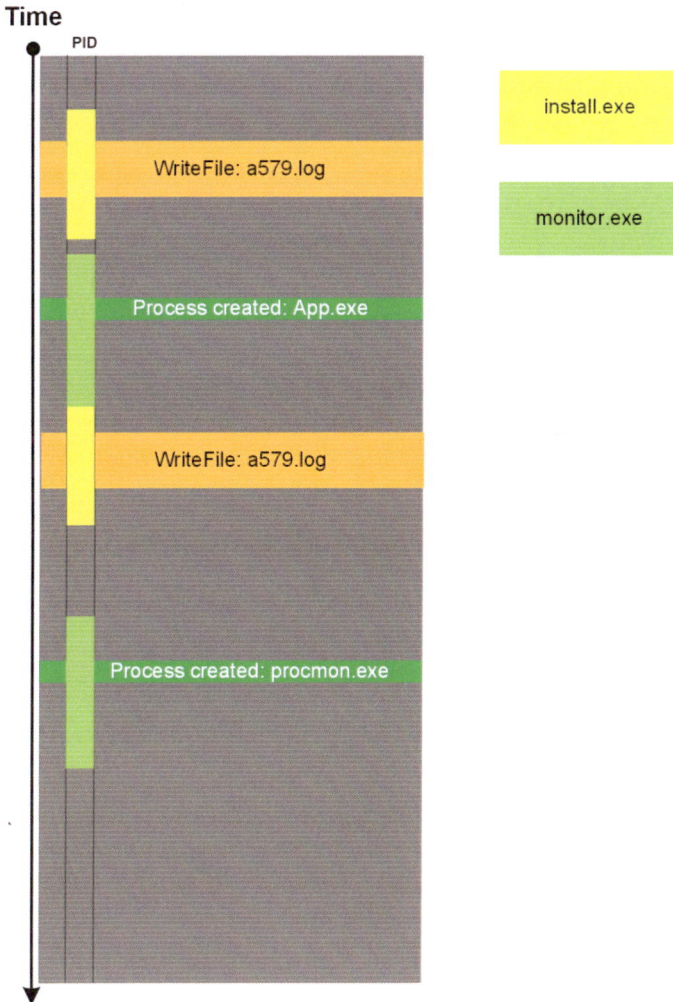

Tensor Trace

The idea of the **Tensor Trace** analysis pattern initially appeared in the context of memory dumps as general traces[161] with several special traces inside but then developed further when working on **Singleton Trace** (page 275) analysis pattern when we realized that several **Singleton Traces** might form a new separate log:

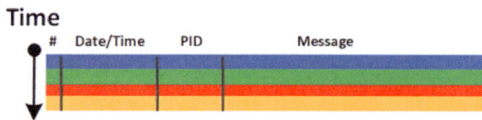

Therefore, we may combine several traces and logs into one global trace where each message references separate local traces and logs:

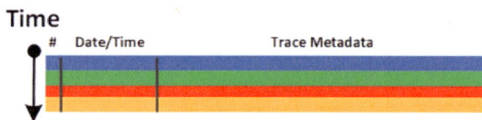

A typical example is repeated tracing. Each trace has an i-th index spanning the number of trace messages. We say it has T_i components. Each individual logging has a j-th index, and overall, the global log has T^j components. Together they form the second-rank tensor[162]:

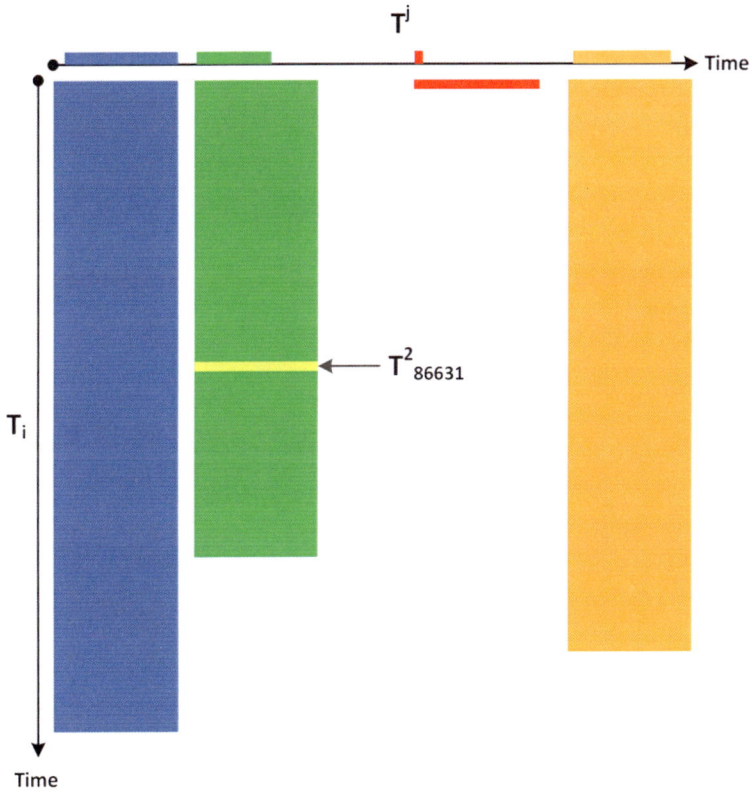

T^j

T^2_{86631}

T_i

Time

There can be **Tensor Traces** of the higher ranks; for example, the 3rd component can be spanning computers:

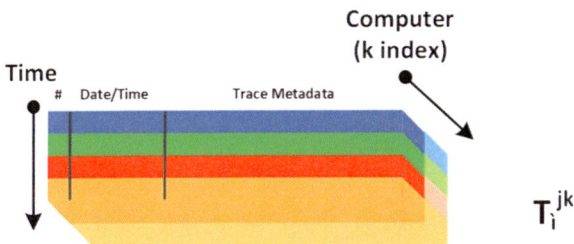

Computer
(k index)

Time

\#   Date/Time   Trace Metadata

T_i^{jk}

This analysis pattern differs from **Meta Trace** (page 204), where the latter is about trace evolution during software development. It also differs from **Trace Dimension** (page 309), which is about one trace (**Tensor Trace** of rank 1).

Text Trace

Trace and log analysis patterns may be additionally applied not only to a database like tables but also to texts (as an example of general trace and log analysis [163]). Sentences may form trace messages with paragraphs and chapters corresponding to traditional ATIDs (IDs for **Adjoint Threads of Activity**, page 48) such as TID and PID in the most simple syntax mapping case, and certain sentences may be interpreted as **Silent Messages** (page 272).

Examples of trace and log ATIDs:

PID, TID, Module
Chapter, Paragraph, Note
Domain, Topic, Author
Vocabulary, Semantic Field

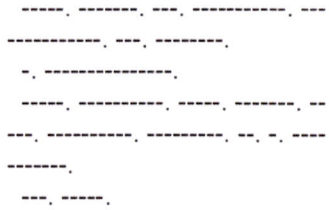

Text 2 Trace conversion may require Paratexts for richer traces. Trace 2 Text may require Paratext generation.

Different attribute generation schemas may be used; for example, selected vocabulary may be used to assign TID numbers. More complex cases may require paratexts and supplementary texts providing additional structure and semantic information, like in the **Paratext** memory analysis pattern[164] and the case of extended traces[165].

The opposite process of converting traces and logs to text is also possible with additional paratext generation if necessary. We call this two-way analysis pattern **Text Trace**. After converting texts to logs, it is possible to apply most trace and log analysis patterns from this reference.

Thread of Activity

When we have software traces that record process identifiers (PID) and thread identifiers (TID), it is important to differentiate between trace statements sorted by time and **Thread of Activity**. The latter is simply the flow of trace messages sorted by TID, and it is very helpful in cases with dense traces coming from hundreds of processes and components. Here is an example from the MessageHistory [166] bulk trace fragment showing different **Threads of Activity** in different font styles:

```
Start time: 21:5:36:651
Format time: 21:5:43:133
Number of messages sent: 24736
Number of messages posted: 905


[...]
21:5:41:990 S PID: a7c TID: 554 HWND: 0x0000000000010E62  Class:
"ToolbarWindow32" Title: "" WM_USER+4b (0x44b) wParam: 0x14 lParam: 0x749e300
21:5:41:990 S PID: a7c TID: 554 HWND: 0x00010E4A  Class: "CtrlNotifySink"
Title: "" WM_NOTIFY (0x4e) wParam: 0x0 lParam: 0x749efa8
21:5:41:990 S PID: a7c TID: 554 HWND: 0x00010E62  Class: "ToolbarWindow32"
Title: "" WM_USER+3f (0x43f) wParam: 0x14 lParam: 0x749e1e0
21:5:41:990 S PID: a7c TID: 554 HWND: 0x00010E62  Class: "ToolbarWindow32"
Title: "" WM_USER+4b (0x44b) wParam: 0x14 lParam: 0x749e300
21:5:41:990 S PID: a7c TID: 554 HWND: 0x00010E62  Class: "ToolbarWindow32"
Title: "" WM_USER+19 (0x419) wParam: 0x14 lParam: 0x0
21:5:41:990 S PID: a7c TID: 554 HWND: 0x00010E62  Class: "ToolbarWindow32"
Title: "" WM_USER+61 (0x461) wParam: 0x6 lParam: 0x0
21:5:41:990 S PID: a7c TID: 554 HWND: 0x00010E62  Class: "ToolbarWindow32"
Title: "" WM_USER+56 (0x456) wParam: 0x0 lParam: 0x0
21:5:41:990 S PID: a7c TID: 554 HWND: 0x00010E4A  Class: "CtrlNotifySink"
Title: "" WM_NOTIFY (0x4e) wParam: 0x0 lParam: 0x749f290
21:5:41:990 S PID: a7c TID: 554 HWND: 0x000E04A8  Class: "CtrlNotifySink"
Title: "" WM_NCPAINT (0x85) wParam: 0xffffffffcc043bdb lParam: 0x0
21:5:41:990 P PID: a7c TID: 554 HWND: 0x000E04A8  Class: "CtrlNotifySink"
Title: "" WM_PAINT (0xf) wParam: 0x0 lParam: 0x0
21:5:42:007 S PID: 1a8 TID: 660 HWND: 0x0001003C  Class: "CiceroUIWndFrame"
Title: "TF_FloatingLangBar_WndTitle" WM_WINDOWPOSCHANGING (0x46) wParam: 0x0
lParam: 0x29af030
21:5:42:007 P PID: a7c TID: 9b4 HWND: 0x00010084  Class: "CiceroUIWndFrame"
Title: "TF_FloatingLangBar_WndTitle" WM_TIMER (0x113) wParam: 0x6 lParam: 0x0
21:5:42:007 P PID: 1a8 TID: 660 HWND: 0x0001003C  Class: "CiceroUIWndFrame"
Title: "TF_FloatingLangBar_WndTitle" WM_TIMER (0x113) wParam: 0x8 lParam: 0x0
21:5:42:007 P PID: a7c TID: 9b4 HWND: 0x00010084  Class: "CiceroUIWndFrame"
Title: "TF_FloatingLangBar_WndTitle" WM_TIMER (0x113) wParam: 0x9 lParam: 0x0
21:5:42:022 P PID: a7c TID: a28 HWND: 0x0001061A  Class: "WPDShServiceObject"
Title: "WPDShServiceObject_WND" WM_TIMER (0x113) wParam: 0xd lParam: 0x0
21:5:42:022 P PID: a7c TID: 9b4 HWND: 0x00010084  Class: "CiceroUIWndFrame"
Title: "TF_FloatingLangBar_WndTitle" WM_TIMER (0x113) wParam: 0x8 lParam: 0x0
21:5:42:022 P PID: a7c TID: 9b4 HWND: 0x00010084  Class: "CiceroUIWndFrame"
```

```
Title: "TF_FloatingLangBar_WndTitle" WM_PAINT (0xf) wParam: 0x0 lParam: 0x0
21:5:42:036 P PID: 1a8 TID: 660 HWND: 0x0001003C  Class: "CiceroUIWndFrame"
Title: "TF_FloatingLangBar_WndTitle" WM_TIMER (0x113) wParam: 0x5 lParam: 0x0
21:5:42:054 S PID: a7c TID: 9b4 HWND: 0x0001006C  Class: "ReBarWindow32" Title:
"" WM_USER+10 (0x410) wParam: 0x2 lParam: 0x0
21:5:42:054 S PID: a7c TID: 9b4 HWND: 0x0001006C  Class: "ReBarWindow32" Title:
"" WM_USER+18 (0x418) wParam: 0x2 lParam: 0x1041a
21:5:42:054 S PID: a7c TID: 9b4 HWND: 0x0001006C  Class: "ReBarWindow32" Title:
"" WM_USER+1a (0x41a) wParam: 0x0 lParam: 0x1041c
21:5:42:054 S PID: a7c TID: 9b4 HWND: 0x0001006C  Class: "ReBarWindow32" Title:
"" WM_USER+19 (0x419) wParam: 0x0 lParam: 0x0
21:5:42:054 S PID: a7c TID: 9b4 HWND: 0x00010084  Class: "CiceroUIWndFrame"
Title: "TF_FloatingLangBar_WndTitle" WM_WINDOWPOSCHANGING (0x46) wParam: 0x0
lParam: 0x2bef960
21:5:42:054 P PID: a7c TID: 9b4 HWND: 0x00010084  Class: "CiceroUIWndFrame"
Title: "TF_FloatingLangBar_WndTitle" WM_TIMER (0x113) wParam: 0x10 lParam: 0x0
21:5:42:054 P PID: a7c TID: 9b4 HWND: 0x00010084  Class: "CiceroUIWndFrame"
Title: "TF_FloatingLangBar_WndTitle" WM_TIMER (0x113) wParam: 0x5 lParam: 0x0
21:5:42:074 S PID: a7c TID: 554 HWND: 0x00010E32  Class: "DirectUIHWND" Title:
"" WM_NCHITTEST (0x84) wParam: 0x0 lParam: 0x640406
21:5:42:074 S PID: a7c TID: 554 HWND: 0x00010E30  Class: "DUIViewWndClassName"
Title: "" WM_NCHITTEST (0x84) wParam: 0x0 lParam: 0x640406
21:5:42:074 S PID: a7c TID: 554 HWND: 0x00010E32  Class: "DirectUIHWND" Title:
"" WM_SETCURSOR (0x20) wParam: 0x10e32 lParam: 0x2000001
21:5:42:074 S PID: a7c TID: 554 HWND: 0x00010E30  Class: "DUIViewWndClassName"
Title: "" WM_SETCURSOR (0x20) wParam: 0x10e32 lParam: 0x2000001
21:5:42:074 S PID: a7c TID: 554 HWND: 0x00010E20  Class: "ShellTabWindowClass"
Title: "Release" WM_SETCURSOR
[...]
```

Usually, when we see an error indication, we select its current **Thread of Activity** and investigate what happened in this process and thread before. Here is a synthesized example from real ETW traces:

```
No    PID  TID  Time          Message
[...]
165797 4280 5696 07:07:23.709 FreeToken Handle 00000000
165798 4660 7948 07:07:23.709 EnumProcesses failed. Error=-2144534527
165799 7984 6216 07:07:23.749 GetData threw exception
165800 7984 6216 07:07:23.750 === Begin Exception Dump ===
[...]
```

We sort by TID 7948 to see what happened before the error and get additional information like the server name:

```
No    PID  TID  Time          Message
[...]
165223 4660 7948 07:07:23.704 GetServerName: Exit. ServerName = SERVER02
165224 4660 7948 07:07:23.704 GetServerProcesses: ServerName is SERVER02
165798 4660 7948 07:07:23.709 EnumProcesses failed. Error=-2144534527
[...]
```

Time Delta

Time Delta is a time interval between **Significant Events** (page 270) or any messages of interest in general. For example:

```
#     Module PID  TID  Time         File     Function Message
1                      10:06:18.994                   (Start)
[...]
6060  dllA   1604 7108 10:06:21.746 fileA.c  DllMain  DLL_PROCESS_ATTACH
[...]
24480 dllA   1604 7108 10:06:32.262 fileA.c  Exec     Path: C:\Program
Files\CompanyA\appB.exe
[...]
24550 dllB   1604 9588 10:06:32.362 fileB.c  PostMsg  Event Q
[...]
28230                  10:07:05.170                   (End)
```

Such **Time Deltas** are useful in examining delays. For example, in the trace fragment above, we are interested in the *dllA* activity from its load until it launches *appB.exe*. We see that the time delta was only 10 seconds. Message #24550 was the last message from the process ID 1604, and after that, we did not "hear" from that PID for more than 30 seconds until the tracing was stopped.

Time Scale

A software trace or log can be analyzed using different **Time Scales**. The coarser the scale, the more messages are included in time intervals. Such per interval **Message Sets** (page 202) can be analyzed and transformed into one message using analysis patterns such as **Significant Event** (page 270), **Motivic Trace** (page 215), **Background and Foreground Components** (page 57), and **Renormalization** (page 254). The resulting new trace is a scaled version of the original trace, as depicted in the following diagram:

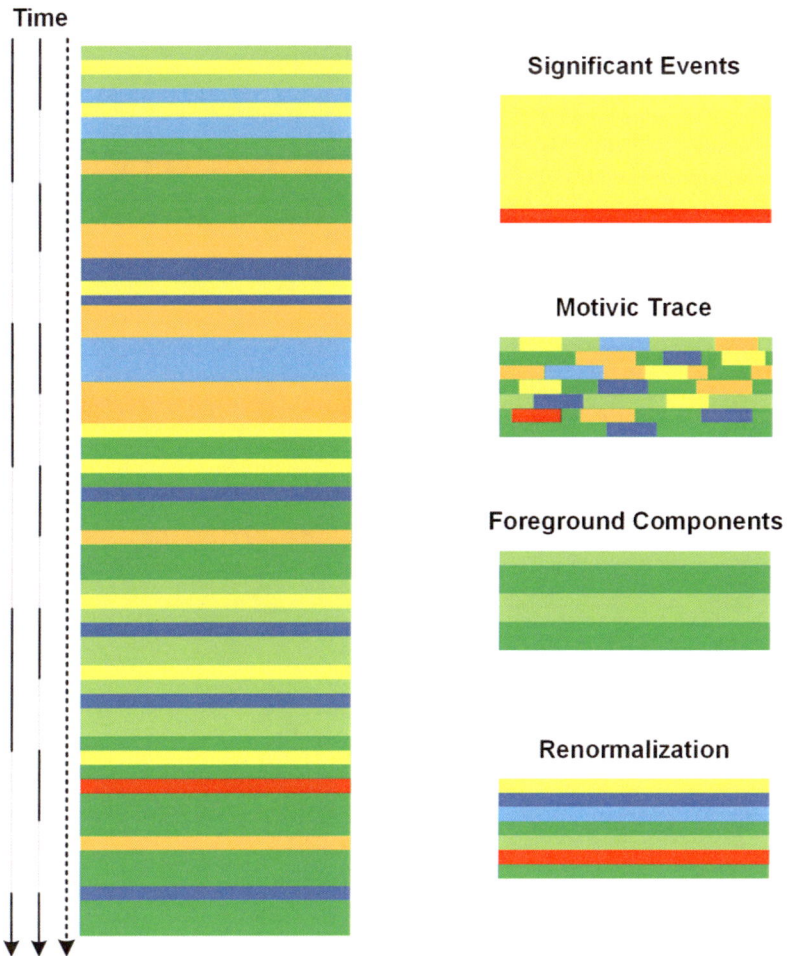

Timeout

Some **Discontinuities** (page 115) may be **Periodic** (page 233) as **Silent Messages** (page 272). If such **Discontinuities** belong to the same **Thread of Activity** (page 296) and their **Time Deltas** (page 298) are constant, we may see the **Timeout** pattern. When **Timeouts** are followed by **Error Message** (page 123), we can identify them by **Back Tracing** (page 56). **Timeouts** differ from **Blackouts** (page 63), where the latter are usually **Singleton Events** (page 274) and have large **Time Deltas**.

Here is a generalized graphical case study. An error message was identified based on the incident **Basic Facts** (page 60):

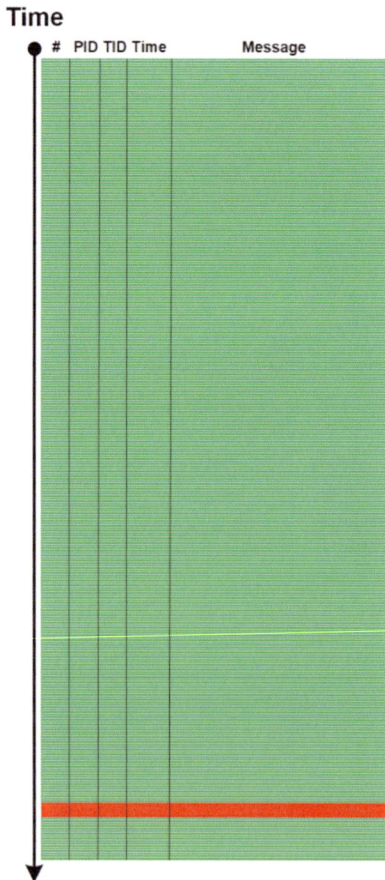

We filtered the trace for the error message TID and found three **Timeouts** 30 minutes each:

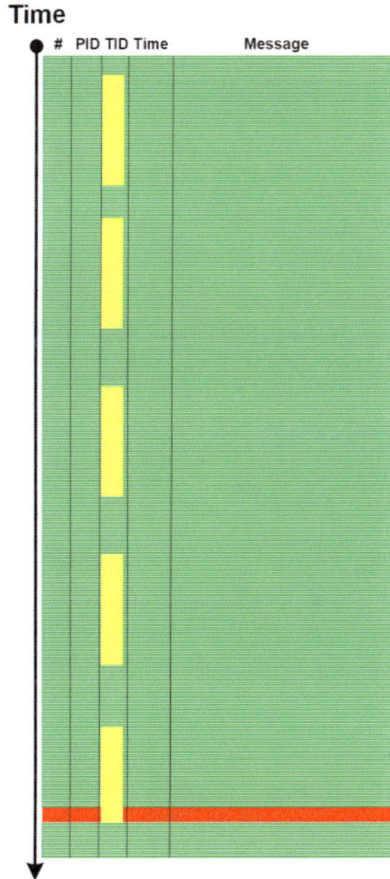

Time

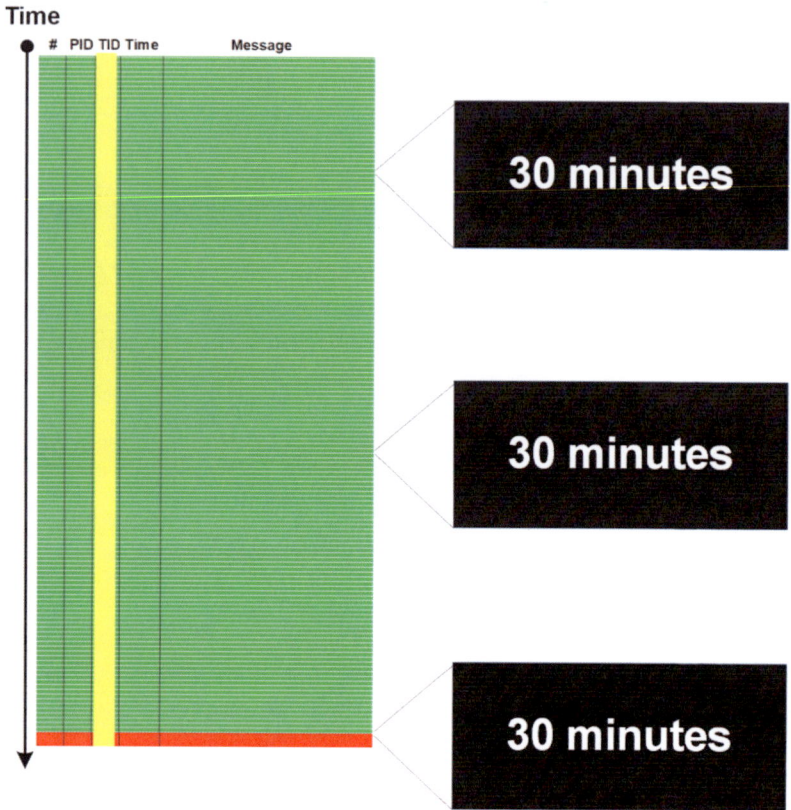

30 minutes

30 minutes

30 minutes

Trace Acceleration

Sometimes we have a sequence of **Activity Regions** (page 41) with increasing values of **Statement Current** (page 286) like depicted here:

Statement current $J_{mi} < J_{mj}$, $i < j < N$

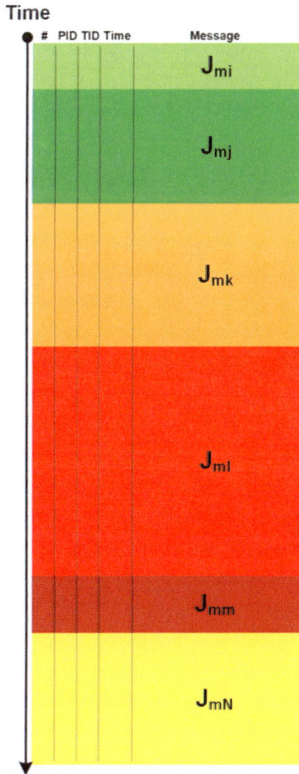

The boundaries of regions may be blurry and arbitrarily drawn. Nevertheless, **Statement Current** is visibly increasing or decreasing, hence the name of this pattern by analogy with physical acceleration, a second-order derivative. We can also metaphorically use here the notion of a partial derivative for trace **Statement Current** and **Acceleration** for **Threads of Activity** (page 296) and **Adjoint Threads of Activity** (page 48), but whether it is useful remains to be seen.

Trace Braidoids

(**Adjoint**, page 48) **Threads of Activity** (page 296) can be interpreted as braids (see multibraiding[167]). This braid analogy assumes that all (adjoint) threads implicitly start and end outside the trace boundaries. However, some (adjoint) threads may start after the beginning of the tracing or end before the finishing of the tracing. Such modified braids are called braidoids[168]. There can be several braidoids per trace based on the chosen (A)TIDs. We call this analysis pattern **Trace Braidoids**, and one, based on TID, is illustrated in the following diagram:

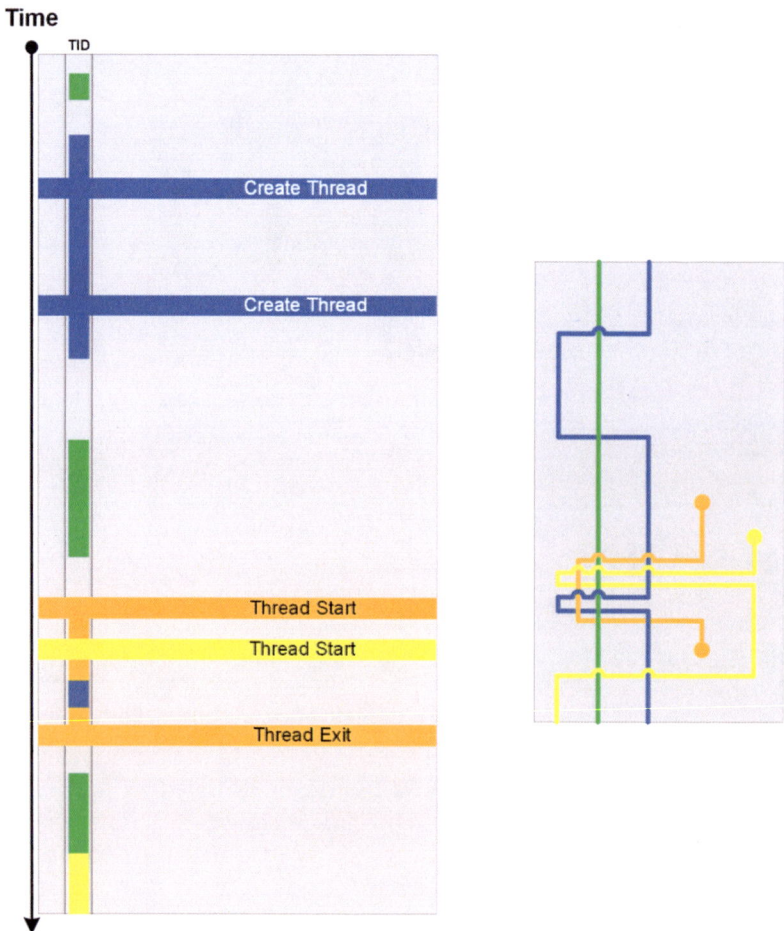

We added arc crossings when a different TID becomes current. Please also compare these crossings with other analysis patterns, such as **Braid Group** (page 65) and **Braid of Activity** (page 66).

Trace Constants

Every trace or log has its own set of constants, values that belong to a global namespace such as TRUE/FALSE, NULL, **Abnormal Values** (page 33), and common error constants such as "access denied." In addition, **Trace Constants** may depend upon **Implementation Discourse** (page 157). There are also constant values that are local to each trace, for example, usernames and IP addresses. They may be constantly repeated in one log but may change for another log. Constants that belong to the local namespace may be a part of the **Vocabulary Index** (page 362) and **Basic Facts** (page 60). Usually, **Trace Constant** is not considered **Message Invariant** (page 198).

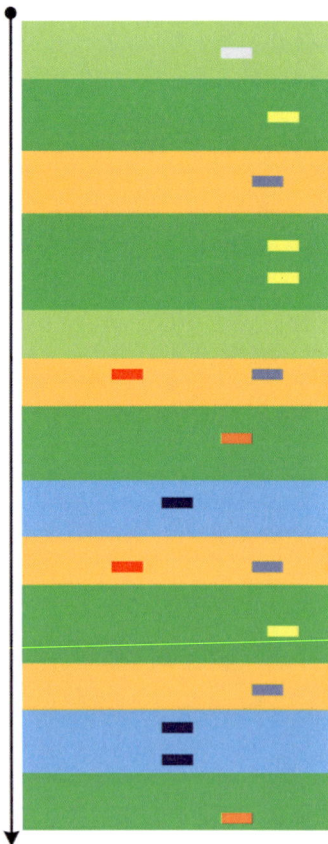

Time

Global Namespace

0x00000000

false

5

FFFFFFFF

Local Namespace

User123

127.0.1.1

Trace Contour

If we take **Combed Trace** (page 82) for **Threads of Activity** (page 296) or some **Adjoint Threads of Activity** (page 48), strip other message content, and then trace all non-empty values, we get **Trace Contour**:

Trace D'Enfant

Causal History (page 73) messages (black circles) pass through **Activity Regions** (page 41), which can be marked as hollow circles:

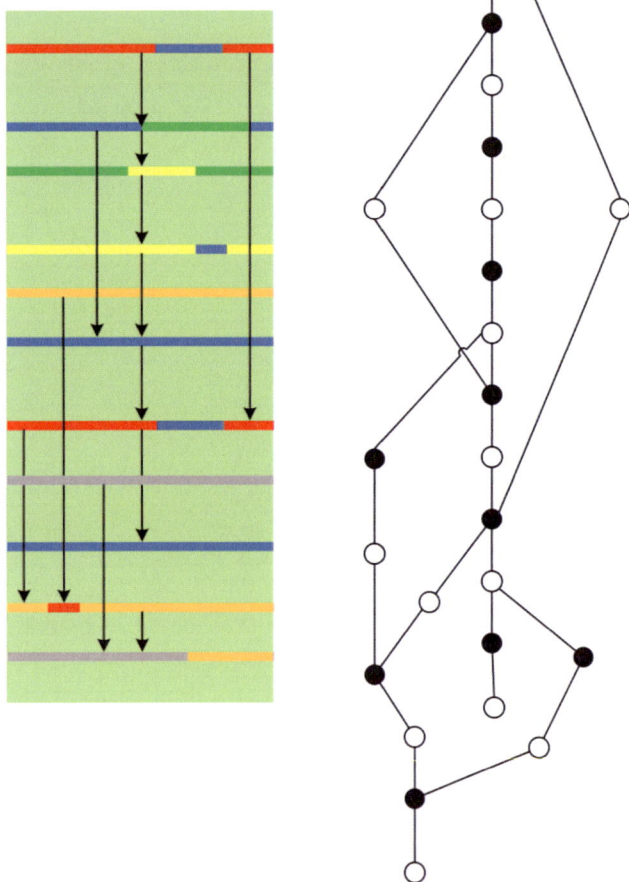

We call this analysis pattern **Trace D'Enfant** by analogy with **dessin d'enfant**[169] in mathematics, a bipartite graph embedded in an oriented surface, so in theory, **Traces D'Enfants** can be studied algebraically.

Trace Dimension

We want to introduce the **Trace Dimension** pattern to address the emerging complexity of logs from distributed environments. By a distributed environment, we mean not only a collection of multiple computers (for example, client-server) but also terminal services environments with several different user sessions on one computer (OS) and even multiple user processes (IPC) in some cases. If some task can be performed on one machine or session or inside one process, then splitting it across several computers, sessions, or processes usually results in logs with added Distributed Infrastructure Messages (DIM) such as from proxies and channels:

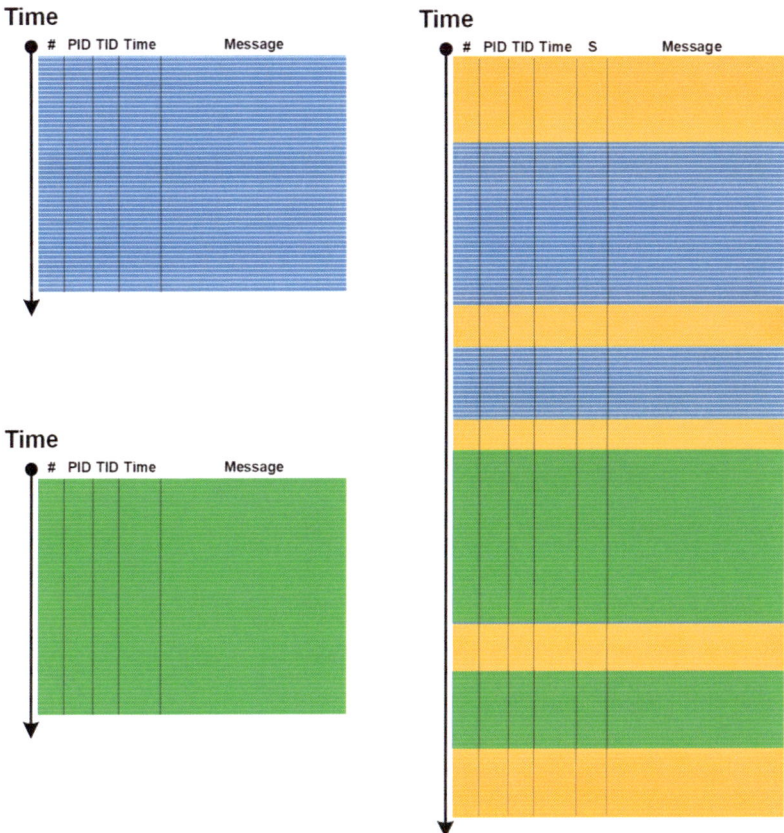

So, one of the trace simplification strategies is to request the reproduction and its tracing in a simplified environment (such as inside one terminal services session) to eliminate DIMs. In one case, we analyzed a trace for a clipboard paste problem in the Windows terminal services environment. After a clipboard copy, different data was pasted into different applications. The same behavior was observed for application processes running inside different sessions and processes running within one session. However, the log was collected for the more complex multiple session scenario with many **False Positive Errors** (page 134), which completely disappeared from one session scenario log.

DIM abbreviation played a role in naming this pattern. Additionally, if sessions can be considered a second dimension, then separate VMs can be considered as a third dimension and separate clouds as a 4th dimension.

Trace Extension

Trace Extension is an obvious log analysis pattern that is about trace messages that refer to some other trace or log that may or may not exist. Sometimes, there can be instructions to enable additional tracing that is not possible to cover by the current trace source. We have seen this in some trace statements from .NET **Exception Stack Traces** (page 129).

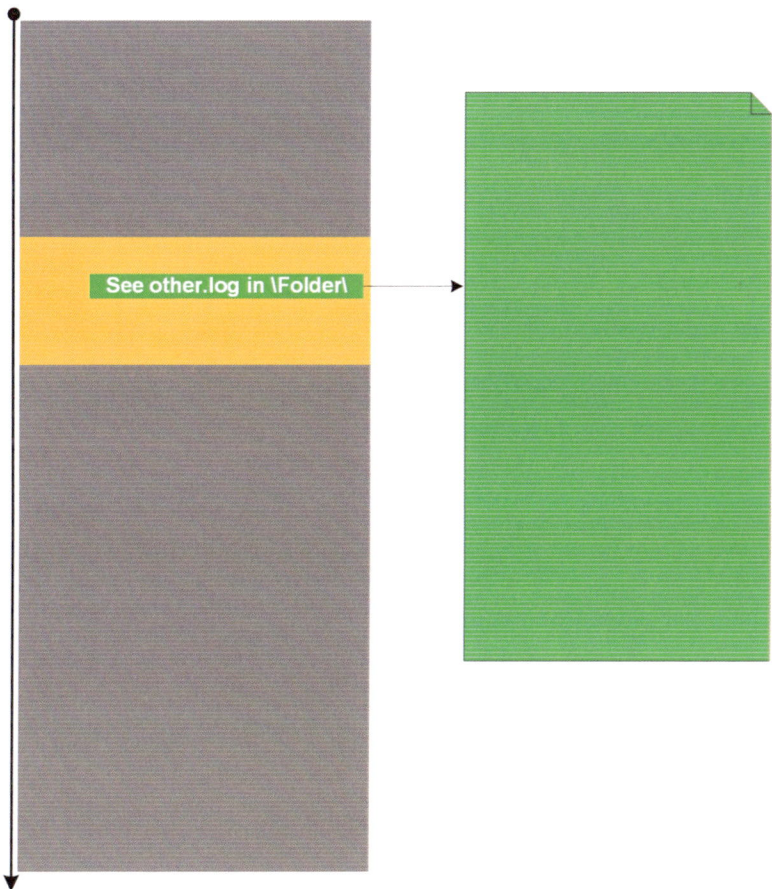

Trace Fabric

If we take **Combed Trace** (page 82) for **Threads of Activity** (page 296) or some **Adjoint Threads of Activity** (page 48) and strip other message content as we did for the **Trace Contour** (page 307) log analysis pattern, we get individual braids that form **Trace Fabric**:

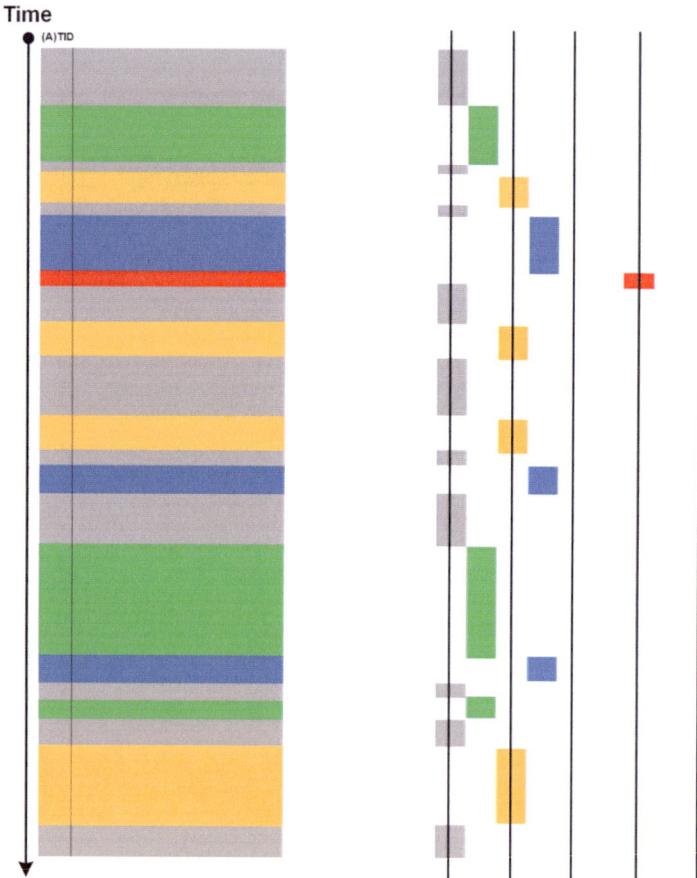

We can also get a stave representation of individual braids after a counter-clockwise 90-degree rotation:

Bars can be added with the help of **Silent Messages** (page 272). Conversely, a musical piece can be transformed into some trace.

We mentioned the "fabric" metaphor already when we introduced *multibraiding*[170].

Trace Field

We can associate a function with a domain of trace messages (M) to some other range, either continuous (T) or discreet (D). We call this analysis pattern **Trace Field** by analogy with fields[171] in physics:

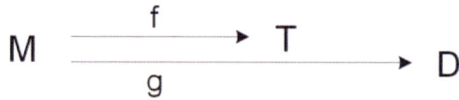

Alternatively, in general, **Trace Field** is a functor[172] between the domain of the category of trace messages (M) and a codomain of some other category, not necessarily numerical. Typical examples include **Trace Presheaves** (page 330) and **Fiber Bundles** (page 136). For generalized logs, another example is **Memory Fibration**[173] taken to the extreme.

Trace Flux

We call the association of external global variables, for example, the number of threads in the system and context switches, the **Trace Flux** analysis pattern. Such variables can be discreet or continuous. Here we adopt the definition of flux as "a global physical variable associated with a surface and a time instant" from Enzo Tonti's book "The Mathematical Structure of Classical and Relativistic Physics."

$G_{threads}$ G_{cs}

Time

This analysis pattern is different than the internal functional association, **Thread Field** (page 312).

Trace Foliation

It is possible to foliate traces into separate traces having the same structure and scale (we also show the corresponding **Trace Fabric**, page 312, for the original trace):

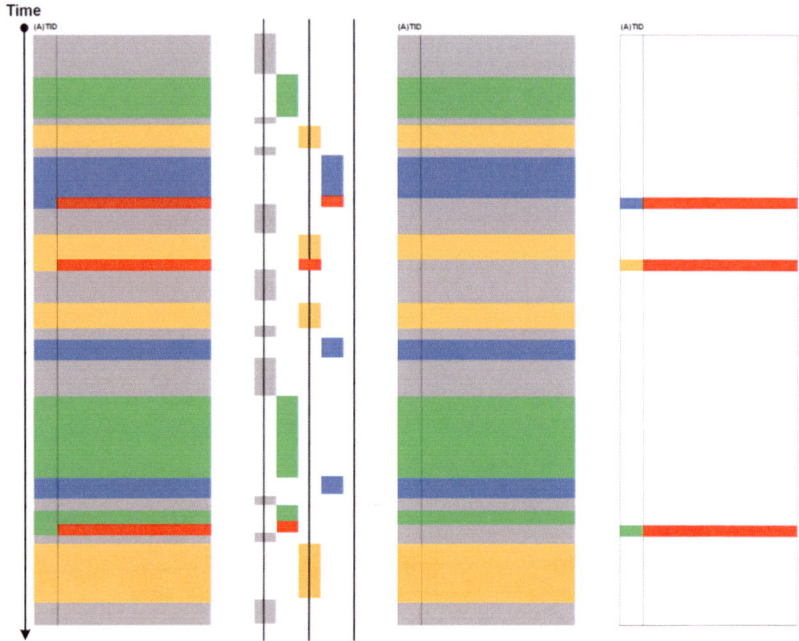

In the diagram above, **Trace Foliation** was done for message type, for example, error and normal messages. The reverse operation of **Trace Mask** (page 322) would produce the same original trace.

Correspondingly, **Trace Fabric** can be foliated too, giving rise to "orchestra" representation and vice versa via **Trace Mask**:

Bars can be added with the help of **Silent Messages** (page 272).

The name of this analysis pattern was also inspired by foliations[174] in mathematics.

Trace Frames

The narrative theory distinguishes between frame types such as (Fludernik, McHale, Nelles, Wolf):

- Introductory framing (missing end frame) [———————————-
- Terminal framing (missing opening frame) ——————————-]
- [——————————-]
- Interpolated framing [—-[ ]—-[ ]———]

At the level of the software trace or **Adjoint Thread** (page 48) as a whole, the first three types correspond to various types of the pattern **Trace Partition** (page 327) where certain parts are missing, such as Head, Prologue, Core, Epilogue, or Tail. The first two types can also be instances of the **Truncated Trace** pattern (page 352). Interpolated framing can be an instance of multiple **Discontinuities** (page 115). All 4 types also correspond to **Foreground Component** messages (page 57), and in general, we have multiple **Trace Frames** as depicted:

Time

Trace Homotopy

We have analysis patterns that compare changes in software traces and logs during different **executions** (**Master Trace**, page 182) and during the evolution of the software itself (**Meta Trace**, page 204). Such patterns are general enough, and often we are interested in their restriction to different execution paths or changes in code that leave start and end software states invariant:

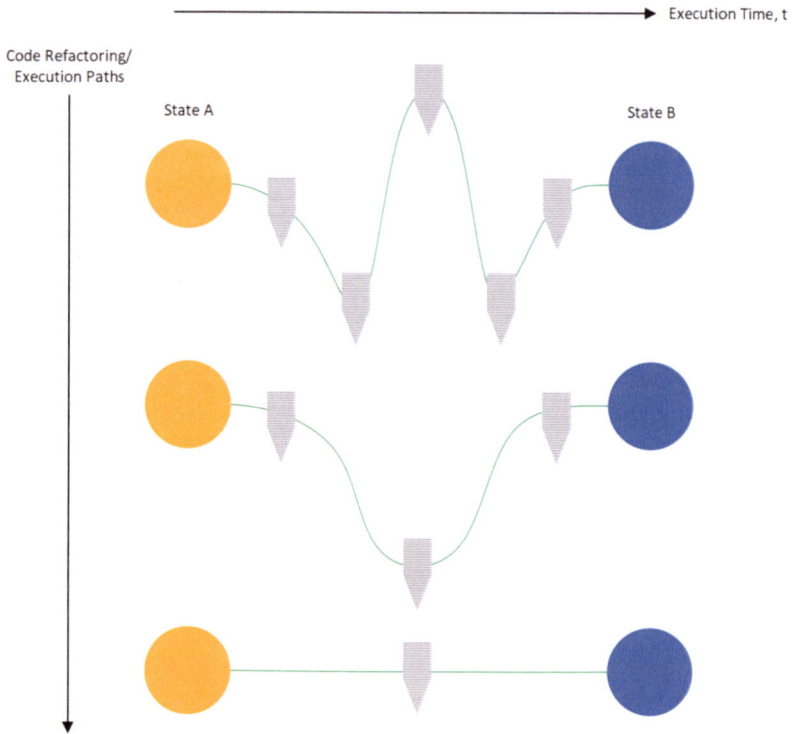

We call such analysis pattern **Trace Homotopy** by analogy with homotopy[175] in mathematics, where a curve or sequence of operations can vary with constant endpoints.

Trace Join

When we have different traces and logs not necessarily with the same **Trace Schema** (page 333) and select only messages that have some condition, for example, the same ATID (see **Adjoint Thread of Activity**, page 48) or FID (see **Feature of Activity**, page 135) value, we get the new trace that we call **Trace Join**. A combination of ATID from one trace or **Message Set** (page 202) from another is also possible, as illustrated in this allegorical picture when joining is done by "Plato" author value or title containing "Plato" (all case-insensitive):

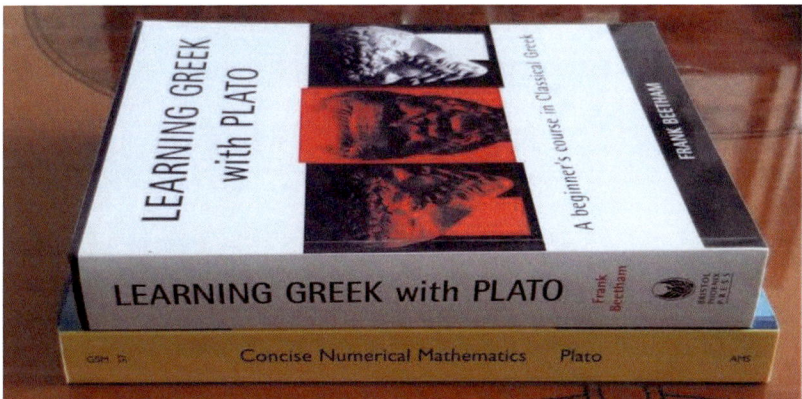

This analysis pattern is very similar to relational data joins. Join of the same trace is possible too. A **Dia|gram** (see *Graphical Diagnostic Analysis Language*[176]) picture (similar to the previous patterns) is left as an exercise.

We initially wanted to call this analysis pattern **Filtered Mask** but later realized that it might not be possible to do **Trace Mask** (page 322) if there is no global ordering information, such as time. In such a case, **Serial Trace** (page 263) is possible.

Trace Mask

Trace Mask is a superposition of two (or many) different traces. This differs from the **Inter-Correlation** (page 167) pattern, where we may only search for certain messages without synthesizing a new log. The most useful **Trace Mask** is when we have different time scales (or significantly different **Statement Currents**, page 286). Then we impose an additional structure on one of the traces:

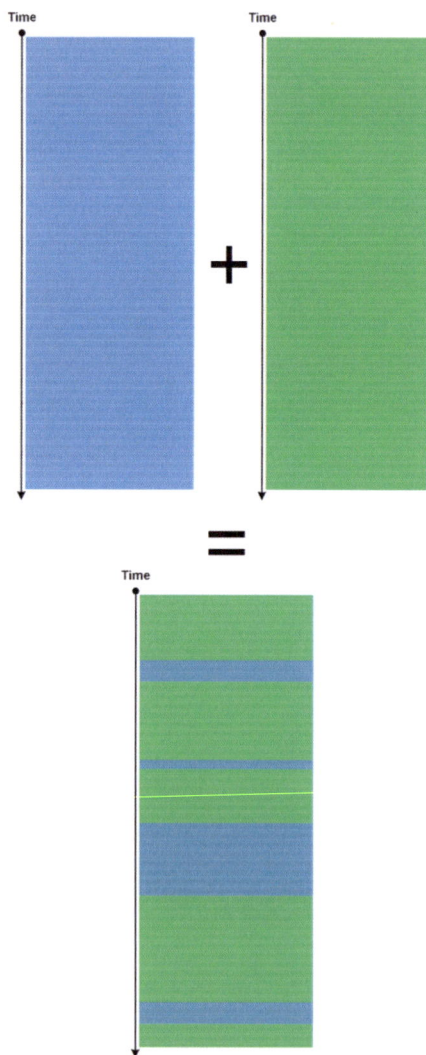

We got the idea from *Narrative Masks* discussed in Miroslav Drozda's book "Narativní masky ruské prózy" ("Narrative Masks in Russian Prose").

A very simple example of the **Trace Mask** is shown in Debugging TV[177] Episode 0x15.

Trace Molecule

For any **Message Complex** (page 189), we can choose the corresponding **Tracemes** (page 347) and assign them to points. If we keep ourselves only to line segments, we call these arrangements **Trace Molecules**. One example is illustrated in the following diagram:

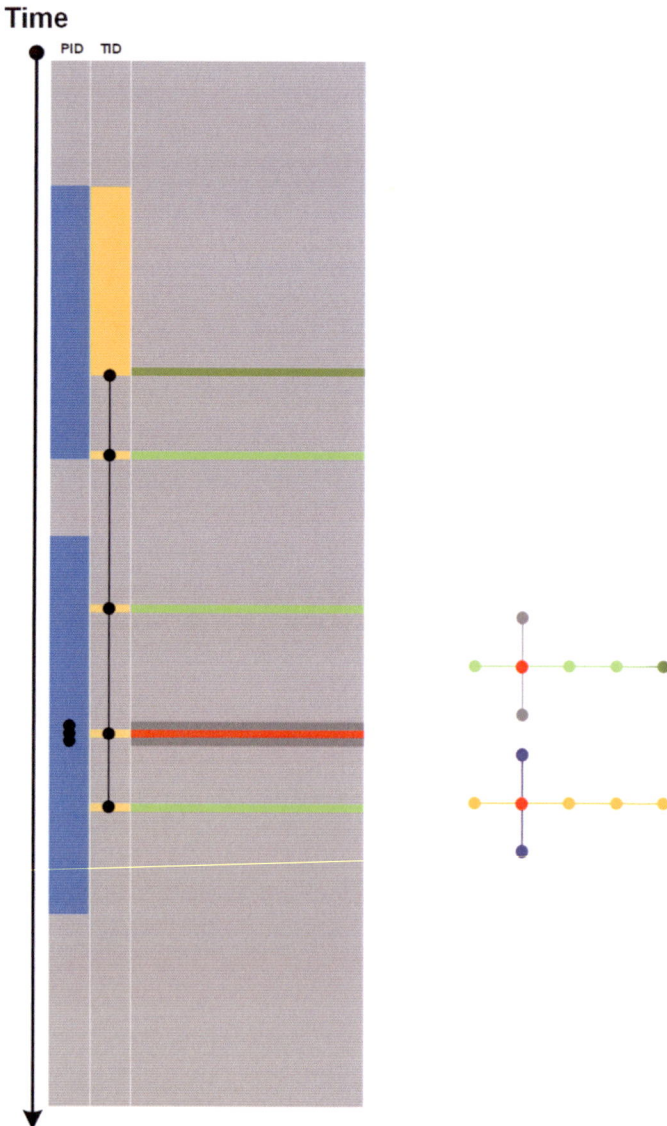

This molecular approach was inspired by semic molecules in semic analysis[178]. On the other hand, ultimately, the whole trace is one giant molecule similar to the traces and logs as a protein metaphor[179]. This approach differs from the earlier artificial chemistry approach to trace and log analysis[180] where molecules are patterns.

Trace Nerve

Trace Nerve is **Thread of Activity** (page 296) or **Adjoint Thread of Activity** (page 48) that runs through all **Activity Regions** (page 41). An example is illustrated in the following diagram:

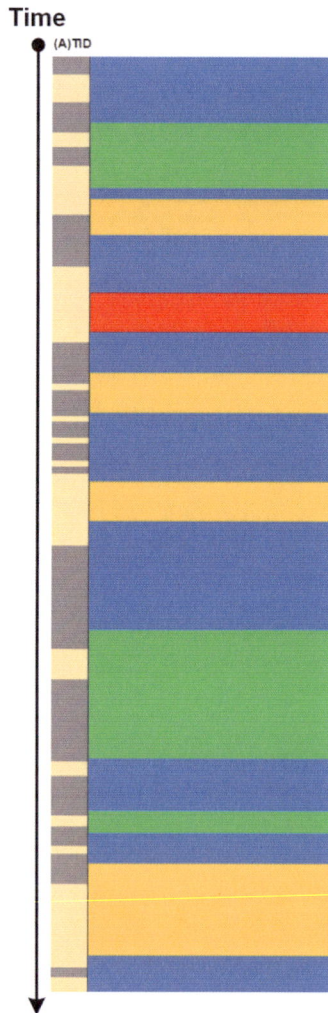

Of course, depending on trace or log, there can be several **Trace Nerves**. This analysis pattern was inspired by nerve complexes [181] in topology.

Trace Partition

Here we introduce a software narratological partitioning of a trace into Head, Prologue, Core, Epilogue, and Tail segments. It is useful for comparative software trace analysis. Suppose a trace started just before the reproduction steps, or a start marker was injected (by CDFMarker[182], for example) and finished just after the last repro steps or after an end marker was injected. Then its core trace messages are surrounded by prolog and epilog statements. What is before and after are not necessary for analysis and usually distract an analyst. They are shown as gray areas in the following picture where the left trace is for a working (non-working) scenario, and the right trace is for a non-working (working) scenario:

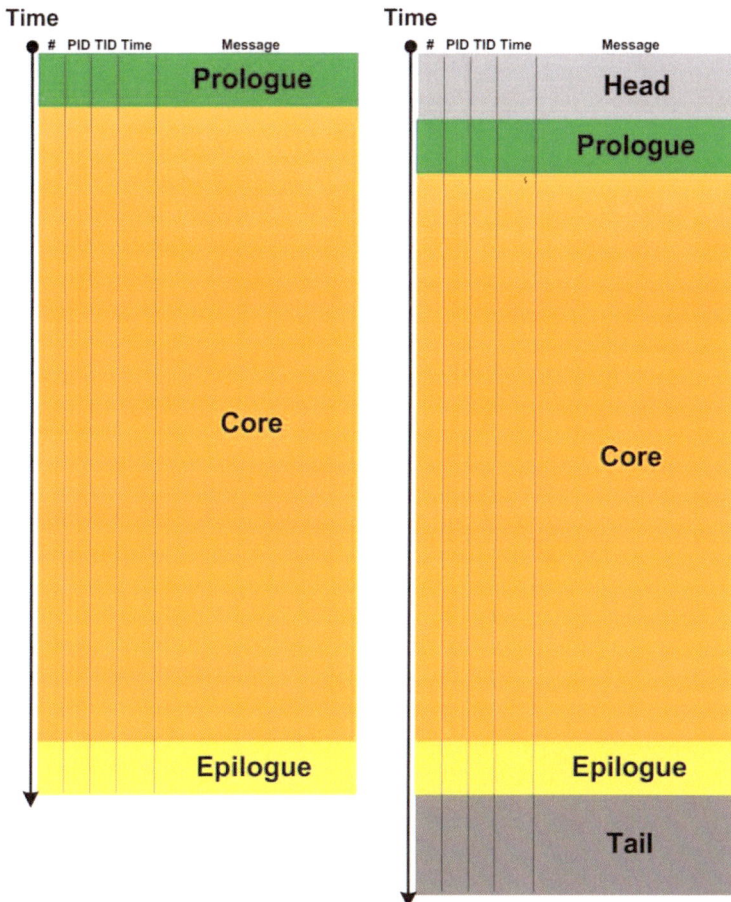

The size of a core segment need not be the same because environments and executed code paths might differ. However, often, some traces are truncated. Also, sometimes it is difficult to establish whether the first trace is normal and the second has a tail, or the first one is truncated, and the second one is normal with an optional tail. Here artificial markers are important.

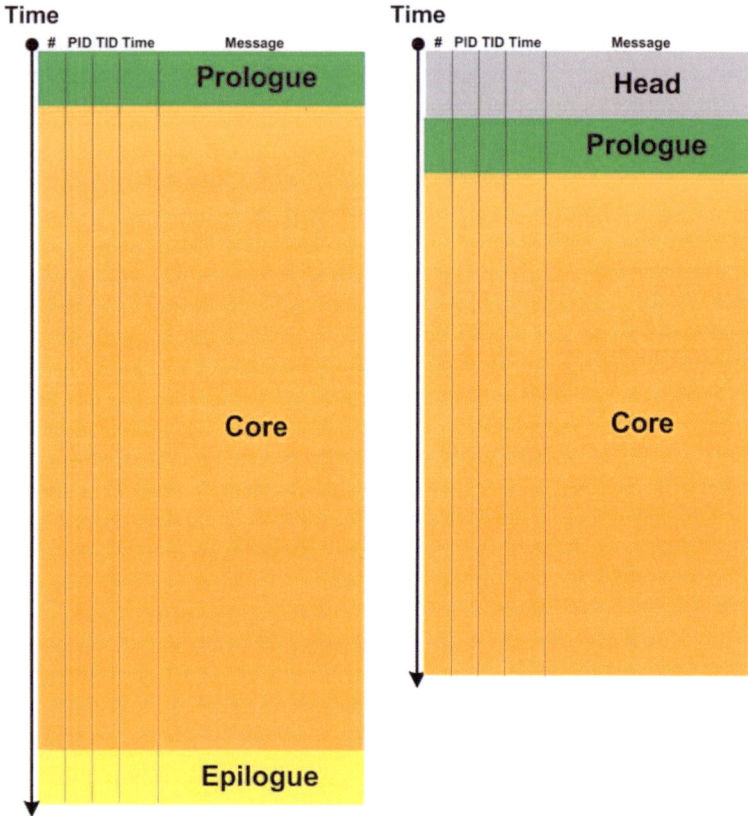

Trace Path

Trace analysis gestures [183] that result in **CoTrace** (page 88) analysis also produce **Trace Path** between messages of interest:

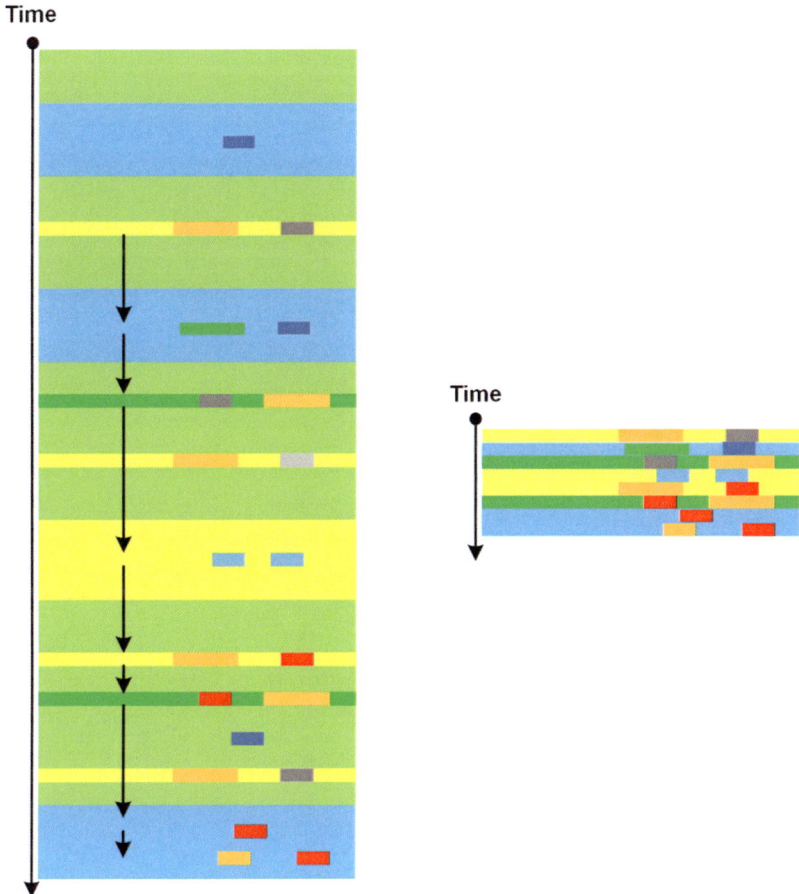

Such **Trace Paths** can also be useful for **Trace Homotopy** (page 320) analysis. They also provide the basis for **Explanation Traces** (page 131).

Note that **Trace Path** is also the reverse of the **Back Trace** (page 56) analysis pattern. Both are usually selected from **Working Set** (page 367).

Trace Presheaf

Adjoint Space (page 45) and **Memory Fibration**[184] analysis patterns may be useful in cases where complementing traces with memory dumps (and vice versa) provides better insight into software behavior. Ideally, every trace statement should have **Adjoint Space,** but this is not feasible practically. The solution is to save memory regions surrounding trace message data, for example, structures referenced by pointers. This solution can be done either for each message or selected **Message Sets** (page 202). Such memory data can be embedded inside logs such as **State Dump** (page 285), **Trace Extension** (page 311), or **Inter-Correlation** (page 167) with a binary log of such memory fragments. It looks like a mapping between trace messages and memory objects. We call this analysis pattern **Trace Presheaf** by analogy with presheaves [185] in mathematics. If **Adjoint Spaces** are available (for example, memory dumps), such memory buffers can be written to memory by a debugger (in Windows by **.readmem** WinDbg command) and examined in association with the rest of **Adjoint Space**. This analysis pattern is illustrated in the following diagram:

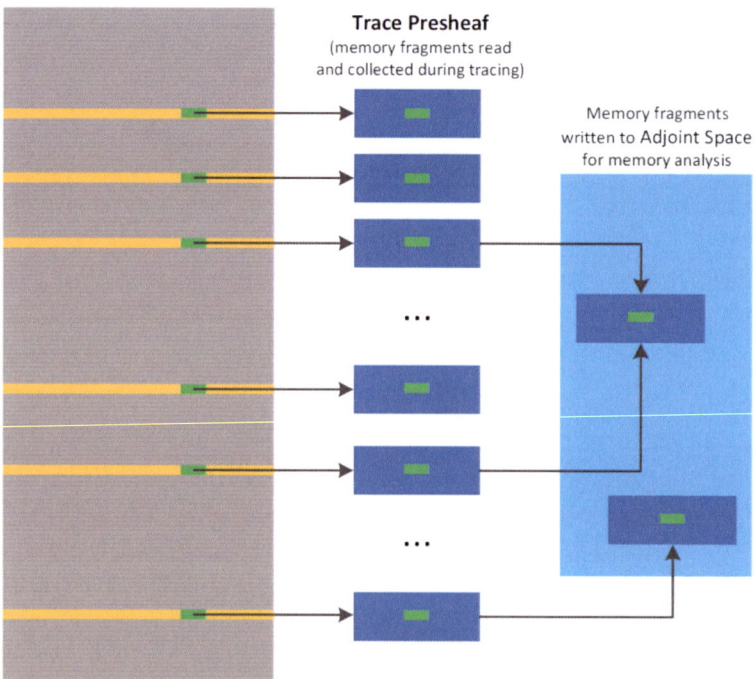

Trace Presheaf
(memory fragments read
and collected during tracing)

Memory fragments
written to Adjoint Space
for memory analysis

Trace Quilt

Trace **Intra-Correlation** (page 170) may be quite elaborate and include analysis of 2-dimensional **Weaves of Activity** (page 366). A similar 2-dimensional metaphor can be applied to **Inter-Correlation** (page 167) between several artifacts such as traces and logs, configuration information including infrastructure as code (**Small DA+TA**, page 276), telemetry and event streams, memory dumps (**Adjoint Spaces**, page 45, **Trace Presheaf**, page 330, **Memory Fibration**[186], **State Dump**, page 285). All these memory patches, layers, and **Trace Fabrics** (page 312) are "sewn" together by **Braids** (page 66), **Threads** (page 296), **Adjoint Threads** (page 48), **Strands** (page 290), **Cords** (page 84), and **Weaves** (page 366) of Activities. We call this pattern **Trace Quilt** but the analogy with quilting and quilts[187].

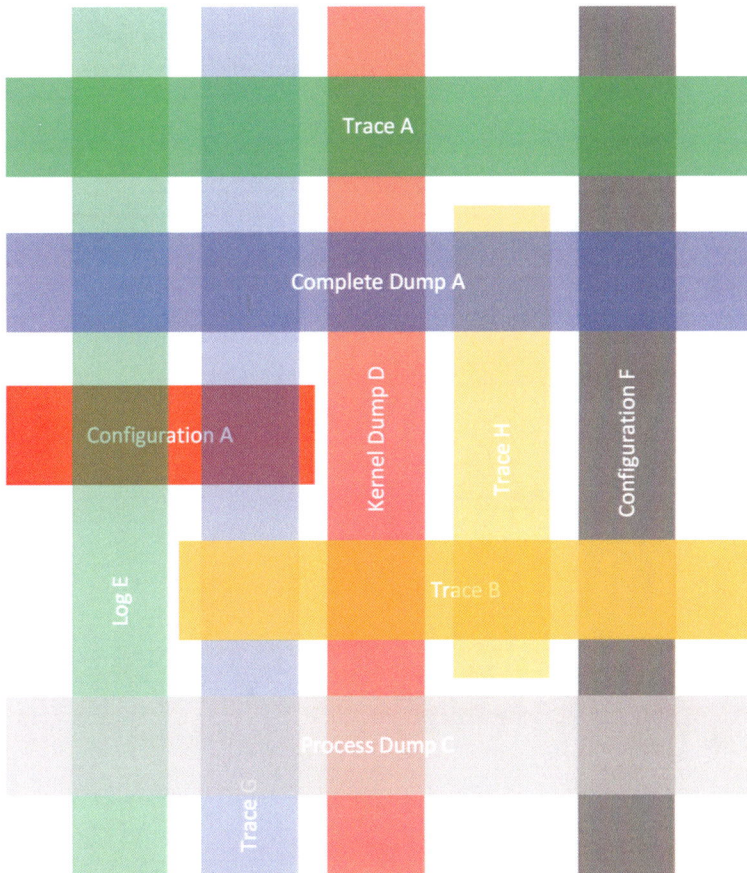

Trace Retract

In addition to **Trace Skeleton** (page 339), we can insert **Silent Messages** (page 272), treat non-silent messages as instances of some template message, and even take **Quotient Trace** (page 250) of them, leaving the position of final non-silent messages intact. This procedure is similar to retraction[188] in topology, so we name this analysis pattern **Trace Retract** and illustrate it in the following diagram:

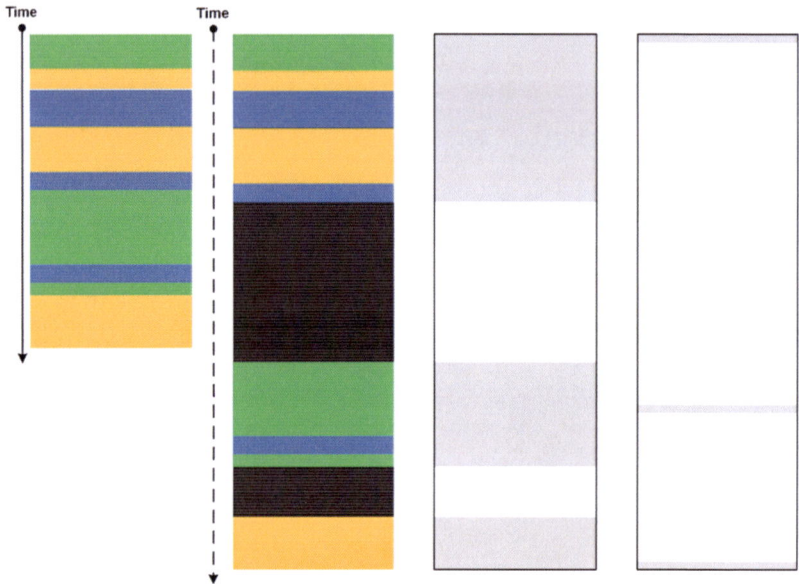

Trace Schema

Most of the trace and log analysis pattern illustrations using **Dia|gram** language[189] are of these two general forms:

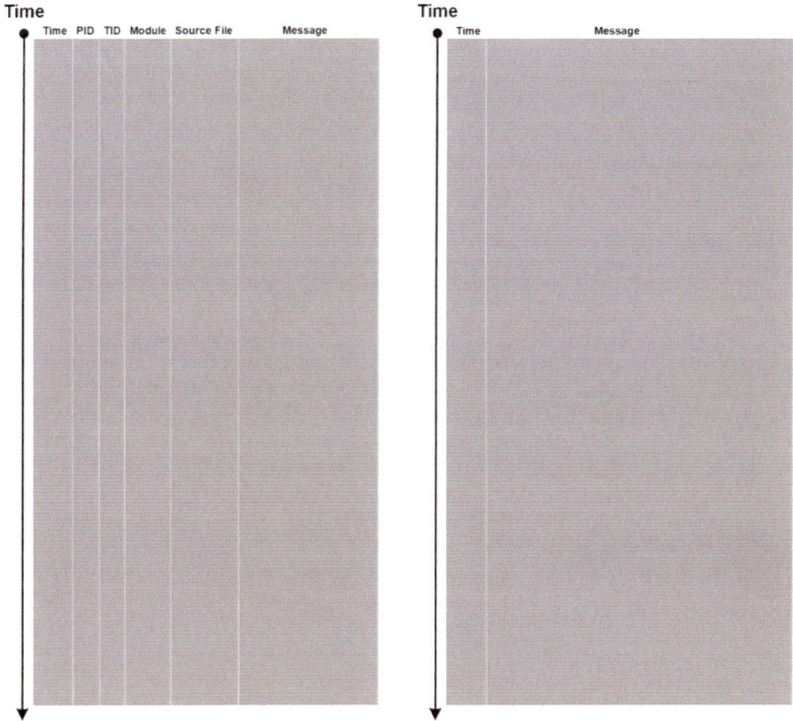

Although the first form represents typical ETW trace attributes (Event Tracing for Windows), the analysis pattern descriptions are usually independent of attribute name semantics. It, therefore, makes sense to generalize such forms into the following **Trace Schema** forms, with ATIDs for **Adjoint Threads of Activity** (page 48) for the first form and with FIDs for **Features of Activity** (page 135) for the second form:

Time

Time	TID	ATID$_1$	ATID$_2$	ATID$_3$	Message

Time

Time	FID$_1$	FID$_2$	FID$_3$	Message

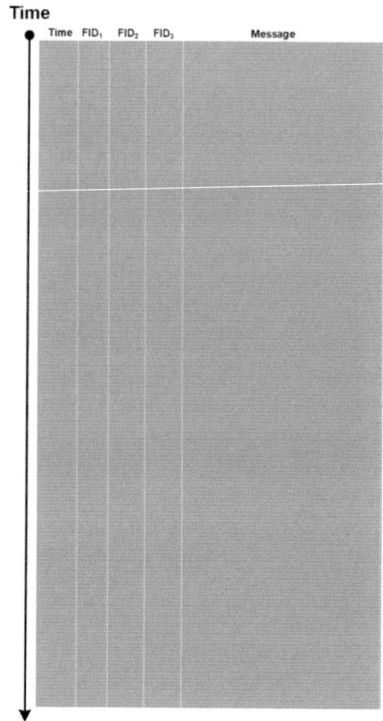

Such **Trace Schemas** are useful for various trace and log joins other than **Trace Mask** (page 322).

Trace Shape

Traces and logs from diverse software systems doing different things may have similar **Trace Shape** despite completely different message content, especially for specific **Threads of Activity** (page 296) or **Adjoint Threads of Activity** (page 48):

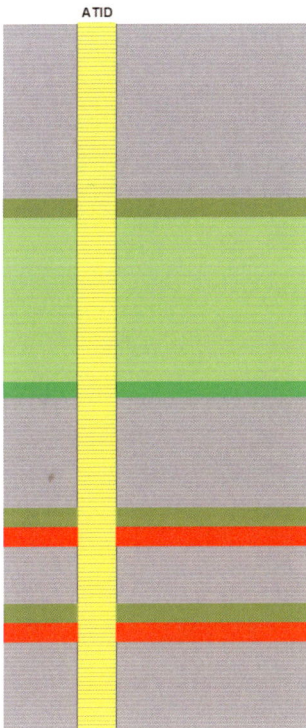

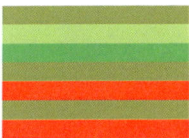

Similarities may be apparent when we compare the Trace Shape of the **Quotient Trace** (page 250).

Trace Sharding

When we have very large traces (including **Split Traces**, page 282), we can use the concept of sharding[190] to split a log into several shards for parallel processing. However, some patterns may require analysis across the boundary of shards. **Trace Sharding** is illustrated in the following diagram:

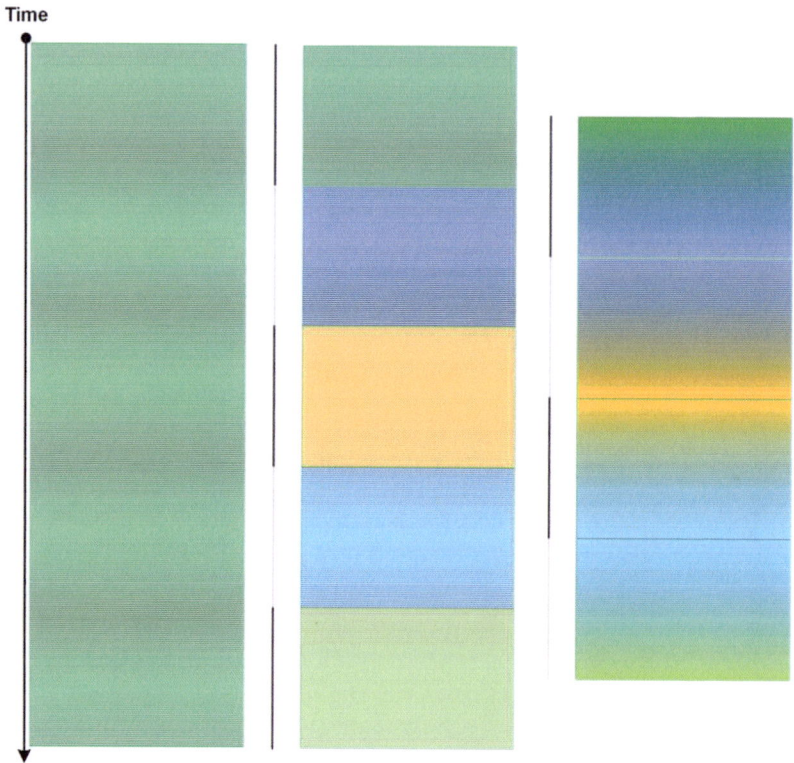

Trace Similarity

Trace Similarity analysis pattern uses various similarity measures [191] to assess the closeness of one trace or log to another. Here we provide an illustrative example using the Jaccard index[192]. Consider three simple logs where sample sets consist of **Activity Regions** (page 41):

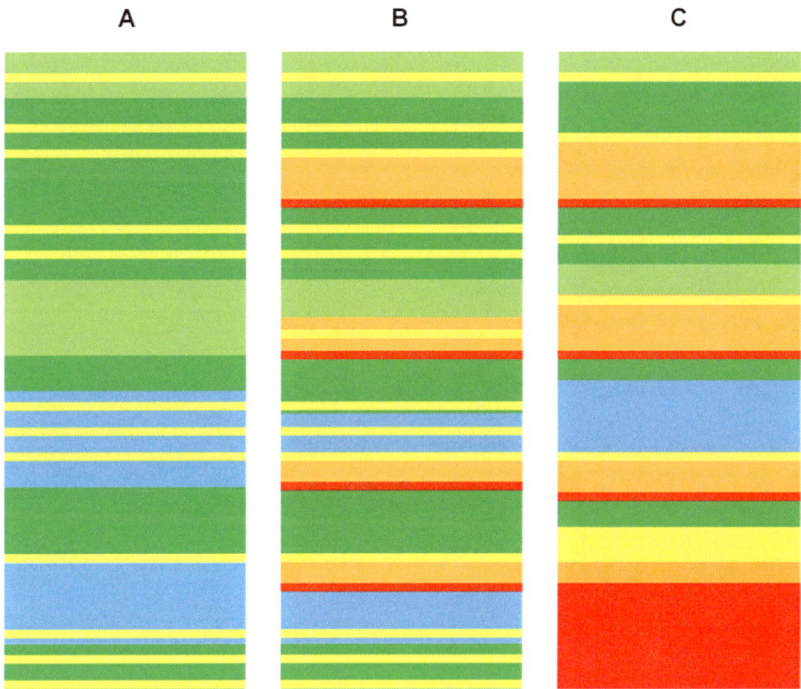

The following table shows the calculation of similarity between A and B, A and C, and B and C:

|Region|		Trace A	Trace B	Trace C	A∩B	A∩C	B∩C	J(A,B)	J(A,C)	J(B,C)
		12	13	6	12	2	5	0.9230769	0.125	0.35714286
		3	3	2	3	2	2	1	0.66666667	0.66666667
		9	9	5	9	4	4	1	0.4	0.4
		5	3	1	3	1	1	0.6	0.2	0.33333333
		0	5	4	0	0	4	0	0	0.8
		0	4	4	0	0	4	0	0	1
Mean								0.5871795	0.23194444	0.59285714

It's possible to use sample sets consisting of messages instead. For our toy example, we get similar index numbers:

Message based:	J(A,B) = 0.463	J(A,C) = 0.258	J(B,C) = 0.482
Activity Region based:	J(A,B) = 0.587	J(A,C) = 0.232	J(B,C) = 0.592

We get different indexes though for individual regions and messages, for example:

Error message (red) based:	J(A,B) = 0	J(A,C) = 0	J(B,C) = 0.333
Error activity (red) based:	J(A,B) = 0	J(A,C) = 0	J(B,C) = 1

Trace Skeleton

When we disregard the length of message blocks having the same attribute (ATID), we get **Quotient Trace** (page 250). But when we disregard the content of these message blocks (and replace each message with the same "empty" non-**Silent Message**, page 272) but preserve their length, we get **Trace Skeleton**.

Different **Trace Shapes** (page 335) may have different Trace Skeletons, but we can generate similar shapes from one skeleton.

We can also apply a music metaphor and consider it as **Trace Rhythm**:

Trace String

Log message "frequencies" in the time domain (**Statement Current** part, page 286) are addressed by **Fourier Activity** (page 142) analysis pattern. However, we may have varying message density (**Statement Density** part, page 286) across different trace runs (space domain, irrespective of time irregularities):

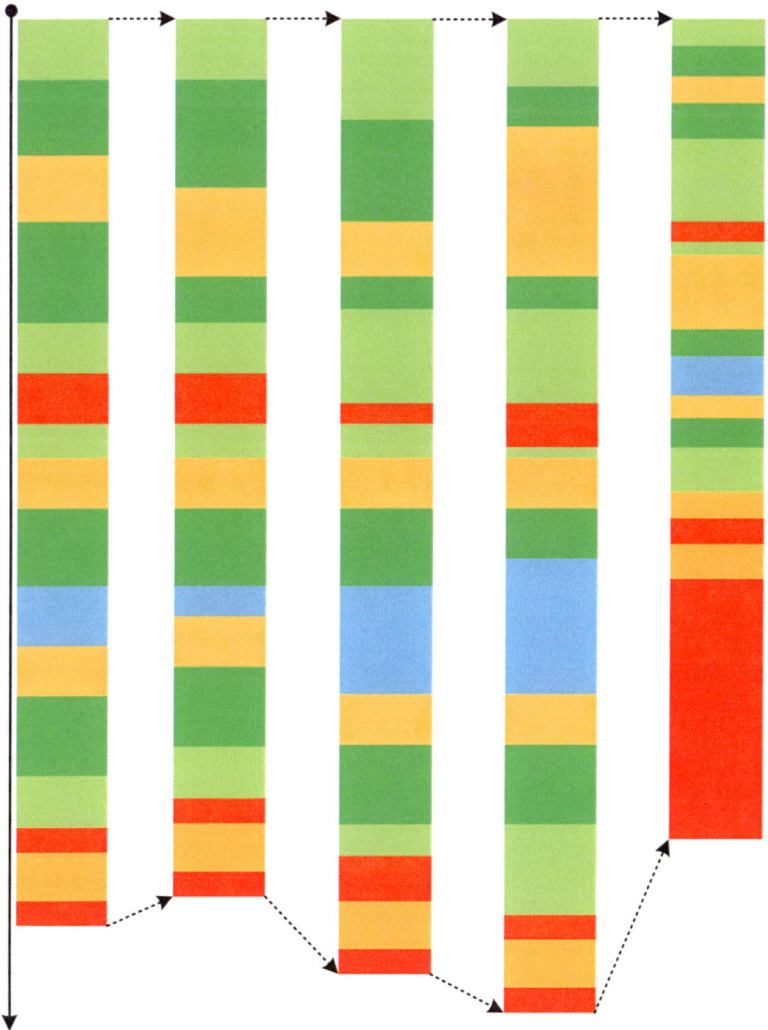

According to OED, in computing and mathematics, a string means "a linear sequence of records or data" and "a sequence of symbols or linguistic elements in a definite order." So we propose to name this pattern that analyzes densities of messages or **Activity Regions** (page 41) as **Trace String**. Such longitudinal "vibrations" can be compared and analyzed for anomalies across different log runs (**Inter-Correlation**, page 167) or similar regions in the same log (**Intra-Correlation**, page 170). Here we consider message density change as a one-dimensional displacement. The analogy for this pattern came from one-dimensional vibrating strings (dual resonance model[193] from 1969-70 by Nambu, Nielsen, and Leonard Susskind).

Trace Summary

Some trace acquisition methods and analysis workflows may require **Trace Summaries** having some timing and other statistical information to play the role of **Indexical Trace** (page 160) when combined:

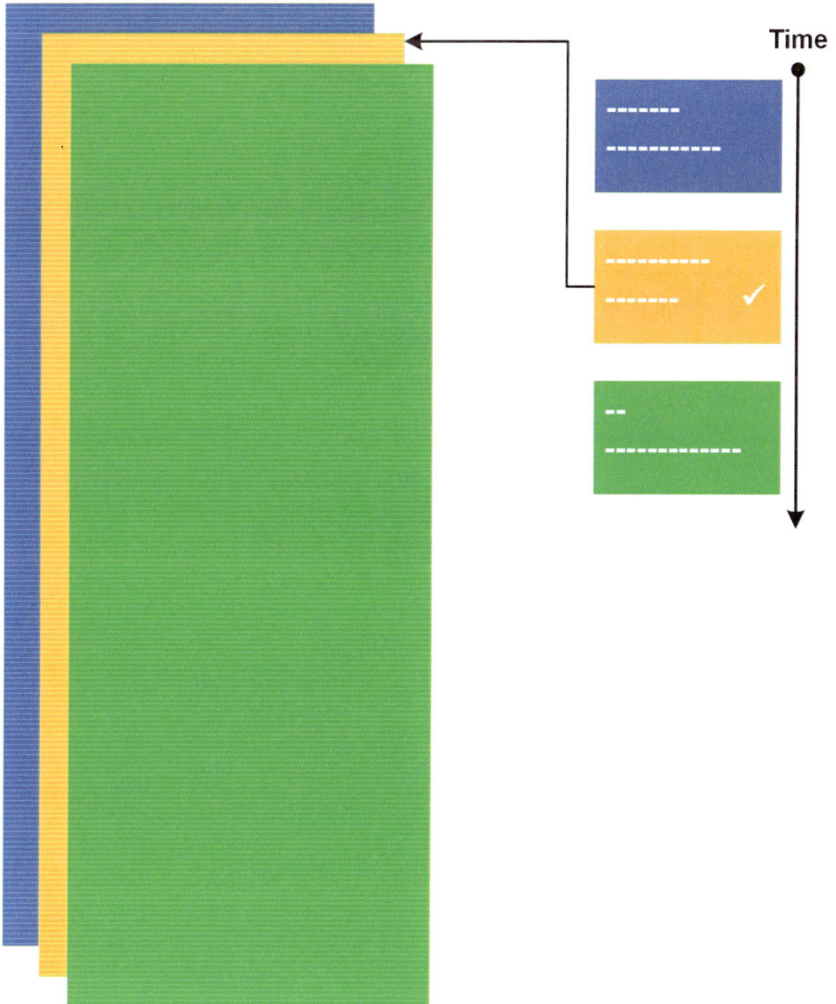

Trace Viewpoints

Reading Boris Uspensky[194]'s book "A Poetics of Composition: The Structure of the Artistic Text and Typology of a Compositional Form" (in its original Russian version) led me to borrow the concept of viewpoints. The resulting analysis pattern is called **Trace Viewpoints**. The viewpoints are "subjective" (semantically laden from the perspective of a trace and log reader) and can be (not limited to):

- Error viewpoints (see also **False Positive Error**, page 134, **Periodic Error**, page 231, and **Error Distribution**, page 121)
- Use case (functional) viewpoints (see also **Use Case Trail**, page 354)
- Architectural (design) viewpoints (see also **Milestones**, page 205)
- Implementation viewpoints (see also **Implementation Discourse**, page 155, **Macrofunctions**, page 180, and **Focus of Tracing**, page 141)
- Non-functional viewpoints (see also **Counter Value**, page 91, and **Diegetic Messages**, page 113)
- Signal/noise viewpoints (see also **Background and Foreground Components**, page 57)

Time

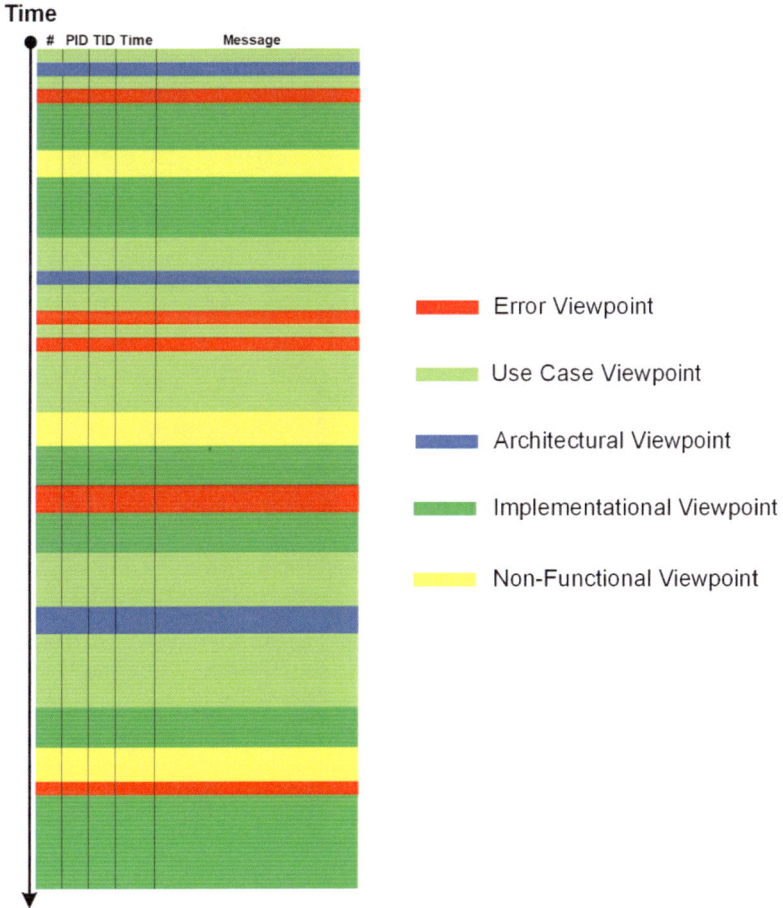

Error Viewpoint

Use Case Viewpoint

Architectural Viewpoint

Implementational Viewpoint

Non-Functional Viewpoint

In comparison, **Activity Regions** (page 41), **Data Flow** (page 95), **Thread of Activity** (page 296), and **Adjoint Thread of Activity** (page 48) are "objective" (structural, syntactical) viewpoints.

Trace Window

Trace Windows, the obvious analysis pattern that was always implicit, is added now due to the proliferation of stream processing nowadays. However, it captures not only horizontal windows but vertical ones, similar to subspaces if we consider messages as vectors. Both types of windows can be combined. This analysis pattern is illustrated in the following diagram:

Traceme

Consider the following trace message:

```
object: 0x77F468AB100 ref: 2
```

It contains several **Tracemes**, the smallest units of tracing (trace meaning, by analogy with semes[195]), corresponding to **Message Invariants** (page 198) and their data: //object memory address// and //reference count//. However, they are structurally higher in the semantic hierarchy when compared with sememes[196]. **Traceme** is pronounced /tɹeɪˈsiːm/ and can also be interpreted as *trace me*.

Traces of Individuality

If **Implementation Discourse** (page 155) focuses on objective technology-specific discourse, then this pattern focuses on subjective elements in a software log and its messages. Here we mean some specific naming or logging conventions from an individual engineer habit or a corporate coding standard. As an example of it, consider a trace message from a catch statement:

```
"Surprise, surprise, should have never been caught."
```

Translated Message

Sometimes we have messages that report about the error but do not give exact details. For example, "Communication error. The problem on the server." or "Access denied error." And It may be the case of **Translated Messages**. Such messages are plain language descriptions or interpretations of flags, errors, and status codes contained in another log message. These descriptions may be coming from system API, for example, *FormatMessage* from Windows API, or maybe from the custom formatting code. Since the code translating the message is close to the original message code, both messages usually follow each other with zero or very small **Time Delta** (page 298), come from the same component, file, and function, and belong to the same **Thread of Activity** (page 296):

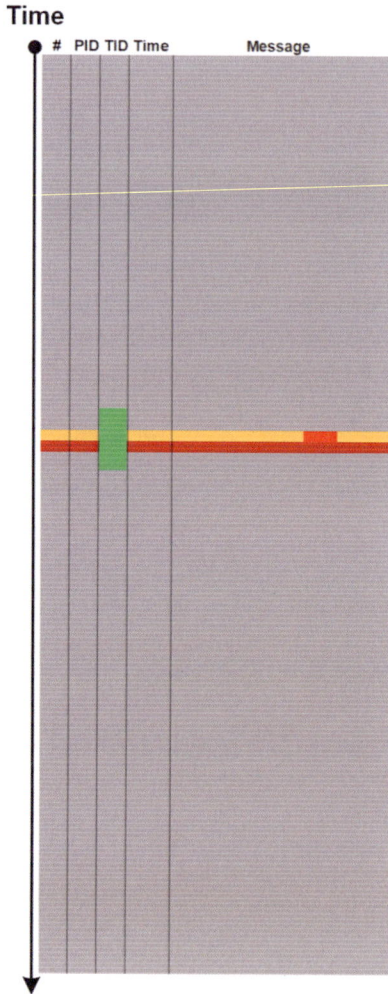

This pattern is different from **Gossip** (page 148) because the latter messages come from different modules, and although they reflect some underlying event, they are independent of each.

Truncated Data

The data in individual messages and **State Dump** (page 285) message blocks may be truncated. This analysis pattern is similar to **Visibility Limit** (page 360) at the log message level. When data values are sorted and resorted, this may result in "hidden" data replacing the previously "visible" data and vice versa, as shown in the following diagram:

Time

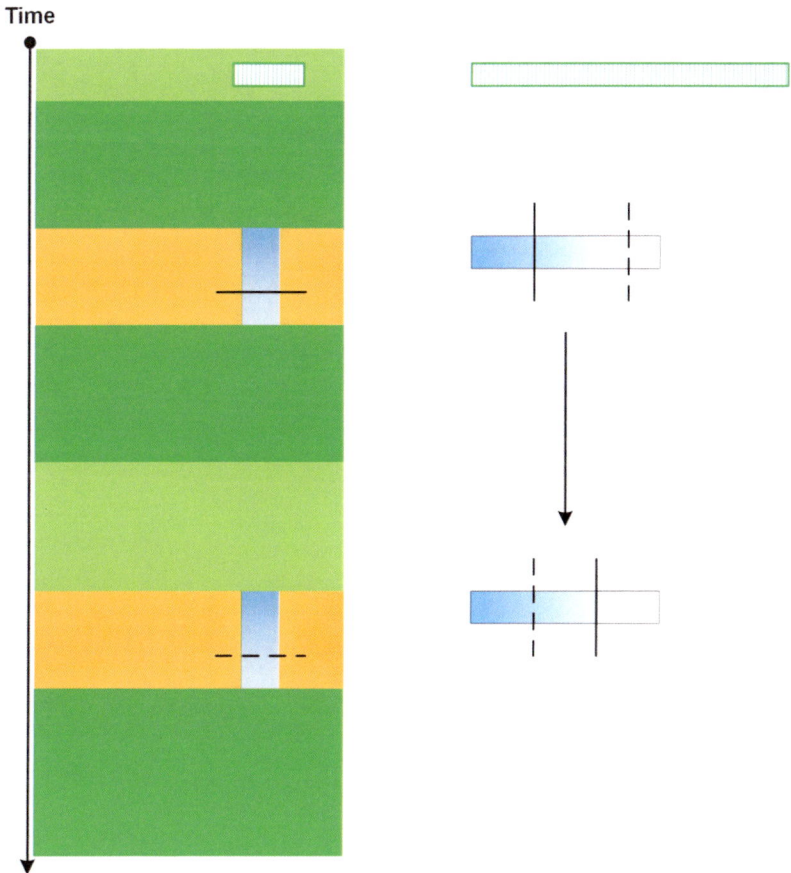

Truncated Trace

Sometimes a software trace is truncated when the trace session was stopped prematurely, often when a problem did not manifest itself visually. We can diagnose such traces by their short time duration, missing **Anchor Messages** (page 53), or **Missing Components** (page 207) necessary for analysis. My favorite example is user session initialization in a terminal services environment when problem effects are visible only after the session is fully initialized and an application is launched, but a truncated trace only shows the launch of *winlogon.exe* despite the presence of a process creation trace provider or other components that record the process launch sequence[197]. The trace itself lasts only a few seconds after that.

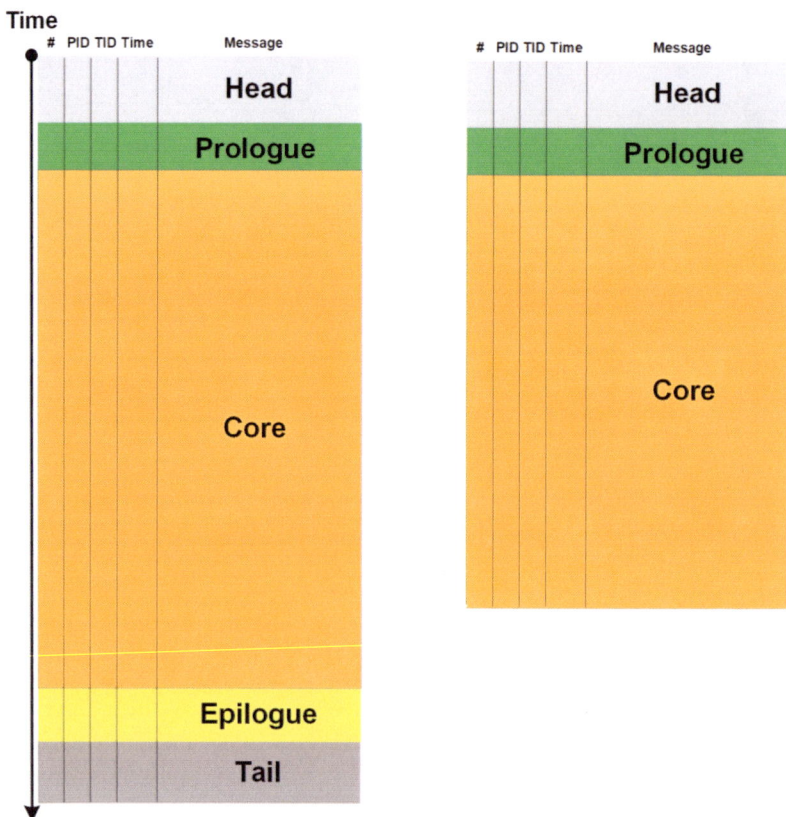

U

UI Message

This pattern is very useful for troubleshooting system-wide issues because we can map visual behavior to various **Activity Regions** (page 41) and consider such messages as **Significant Events** (page 270).

```
#    Module  PID  TID  Time         Message
[...]
2782 ModuleA 2124 5648 10:58:03.356 CreateWindow: Title "..." Class "..."
[...]
3512 ModuleA 2124 5648 10:58:08.154 Menu command: Save Data
[...]
3583 ModuleA 2124 5648 10:58:08.155 CreateWindow: Title "Save As" Class "Dialog"
[... Data update and replication-related messages ...]
4483 ModuleA 2124 5648 10:58:12.342 DestroyWindow: Title "Save As" Class "Dialog"
[...]
```

By filtering the emitting module, we can create **Adjoint Thread** (page 48):

```
#    Module  PID  TID  Time         Message
[...]
2782 ModuleA 2124 5648 10:58:03.356 CreateWindow: Title "..." Class "..."
3512 ModuleA 2124 5648 10:58:08.154 Menu command: Save Data
3583 ModuleA 2124 5648 10:58:08.155 CreateWindow: Title "Save As" Class "Dialog"
4483 ModuleA 2124 5648 10:58:12.342 DestroyWindow: Title "Save As" Class "Dialog"
[...]
```

Ultrasimilar Messages

Certain types of blind SQL injection[198] attacks may leave log messages with a one-byte difference. We call with analysis pattern **Ultrasimilar Messages** by analogy with ultrametric spaces[199] in mathematics and the interpretation of messages as p-adic numbers[200]. Since such messages may be scattered in a log, we can choose **Message Pattern** (page 201) based on some **Message Invariant** (page 198, for example, parts of SQL request) and then analyze its **Fiber of Activity** (page 138, for example, **Data Flow**, page 95, of its variable part). A log with two different types of **Ultrasimilar Messages** is shown in the following diagram:

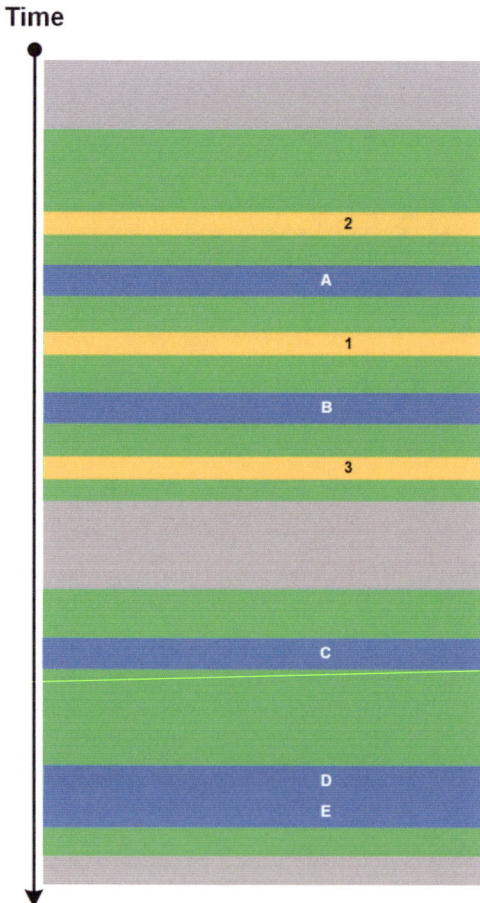

Unsynchronized Messages

Even if traces and logs are perfectly synchronized (**Unsynchronized Traces**, page 357), we may still get **Unsynchronized Messages** because if respective message times are the same (can depend on time resolution), we don't know which one was first. It is visible if we do **Trace Mask** (page 322) using different order:

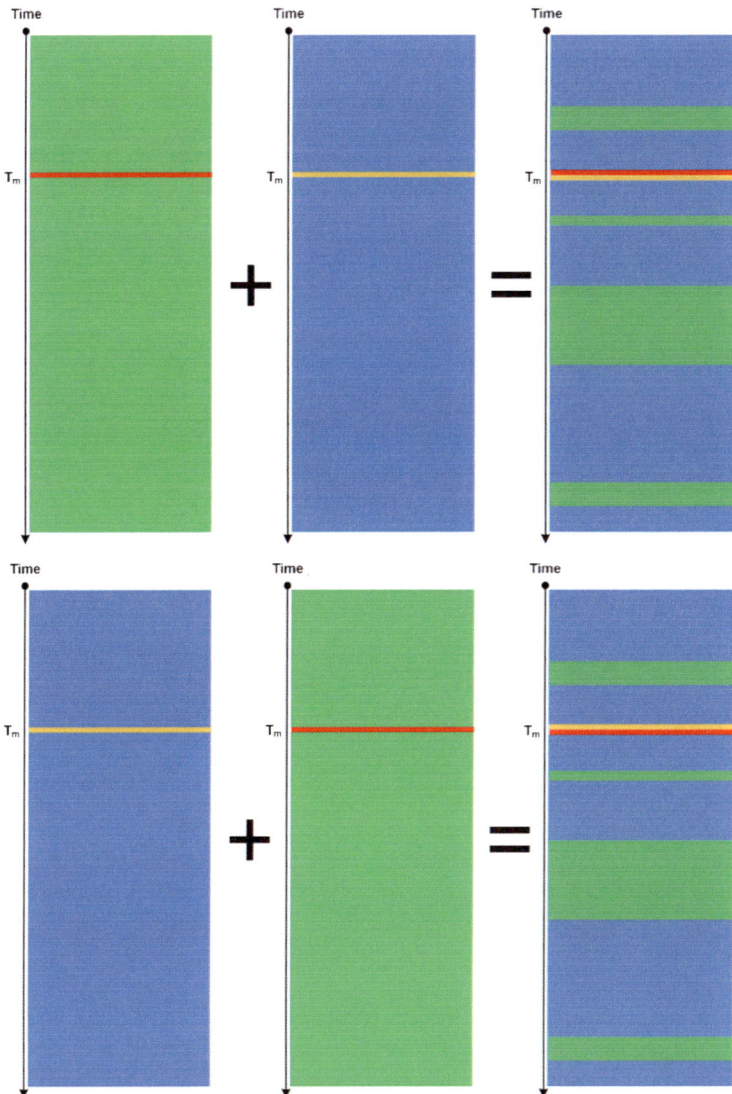

If both messages belong to the same **Thread of Activity** (page 296), we may be able to reorder them correctly based on additional message semantics, such as module hierarchy (for example, OS runtime library and application code that are traced separately).

Unsynchronized Traces

Often, for **Inter-Correlational** (page 167) trace and log analysis, we need to make sure that we have synchronized traces. The one version of the **Unsynchronized Traces** analysis pattern is depicted in the following diagram, where one trace ends (possibly **Truncated Trace**, page 352) before the start of another trace, and both were traced within one hour:

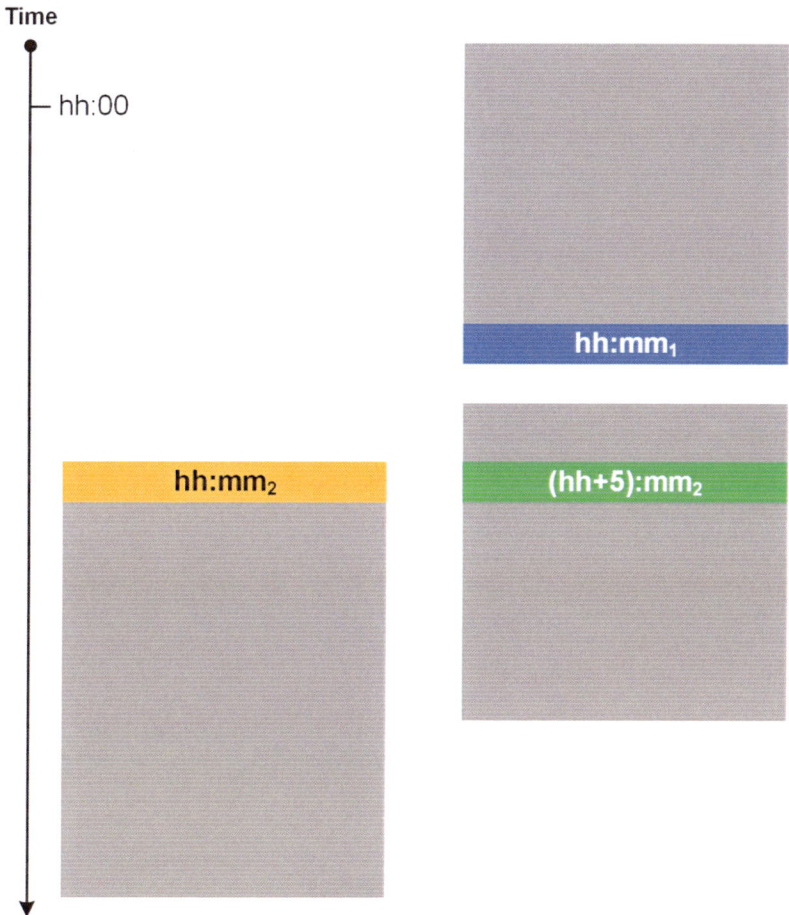

If tracing was done in different time zones with different local times specified in logs, we could determine whether the traces are synchronized (when time zone information is not available in **Basic Facts**, page 60) by looking at minutes, as shown in the third trace in the diagram above. This technique can also be used in trace calibration (see **Calibrating Trace**, page 68).

There is a similar analysis pattern for memory dump analysis called **Unsynchronized Dumps**[201].

Use Case Trail

Use cases[202] are implemented in various components, such as subsystems, processes, modules, and source code files. Most of the time, with good logging implementation, we can see **Use Case Trails**: log messages corresponding to use case scenarios. For simple systems, one log may fully correspond to just one use case, but for complex systems, especially distributed client-server ones, there may be several use case instances present simultaneously in one log. One way to disentangle them in the absence of UCID (Use Case ID) or some other grouping tag is to use **Event Sequence Phase** (page 127).

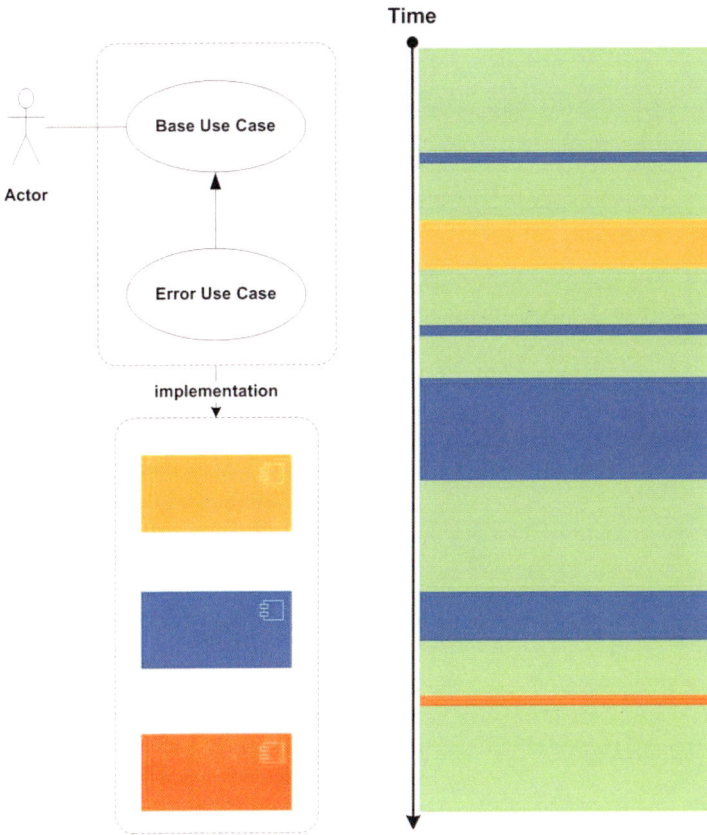

Master Traces (page 182) may also correspond to use cases, but they should ideally correspond to only one use case instance.

V

Visibility Limit

Often it is not possible to trace from the very beginning of the software execution. Internal application tracing cannot trace anything between that application's start and its early initialization. The same is for system-wide tracing, which cannot trace before the logging subsystem or service starts. For this reason, each log has its visibility limit in addition to possible **Truncation** (page 349) or **Missing Components** (page 207):

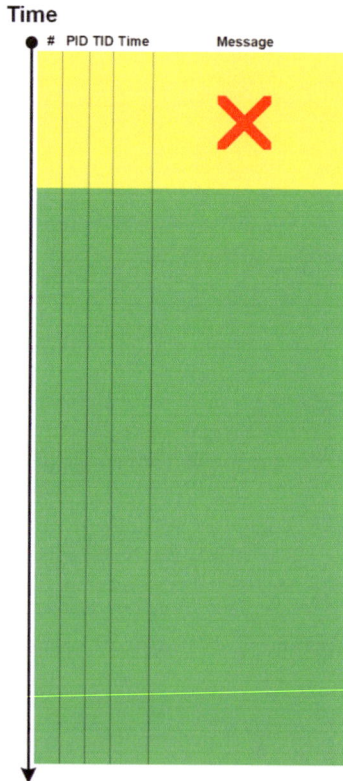

One of the solutions would be to use different logging tools and **Inter-Correlation** (page 167) to glue activities, for example, Process Monitor and CDFControl[203] for terminal services environments.

Visitor Trace

Some traces and logs may have **Periodic Message Blocks** (page 233) with very similar message structure and content (mostly **Message Invariants**, page 198). The only significant difference between them is some unique data. We call such a pattern **Visitor Trace** by analogy with the Visitor design pattern[204] where tracing code "visits" each object data or data part to log its content or status.

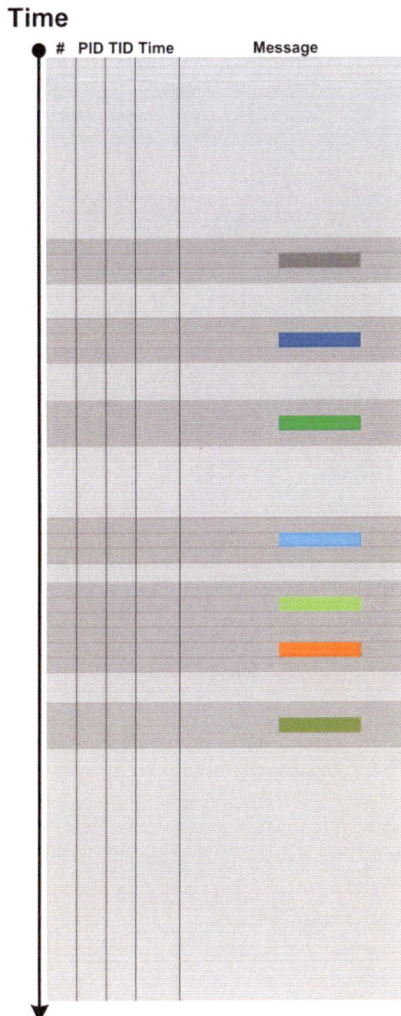

Vocabulary Index

What will you do when confronted with one million trace messages recorded between 10:44:15 and 10:46:55 with an average trace **Statement Current** (page 286) of 7,000 msg/s from dozens of modules and having a one-sentence problem description? One solution is to try to search for a specific vocabulary relevant to the problem description. For example, if a problem is intermittent re-authentication, then we might try to search for the word "password" or a similar one drawn from a troubleshooting domain vocabulary. So, it is useful to have **Vocabulary Index** to search for. In our trace example, the search for "password" jumps straight to a small **Activity Region** (page 41) of authorization modules starting from the message number #180,010, and the last "password" occurrence is in the message #180,490 that narrows initial analysis region to just 500 messages. Note the similarity here between a book and its index and a trace as a software narrative and its vocabulary index.

Watch Thread

When we do tracing and logging, much of the computational activity is not visible. For live tracing and debugging, this can be alleviated by adding **Watch Threads**. These are selected memory locations that may or may not be formatted according to specific data structures and are inspected at each main trace message occurrence or after specific intervals or events:

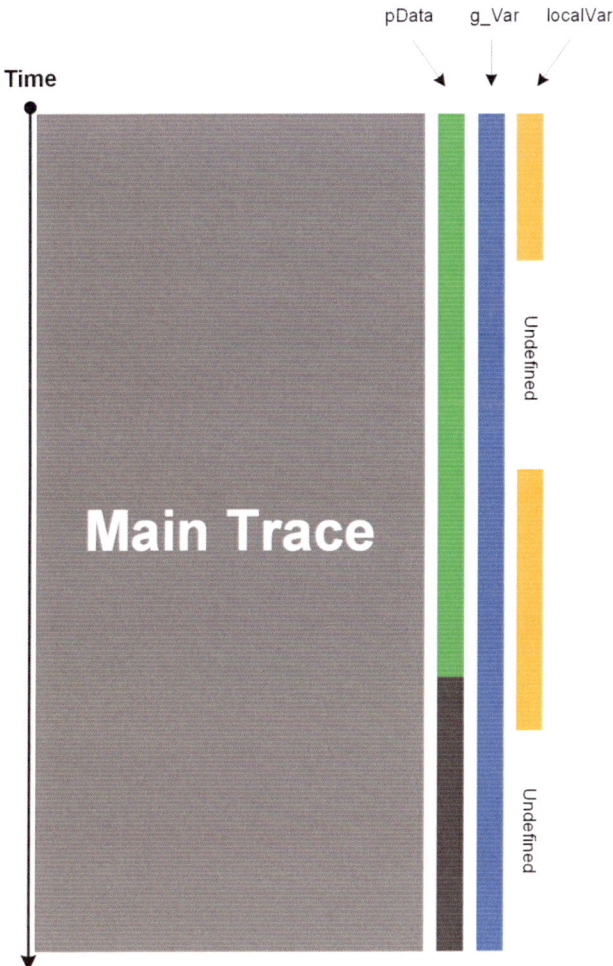

This analysis pattern differs from **State Dump** (page 285), which is about intrinsic tracing where the developer of logging statements already incorporated variable watch in the source code. **Watch Threads** are completely independent of original tracing and may be added independently. **Counter Value** (page 91) is the simplest example of **Watch Thread** if done externally because the former usually doesn't require source code and often means some OS or **Module Variable**[205] independent of product internals. **Watch Thread** is also similar to the **Data Flow** (page 95) pattern, where specific data we are interested in is a part of every trace message.

Whisker Trace

Looking at software traces and logs as 2-categories[206] allows us to consider **Whisker Traces** (horizontal composition) in addition to vertical composition such as **Serial Traces** (page 263), **Trace Mask** (page 322), and **Container Traces** (page 83). The same ATIDs can be combined, and if there is a time mismatch, additional message copies need to be added (whiskering). The process is illustrated in the following diagram:

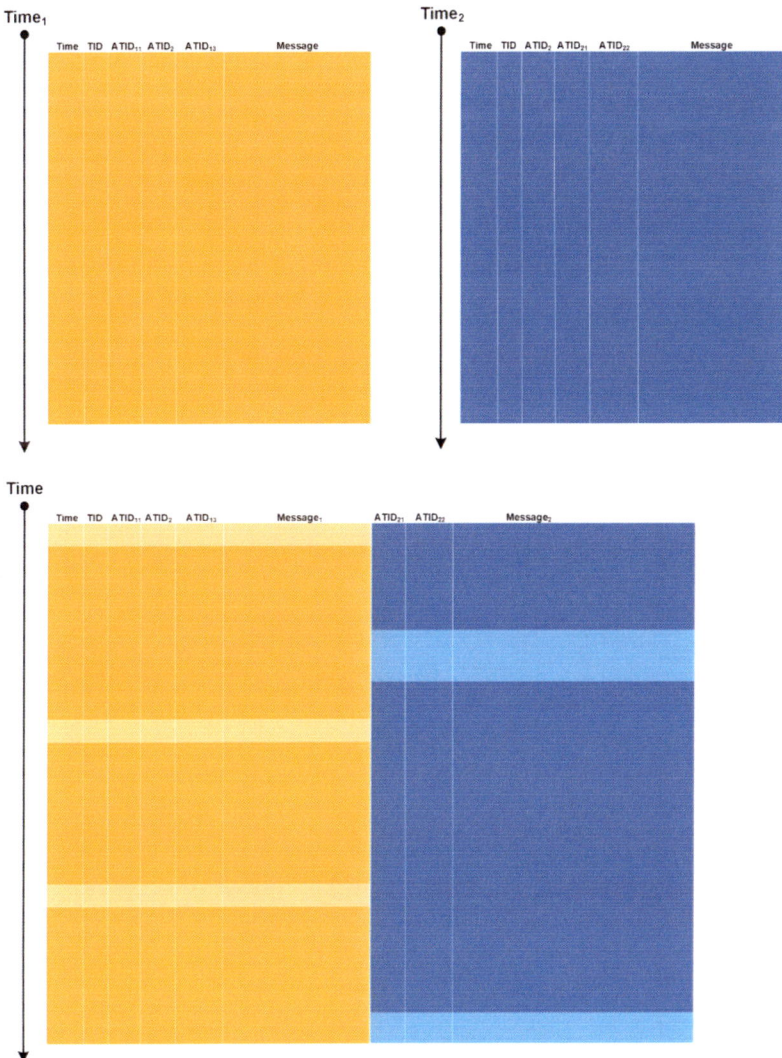

Weave of Activity

If messages from (**Adjoint**, page 48) **Thread of Activity** (page 296) also have associated traces (**Fiber Bundle**, page 136), then the latter messages data, for example, module names, can be interlinked with corresponding **Adjoint Threads of Activity**, thus forming "two-dimensional" **Weave of Activity**.

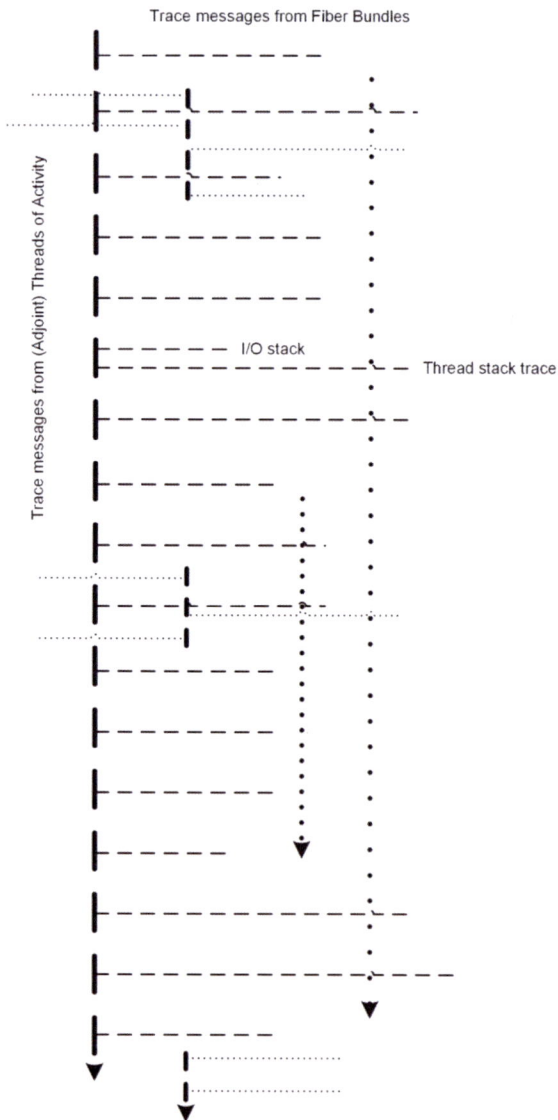

Trace messages from Fiber Bundles

Trace messages from (Adjoint) Threads of Activity

I/O stack

Thread stack trace

Working Set

When we analyze traces and logs, we work with only a small subset of log messages. We call any such current subset **Working Set** by analogy with working sets in operating system memory paging implementations:

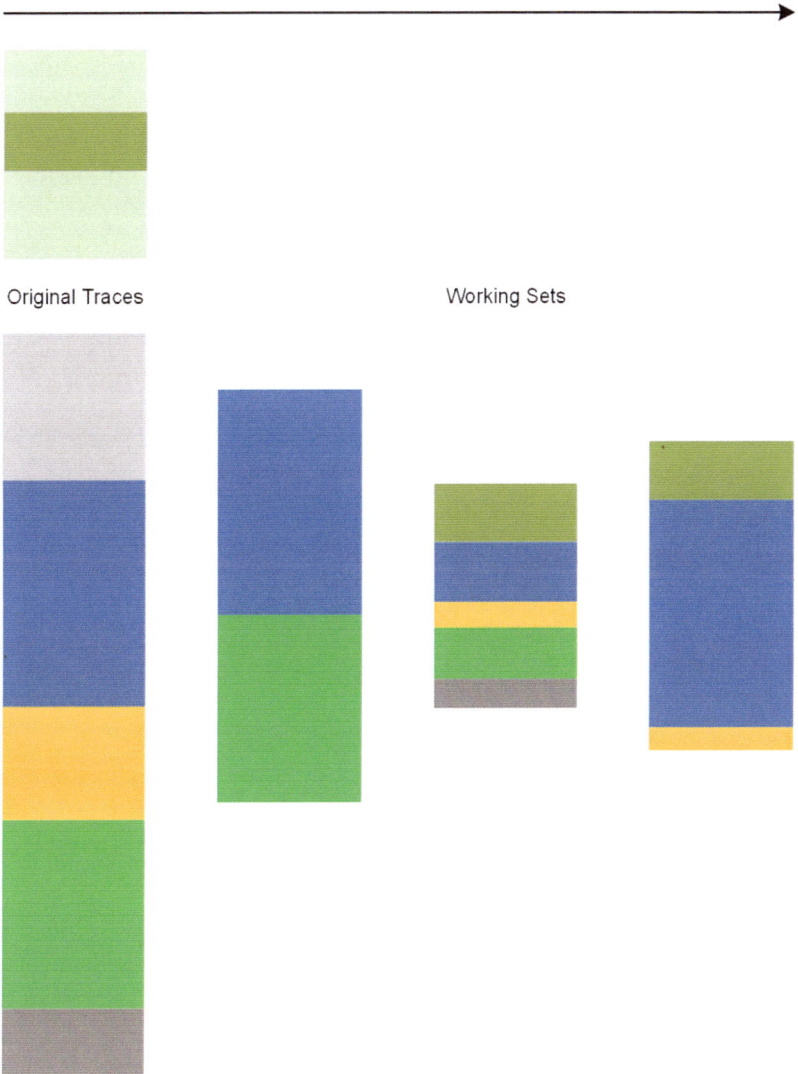

Original Traces   Working Sets

This analysis pattern can also be reconciled with an operadic approach to trace and log analysis by chaining appropriate diagnostic operads[207] from the original traces to the desired working sets:

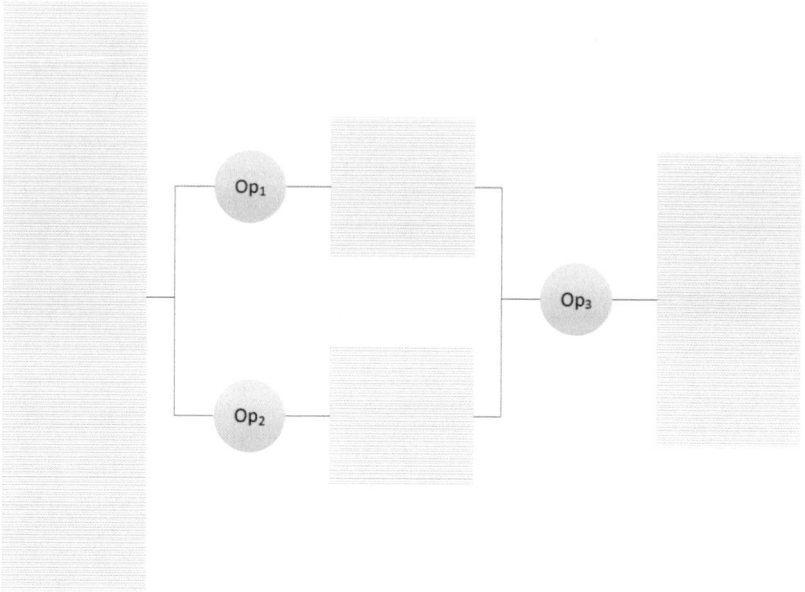

Appendix

Classification

This updated classification was originally introduced as a part of the Accelerated Windows Software Trace Analysis training course[208]. Therefore, the preliminary classification may be changed in the subsequent editions. Also, some analysis patterns may belong to different categories, but we chose only one for them.

Activity

Activity Disruption (page 34)
Activity Divergence (page 36)
Activity Overlap (page 37)
Activity Packet (page 39)
Activity Quantum (page 40)
Activity Region (page 41)
Activity Theatre (page 42)
Adjoint Thread of Activity ↓[1] (page 48)
Blackout ↓ (page 63)
Braid Group ↓ (page 65)
Braid of Activity ↓ (page 66)
Break-in Activity ↓ (page 67)
CoActivity (page 80)
Cord of Activity ↓ (page 84)
Coupled Activities ↓ (page 92)
Delay Dynamics ↓ (page 107)
Discontinuity ↓ (page 115)
Feature of Activity ↓ (page 135)

---

[1] '↓' sign means that a pattern involves time or order dependency.

Fiber of Activity ↓ (page 138)
Flag (page 140)
Glued Activity (page 146)
Last Activity (page 174)
No Activity (page 219)
Phantom Activity (page 234)
Piecewise Activity ↓ (page 238)
Punctuated Activity ↓ (page 249)
Resume Activity ↓ (page 255)
Ruptured Trace ↓ (page 257)
Strand of Activity ↓ (page 290)
Thread of Activity ↓ (page 296)
Time Delta ↓ (page 298)
Timeout ↓ (page 300)
Trace Quilt (page 331)
Weave of Activity ↓ (page 366)

Block

Intra-Correlation (page 170)
Macrofunction (page 180)
Motif (page 214)
Motivic Trace (page 215)
Periodic Message Block (page 233)
Renormalization (page 254)
Significant Interval (page 271)

Data

Back Trace ↓ (page 56)
Counter Value (page 91)
Data Association (page 94)
Data Flow ↓ (page 95)
Data Interval (page 96)
Data Reversal ↓ (page 97)

Error

Large Scale

Message

Trace as a Whole

Trace Skeleton (page 339)
Trace Summary (page 343)
Truncated Trace ↓ (page 352)
Visibility Limit (page 360)

Trace Set

Bifurcation Point (page 61)
Cartesian Trace (page 69)
Correlated Discontinuity ↓ (page 86)
Galois Trace ↓ (page 144)
Indexical Trace (page 160)
Inter-Correlation (page 167)
Master Trace (page 182)
Meta Trace (page 204)
News Value (page 217)
Polytrace (page 246)
Projective Space (page 247)
Relative Density (page 253)
Serial Trace ↓ (page 263)
Shared Point (page 265)
Sheaf of Activities (page 266)
Small DA+TA (page 276)
Split Trace (page 282)
Tensor Trace (page 292)
Trace Dimension (page 309)
Trace Extension (page 311)
Trace Homotopy (page 320)
Trace Join (page 321)
Trace Mask (page 322)
Trace Sharding (page 336)
Trace Similarity (page 337)
Trace String (page 341)
Unsynchronized Traces (page 357)
Whisker Trace (page 365)
Working Set (page 367)

Vocabulary

Memory

Code

Text

Narratological and Mathematical Influences

The following analysis patterns were influenced by semiotics, narratology, rhetoric, literary theory, philosophy of language, and historiography:

Activity Theatre (page 42)
CoActivity (page 80)
Declarative Trace (page 102)
Defamiliarizing Effect (page 103)
Dialogue (page 110)
Diegetic Messages (page 113)
Focus of Tracing (page 141)
Gossip (page 148)
Guest Component (page 149)
Implementation Discourse (page 157)
Layered Periodization (page 175)
Macrofunction (page 180)
Marked Message (page 181)
Master Trace (page 182)
Message Interleave (page 197)
News Value (page 217)
Null Reference (page 223)
Opposition Messages (page 225)
Palimpsest Messages (page 229)
Polytrace (page 246)
Silent Messages (page 272)
Text Trace (page 294)
Trace Frames (page 318)
Trace Partition (page 327)
Trace Retract (page 332)
Trace Viewpoints (page 344)
Traceme (page 347)
Traces of Individuality (page 348)

The following analysis patterns were influenced by mathematics:

Shared Point (page 265)
Sheaf of Activities (page 266)
Significant Interval (page 271)
Tensor Trace (page 292)
Trace Acceleration (page 303)
Trace Braidoids (page 304)
Trace D'Enfant (page 308)
Trace Dimension (page 309)
Trace Field (page 314)
Trace Foliation (page 316)
Trace Homotopy (page 320)
Trace Nerve (page 326)
Trace Path (page 329)
Trace Presheaf (page 330)
Trace Shape (page 335)
Trace Similarity (page 337)
Ultrasimilar Messages (page 354)
Whisker Trace (page 365)

The links to their corresponding concepts can be found in the analysis pattern descriptions. In addition, the currently used mathematical concepts list is also available online[209] and regularly updated.

Traces and Logs as 2-categories

In the past, we looked at software traces and logs as semigroups[210] or monoids[211] as a single object category. In the latter case, the monoid object is a trace or log, and arrows (morphisms) are trace messages.

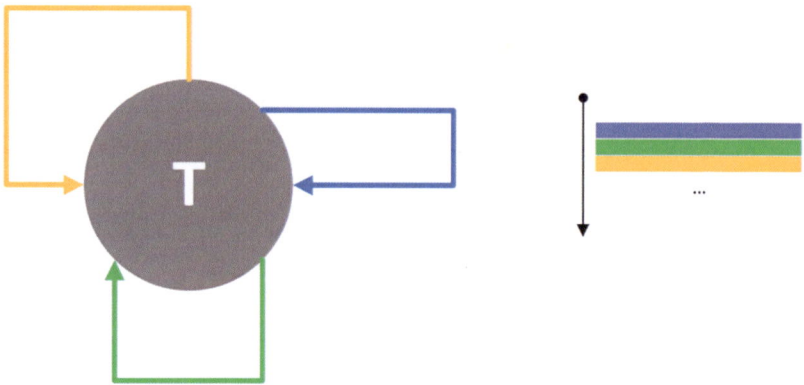

However, we can look at the traces and logs from another perspective. First, the monoid object is a system we trace, and messages are arrows. Then arrows between messages become arrows between arrows (2-morphisms[212]) in a 2-category[213].

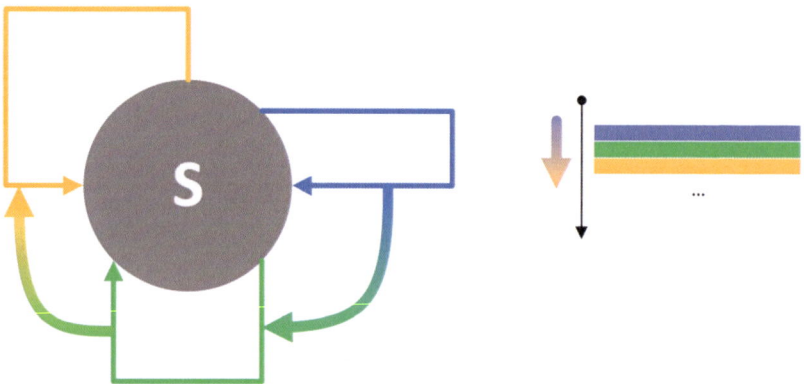

Therefore, we suggest looking at software traces and logs as 2-categories. Some forthcoming trace and log analysis patterns will use such a metaphor. For example, it provides some theoretical justification for the vertical and horizontal composition of traces and logs.

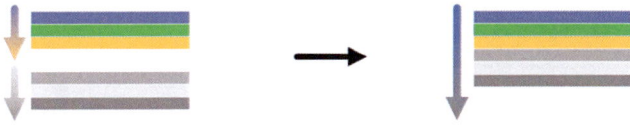

The horizontal composition type also allows the so-called whiskering[214].

Mathematical Concepts

Various analogies and metaphors from mathematics inspired trace and log analysis patterns. The links to definitions of concepts can be found in the corresponding analysis pattern references.

Adjoints (**Adjoint Message**, page 48; **Adjoint Message**, page 43)

Braid groups (**Braid Group**, page 65)

Braids (**Braid of Activity**, page 66)

Cartesian product (**Cartesian Trace**, page 68)

Causal sets (**Causal History**, page 73; **Causal Messages**, page 74; **Causal Chains**, page 71)

Continuous and discontinuous functions (**Discontinuity**, page 115)

Cover (**Message Cover**, page 192)

Critical points, Morse theory (**Critical Point**, page 93)

Curves (**Shared Point**, page 265)

Defect group of a block (**Defect Group**, page 105)

Derivatives, partial derivatives (**Statement Density and Current**, page 286; **Trace Acceleration**, page 303; **Message Change**, page 187; **Data Association**, page 94)

Dessin d'enfant (**Trace D'Enfant**, page 308)

Dimension (**Trace Dimension**, page 309)

Divergence (**Activity Divergence**, page 36)

Duality (**CoActivity**, page 80)

Edge contraction (**Collapsed Message**, page 81)

Equivalence relation (**Equivalent Messages**, page 121)

Fiber bundles (**Fiber Bundle**, page 136)

Flag, filtration (**Flag**, 140)

Foliation (**Trace Foliation**, page 316)

Fourier series (**Fourier Activity**, page 142)

Functor (**Trace Field**, page 314)

Fuzzy sets (**Case Messages**, page 70)

Galois connections (**Galois Trace**, page 144)

Hasse diagrams (**Causal History**, page 73)

Homotopy (**Trace Homotopy**, page 320; **Trace Path**, page 329)

Intervals (**Data Interval**, page 96)

Jaccard index (**Trace Similarity**, page 337)

Index of Patterns

U

V

W

Bibliography

Accelerated Software Trace Analysis, Revised Edition, Part 1: Fundamentals and Basic Patterns (ISBN: 978-1912636310)

Introduction to Pattern-Driven Software Problem Solving (ISBN: 978-1908043177)

Malware Narratives: An Introduction, Revised Edition (ISBN: 978-1912636525)

Memory Dump Analysis Anthology, Volume 3 (ISBN: 978-1906717438)

Memory Dump Analysis Anthology, Volume 4 (ISBN: 978-1906717865)

Memory Dump Analysis Anthology, Volume 5 (ISBN: 978-1906717964)

Memory Dump Analysis Anthology, Volume 6 (ISBN: 978-1908043191)

Memory Dump Analysis Anthology, Volume 7 (ISBN: 978-1908043511)

Memory Dump Analysis Anthology, Volume 8a (ISBN: 978-1908043535)

Memory Dump Analysis Anthology, Volume 8b (ISBN: 978-1908043542)

Memory Dump Analysis Anthology, Volume 9a (ISBN: 978-1908043351)

Memory Dump Analysis Anthology, Volume 9b (ISBN: 978-1908043368)

Memory Dump Analysis Anthology, Volume 10 (ISBN: 978-1908043856)

Memory Dump Analysis Anthology, Volume 11 (ISBN: 978-1912636112)

Memory Dump Analysis Anthology, Volume 12 (ISBN: 978-1912636129)

Memory Dump Analysis Anthology, Volume 13 (ISBN: 978-1912636136)

Memory Dump Analysis Anthology, Volume 14 (ISBN: 978-1912636143)

Mobile Software Diagnostics: An Introduction (ISBN: 978-1908043658)

Pattern-Based Software Diagnostics: An Introduction (ISBN: 978-1908043498)

Pattern-Driven Software Diagnostics: An Introduction (ISBN: 978-1908043382)

Pattern-Oriented Network Forensics: A Patten Language Approach (978-1908043788)

Pattern-Oriented Network Trace Analysis (ISBN: 978-1908043580)

Software Narratology: An Introduction to the Applied Science of Software Stories (ISBN: 978-1908043078)

Software Trace and Memory Dump Analysis: Patterns, Tools, Processes and Best Practices (ISBN: 978-1908043238)

Systemic Software Diagnostics: An Introduction (ISBN: 978-1908043399)

Theoretical Software Diagnostics: Collected Articles, Third Edition (ISBN: 978-1912636334)

Notes

[1] http://www.patterndiagnostics.com/accelerated-windows-software-trace-analysis-book

[2] http://www.DumpAnalysis.org

[3] http://www.DumpAnalysis.org/blog

[4] http://dumpanalysis.org/introduction-malware-narratives

[5] http://en.wikipedia.org/wiki/Divergence

[6] https://en.wikipedia.org/wiki/Wave_packet

[7] Event Tracing for Windows http://msdn.microsoft.com/en-us/library/windows/desktop/aa363668(v=vs.85).aspx

[8] Memory Dump Analysis Anthology, Volume 9a, 149

[9] Ibid., Volume 7, page 173

[10] Ibid., Volume 7, page 225

[11] What is an Adjoint Thread? Theoretical Software Diagnostics, Second Edition, page 287

[12] Memory Dump Analysis Anthology, Volume 1, page 503

[13] Looks like biology keeps giving insights into software, there is even a software phenotype metaphor (http://turingmachine.org/~dmg/papers/dmg2009_iwsc_siblings.pdf) although a bit restricted to code, and we also need an *Extended Software Phenotype*.
http://en.wikipedia.org/wiki/The_Extended_Phenotype

[14] Event Tracing for Windows http://msdn.microsoft.com/en-us/library/windows/desktop/aa363668(v=vs.85).aspx

[15] http://en.wikipedia.org/wiki/Adjoint

[16] Memory Dump Analysis Anthology, Volume 5, page 279

[17] Ibid., Volume 4, page 241

[18] Ibid., Volume 3, page 342

[19] http://en.wikipedia.org/wiki/Catastrophe_theory

[20] Threads as Braided Strings in Abstract Space, Memory Dump Analysis Anthology, Volume 1, page 503

[21] https://en.wikipedia.org/wiki/Braid_group

[22] Extending Multithreading to Multibraiding (Adjoint Threading), Memory Dump Analysis Anthology, Volume 4, page 330

[23] Memory Dump Analysis Anthology, Volume 4, page 330

[24] https://en.wikipedia.org/wiki/Cartesian_product

[25] https://en.wikipedia.org/wiki/Fuzzy_set

[26] https://www.springer.com/gp/book/9783319500812

[27] https://en.wikipedia.org/wiki/Causal_chain

[28] https://en.wikipedia.org/wiki/Causal_sets

[29] https://www.springer.com/gp/book/9783319500812

[30] https://en.wikipedia.org/wiki/Hasse_diagram

[31] Software Diagnostic Space as a General Graph of Software Narratives, Memory Dump Analysis Anthology, Volume 10, page 80

[32] Special and General Trace and Log Analysis, Memory Dump Analysis Anthology, Volume 8b, page 119

[33] Memory Dump Analysis Anthology, Volume 4, page 329

[34] https://en.wikipedia.org/wiki/Duality_(mathematics)

[35] https://en.wikipedia.org/wiki/Edge_contraction

[36] Ibid., page 330

[37] https://en.wikipedia.org/wiki/Ordinal_number

[38] https://en.wikipedia.org/wiki/Cardinal_number

[39] https://link.springer.com/referenceworkentry/10.1007%2F978-3-319-70658-0_73-1

[40] https://link.springer.com/content/pdf/10.1007%2F978-3-319-70658-0_15-1.pdf

[41] http://www.dumpanalysis.org/space-like-narratology

[42] http://www.dumpanalysis.org/pattern-narratives

[43] Memory Dump Analysis Anthology, Volume 7, page 98

[44] Ibid., Volume 1, page 419

[45] https://en.wikipedia.org/wiki/Critical_point_(mathematics)

[46] https://en.wikipedia.org/wiki/Morse_theory

[47] http://en.wikipedia.org/wiki/Partial_derivative

[48] http://en.wikipedia.org/wiki/Interval_(mathematics)

[49] Memory Dump Analysis Anthology, Volume 1, page 356

[50] https://en.wikipedia.org/wiki/Louis_de_Broglie

[51] Software Chorography and Chorology: A Definition, Memory Dump Analysis Anthology, Volume 5, page 229

[52] http://www.dumpanalysis.org/STMDA-book

[53] Special and General Trace and Log Analysis, Memory Dump Analysis Anthology, Volume 8b, page 119

[54] Encyclopedia of Crash Dump Analysis Patterns, 2nd edition, page 1177

[55] Memory Dump Analysis Anthology, Volume 3, page 342

[56] Basic Software PLOTs, Memory Dump Analysis Anthology, Volume 5, page 272

[57] https://en.wikipedia.org/wiki/Modular_representation_theory#Defect_groups

[58] http://en.wikipedia.org/wiki/Diegesis

[59] Memory Dump Analysis Anthology, Volume 2, page 387

[60] Debugged! MZ/PE Volume 1, Issue 3 (ISBN: 978-1906717797)

[61] Memory Dump Analysis Anthology, Volume 2, page 387

[62] https://en.wikipedia.org/wiki/Drone_(music)

[63] https://en.wikipedia.org/wiki/Equivalence_relation

[64] http://www.patterndiagnostics.com/accelerated-windows-software-trace-analysis-book

[65] http://support.citrix.com/article/CTX122741

[66] http://en.wikipedia.org/wiki/Power_set

[67] Memory Dump Analysis Anthology, Volume 2, page 239

[68] Ibid., Volume 1, page 395

[69] http://en.wikipedia.org/wiki/Phase_(waves)

[70] http://en.wikipedia.org/wiki/Quotient_group

[71] http://en.wikipedia.org/wiki/Group_(mathematics)

[72] http://support.citrix.com/article/CTX109235

[73] https://en.wikipedia.org/wiki/Feature_engineering

[74] http://en.wikipedia.org/wiki/Fiber_bundle

[75] https://en.wikipedia.org/wiki/Fiber_(computer_science)

[76] Memory Dump Analysis Anthology, Volume 7, page 437

[77] https://en.wikipedia.org/wiki/Flag_(linear_algebra)

[78] https://en.wikipedia.org/wiki/Filtered_algebra

[79] Dia|gram Graphical Diagnostic Analysis Language, Memory Dump Analysis Anthology, Volume 9b, page 82

[80] https://en.wikipedia.org/wiki/Fourier_series

[81] https://en.wikipedia.org/wiki/Galois_connection

[82] https://en.wikipedia.org/wiki/Galois_connection#.28Monotone.29_Galois_connection

[83] Special and General Trace and Log Analysis, Memory Dump Analysis Anthology, Volume 8b, page 119

[84] https://dumpanalysis.org/generative-software-narratology

[85] http://en.wikipedia.org/wiki/Manifold

[86] https://en.wikipedia.org/wiki/Variadic_function

[87] Memory Dump Analysis Anthology, Volume 1, page 271

[88] Ibid., Volume 7, page 162

[89] http://chentiangemalc.wordpress.com/2014/06/24/case-of-the-outlook-cannot-display-this-view/

[90] Memory Dump Analysis Anthology, Volume 5, page 272

[91] http://support.citrix.com/article/CTX106985

[92] Special and General Trace and Log Analysis, Memory Dump Analysis Anthology, Volume 8b, page 119

[93] http://www.dumpanalysis.org/blog/index.php/2007/02/15/windowhistory-40/

[94] http://en.wikipedia.org/wiki/Periodization

[95] http://en.wikipedia.org/wiki/Roman_Jakobson

[96] http://en.wikipedia.org/wiki/Distinctive_features

[97] http://en.wikipedia.org/wiki/Phonology

[98] Special and General Trace and Log Analysis, Memory Dump Analysis Anthology, Volume 8b, page 119

[99] Generalized Software Narrative and Trace, Memory Dump Analysis Anthology, Volume 7, page 395

[100] https://dumpanalysis.org/unified-computer-diagnostics-hardware-narratology

[101] http://www.dumpanalysis.org/pattern-narratives

[102] https://en.wikipedia.org/wiki/Covalent_bond

[103] https://en.wikipedia.org/wiki/Simplicial_complex

[104] Memory Dump Analysis Anthology, Volume 5, page 279

[105] http://en.wikipedia.org/wiki/Cover_(topology)

[106] Memory Dump Analysis Anthology, Volume 5, page 272

[107] https://en.wikipedia.org/wiki/NetFlow

[108] Memory Dump Analysis Anthology, Volume 5, page 272

[109] https://prometheus.io/

[110] https://prometheus.io/docs/concepts/data_model/

[111] Extending Multithreading to Multibraiding, Memory Dump Analysis Anthology, Volume 4, page 330

[112] Special and General Trace and Log Analysis, Memory Dump Analysis Anthology, Volume 8b, page 119

[113] http://en.wikipedia.org/wiki/Metanarrative

[114] http://en.wikipedia.org/wiki/Milestone_(project_management)

[115] https://en.wikipedia.org/wiki/Minimal_surface

[116] Memory Dump Analysis Anthology, Volume 6, page 54

[117] Ibid., Volume 8a, page 48

[118] https://en.wikipedia.org/wiki/Moduli_space

[119] https://en.wikipedia.org/wiki/Motive_(algebraic_geometry)

[120] Memory Dump Analysis Anthology, Volume 7, page 386

[121] https://en.wikipedia.org/wiki/Motivic_integration

[122] Memory Dump Analysis Anthology, Volume 1, page 298

[123] https://en.wikipedia.org/wiki/Failure_to_refer

[124] http://en.wikipedia.org/wiki/Binary_opposition

[125] http://en.wikipedia.org/wiki/Ferdinand_de_Saussure

[126] https://en.wikipedia.org/wiki/Jean-Fran%C3%A7ois_Lyotard

[127] https://en.wikipedia.org/wiki/Rhetoric

[128] http://en.wikipedia.org/wiki/Palimpsest

[129] Memory Dump Analysis Anthology, Volume 8a, page 121

[130] https://en.wikipedia.org/wiki/Phase_transition

[131] http://en.wikipedia.org/wiki/Piecewise_linear_function

[132] http://www.dumpanalysis.org/blog/index.php/2009/02/17/wait-chain-patterns/

[133] http://mathworld.wolfram.com/SurfaceofSection.html

[134] https://en.wikipedia.org/wiki/Poincar%C3%A9_map

[135] https://en.wikipedia.org/wiki/Projective_space

[136] https://en.wikipedia.org/wiki/Quotient_space_(topology)

[137] https://en.wikipedia.org/wiki/Address_space_layout_randomization

[138] http://en.wikipedia.org/wiki/Relative_density

[139] https://en.wikipedia.org/wiki/Renormalization

[140] Memory Dump Analysis Anthology, Volume 6, page 62

[141] Ibid., Volume 1, page 305

[142] Ibid., Volume 4, page 279

[143] Ibid, Volume 8a, page 121

[144] https://cacm.acm.org/magazines/2010/8/96628-the-emergence-of-cross-channel-scripting/abstract

[145] https://en.wikipedia.org/wiki/Cross-site_scripting

[146] https://en.wikipedia.org/wiki/Semantic_field

[147] http://en.wikipedia.org/wiki/Repeated_sequence_(DNA)

[148] Memory Dump Analysis Anthology, Volume 7, page 178

[149] http://en.wikipedia.org/wiki/Sheaf_(mathematics)

[150] Topological Signal Processing, p. 5 (ISBN: 978-3662522844)

[151] http://www.dumpanalysis.org/introduction-software-narratology

[152] Memory Dump Analysis Anthology, Volume 7, page 396

[153] https://en.wikipedia.org/wiki/Significant_figures

[154] http://en.wikipedia.org/wiki/Singleton_pattern

[155] Special and General Trace and Log Analysis, Memory Dump Analysis Anthology, Volume 8b, page 119

[156] Memory Dump Analysis Anthology, Volume 5, page 272

[157] https://en.wikipedia.org/wiki/Strace

[158] http://support.citrix.com/article/CTX111961

[159] http://www.debugging.tv/Frames/0x14/DebuggingTV_Frame_0x14.pdf

[160] http://www.debugging.tv/

[161] Special and General Trace and Log Analysis, Memory Dump Analysis Anthology, Volume 8b, page 119

[162] https://en.wikipedia.org/wiki/Tensor

[163] Special and General Trace and Log Analysis, Memory Dump Analysis Anthology, Volume 8b, page 119

[164] Memory Dump Analysis Anthology, Volume 7, page 225

[165] The Extended Software Trace, Memory Dump Analysis Anthology, Volume 5, page 277

[166] http://www.dumpanalysis.org/blog/index.php/2007/01/17/messagehistory-20/

[167] Extending Multithreading to Multibraiding, Memory Dump Analysis Anthology, Volume 4, page 330

[168] https://arxiv.org/abs/1908.06053

[169] https://en.wikipedia.org/wiki/Dessin_d%27enfant

[170] Extending Multithreading to Multibraiding, Memory Dump Analysis Anthology, Volume 4, page 330

[171] https://en.wikipedia.org/wiki/Field_(physics)

[172] https://en.wikipedia.org/wiki/Functor

[173] Memory Dump Analysis Anthology, Volume 10, page 20

[174] https://en.wikipedia.org/wiki/Foliation

[175] https://en.wikipedia.org/wiki/Homotopy

[176] Memory Dump Analysis Anthology, Volume 9b, page 82

[177] http://www.debugging.tv/

[178] http://www.signosemio.com/rastier/semic-analysis.asp

[179] https://www.dumpanalysis.org/traces-logs-as-proteins

[180] https://www.dumpanalysis.org/artificial-chemistry

[181] https://en.wikipedia.org/wiki/Nerve_complex

[182] Memory Dump Analysis Anthology, Volume 5, page 276

[183] Introducing Diags, Memory Dump Analysis Anthology, Volume 13, page 83

[184] Memory Dump Analysis Anthology, Volume 10, page 20

[185] https://en.wikipedia.org/wiki/Sheaf_(mathematics)#Presheaves

[186] Memory Dump Analysis Anthology, Volume 10, page 20

[187] https://en.wikipedia.org/wiki/Quilt

[188] https://en.wikipedia.org/wiki/Retraction_(topology)

[189] Memory Dump Analysis Anthology, Volume 9b, page 82

[190] https://en.wikipedia.org/wiki/Shard_(database_architecture)

[191] https://en.wikipedia.org/wiki/Similarity_measure

[192] https://en.wikipedia.org/wiki/Jaccard_index

[193] https://en.wikipedia.org/wiki/History_of_string_theory#1968%E2%80%931974:_dual_resonance_model

[194] http://en.wikipedia.org/wiki/Boris_Uspensky

[195] https://en.wikipedia.org/wiki/Seme_(semantics)

[196] https://en.wikipedia.org/wiki/Sememe

[197] Memory Dump Analysis Anthology, Volume 2, page 387

[198] https://www.owasp.org/index.php/Blind_SQL_Injection

[199] https://en.wikipedia.org/wiki/Ultrametric_space

[200] https://en.wikipedia.org/wiki/P-adic_number

[201] Memory Dump Analysis Anthology, Volume 6, page 113

[202] http://en.wikipedia.org/wiki/Use_case

[203] http://support.citrix.com/article/CTX111961

[204] http://en.wikipedia.org/wiki/Visitor_pattern

[205] Memory Dump Analysis Anthology, Volume 7, page 98

[206] https://dumpanalysis.org/traces-logs-as-2-categories

[207] Ibid., Volume 11, page 63

[208] http://dumpanalysis.org/accelerated-windows-software-trace-analysis-book

[209] http://dumpanalysis.org/mathematical-concepts-software-diagnostics-data-analysis

[210] https://en.wikipedia.org/wiki/Semigroup

[211] https://en.wikipedia.org/wiki/Monoid

[212] https://ncatlab.org/nlab/show/2-morphism

[213] https://ncatlab.org/nlab/show/2-category or https://en.wikipedia.org/wiki/Strict_2-category

[214] https://ncatlab.org/nlab/show/whiskering